BEST of the BEST from

BIG SKY
COOKBOOK

Selected Recipes from the
FAVORITE COOKBOOKS
of Montana and Wyoming

One glance across the Montana landscape and you'll discover why this is known as Big Sky Country.

PHOTO © JOHN REDDY PHOTOGRAPHY, INC.

★ ★

BEST of the BEST
from

BIG SKY
COOKBOOK

Selected Recipes from the
FAVORITE COOKBOOKS
of Montana and Wyoming

Edited by
GWEN McKEE
and
BARBARA MOSELEY

Illustrated by Tupper England

QUAIL RIDGE PRESS
Preserving America's Food Heritage

Recipe Collection© 2003 Quail Ridge Press, Inc.

Reprinted with permission and all rights reserved under the name
of the cookbooks, organizations or individuals listed below.

Amish Country Cooking @1988 by Andy & Millie Yoder; *Best-of-Friends, Festive Occasions Cookbook* @1993 by Darlene Glantz Skees; *The Best of Rural Montana Cookbook* @2001 Montana Electric Cooperatives' Association; *Bitterroot Favorites & Montana Memories* @2002 Bitterroot Favorites & Montana Memories; *Breakfast and More* @1992 Porch Swing Publications; *Cheyenne Frontier Days™ "Daddy of 'em All" Cookbook* @1995 Chuckwagon Gourmet; *The Cool Mountain Cookbook: A Gourmet Guide to Winter Retreats* @2001 by Gwen Ashley Walters; *Cow Country Cookbook* @1993 Clear Light Publishers; *Duck & Goose Cookery* @2001 by Eileen Clarke/Photos Eileen Clarke; *First Ladies' Cookbook* @1996 by Betty L. Babcock; *Game on the Grill* @2001 by Eileen Clarke/Photos (except where noted) Eileen Clarke; *Get Your Buns in Here* @1999 by Laurel A. Wicks; *The Great Entertainer Cookbook* @1992, 2002 Buffalo Bill Historical Center; *The Great Ranch Cookbook: Spirited Recipes & Rhetoric from America's Best Guest Ranches* @1998 by Gwen Ashley Walters; *Irene's Country Cooking: From Farm to Freeway* @2002 by Irene D. Wakefield; *Jackson Hole à la Carte* @1986 Jackson Hole Conservation Alliance; *The Kim Williams Cookbook and Commentary* @1983 by Kim Williams; *Montana Celebrity Cookbook* @1992 American and World Geographic Publishing; *Montana Bed & Breakfast Guide & Cookbook, 2nd Edition* @2000 Janet & Steve Colberg; *Mountain Brook's Wacky Wonders of the Woods* @1995 Mountain Brook Ladies Club; *Potluck: The Archie Bray Foundation Artists Cookbook* @1999 Archie Bray Foundation for the Ceramic Arts; *Pure Food Club of Jackson Hole* @2001 by Judy S. Clayton; *Ranch Recipe Roundup IV* @2001 Maverick Press; *Recipes from Big Sky Country: A Collection of Montana's Finest Bed & Breakfast Recipes* @2001 Tracy Winters; *Salad Sampler from Quilting in the Country* @2000 Quilting in the Country; *Soup's On at Quilting in the Country* @1998 Quilting in the Country; *A Taste of Jackson Hole II* @2001 by Christine Goodman; *A Taste of Montana: A Collection of Our Best Recipes* @1999 Tracy Winters; *Tastes & Tours of Wyoming* @1997 Wyoming Homestay and Outdoor Adventures; *Truly Montana Cookbook* @2002 Bitterroot Valley Public Television; *What's Cooking, Flo?* @1990 STAMPEDE Cartoon, Inc.; *Wheat Montana Cookbook* @1999 Wheat Montana; *Wild, Wild West Cowboy Cookies* @ 1997 Tuda Libby Crews/Photography 1997 Gibbs Smith, Publisher; *With Lots of Love* @2002 Taydie Drummond; *Wonderful Wyoming Facts and Foods* @1989 by Judy Barbour; *Wyoming Cook Book* @1998 Golden West Publishers; *You're Hot Stuff, Flo!* @1995 STAMPEDE, Inc.

Library of Congress Cataloging-in-Publication Data

Best of the best from Big Sky cookbook : selected recipes from the favorite cookbooks of
    Montana and Wyoming / edited by Gwen McKee and Barbara Moseley ; illustrations
    by Tupper England.
        p. cm.
    Includes index.
    ISBN 1-893062-43-0
        1. Cookery, American 2. Cookery—Montana. 3. Cookery—Wyoming. I. McKee,
    Gwen. II. Moseley, Barbara.

TX715.B485645 2003
641.59786—dc21   2003043150

Front cover photos: Pintlar Range & Mule Ranch, Montana © John Reddy Photography, Inc.
Devil's Tower, Wyoming, courtesy of Gillette Convention & Visitor's Bureau.
Back cover photo by Greg Campbell. Design by Cynthia Clark.
Manufactured in the United States of America.

QUAIL RIDGE PRESS
P. O. Box 123 • Brandon, MS 39043 • 1-800-343-1583
email: info@quailridge.com • www.quailridge.com

CONTENTS

PHOTO BY SHAWN MCKEE

Old Faithful, while not the highest, largest or most regularly erupting geyser in Yellowstone National Park, is the most recognized. Old Faithful erupts 18 to 21 times a day.

PREFACE

The sky is not the only thing that is big in Montana and Wyoming. The heritage, the history, the culture, the cuisine . . . it's all big. It's big country! We put these two beautiful states together in this cookbook because they are not only close geographically, but have many similarities of landscape and lifestyle . . . and cooking.

The landscape alone is enough to overwhelm you. One sees the sky so vividly over the boundless miles of rolling plains, where mountain peaks often decorate the horizon with such incredible grandeur . . . looking up simply fills one with awe. There are real cowboys out here, and huge herds of buffalo grazing as far as the eye can see. No, it's not a backdrop for a western movie, this is Montana and Wyoming in all their glory!

An adventurous journey through Montana and Wyoming will take you down the trails forged by Lewis and Clark, as well as early settlers to the West. You can explore the grandeur that is Yellowstone Park, visit authentic ghost towns, hike beautiful trails, fish for trout and hunt for elk, or just slow down a little and enjoy the beauty of this great land.

Montana and Wyoming's major cities with their fine restaurants, and the many cozy bed and breakfast establishments offer wonderful recipes that have become local favorites. But beyond the cities, the rugged elements of everyday living are reflected in their cooking styles. Indeed the early pioneers have passed on to today's ranchers their knack and zest for outdoor grilling and campfire cooking, as well as so many delicious warm dishes waiting at home for hungry cowboys. There may not be a supermarket to run to out there, so staple dishes of meat and game, beans and potatoes, and homemade breads have been preferred and perfected over the years. Here you'll find a taste as big as the land with heaps of hearty dishes like Drovers' Stew, down-home cowboy fare such as Wagon Master Soup, one-dish meals cooked on campfires like Omelet in a Bag, and wondrous wild game and fish such as Montana Stuffed Baked Trout. They brag on their huckleberry dishes, and well they should! And oh my, the breads are the best!

We were pleased to discover many modern dishes, too, easy to prepare from convenient mixes (like Easy Strawberry Cake), and so good (like Chocolate Covered Cherry Pie), you want to share it with everybody you know. There is so much creativity and variety in their cooking. We are truly pleased to share these recipes that help us to Preserve America's Food Heritage. In the pages of *Best of the Best from Big Sky Cookbook,* you'll also encounter photographs and facts about Montana and Wyoming that offer a vivid view of each state. Did you know that the Bitterroot River in Bitterroot Valley, Montana, is one of the few rivers on the continent that flows north? Or that Wyoming, though it is the smallest state in population, was the first to give women the right to vote? These fascinating facts scattered throughout the book reveal much of the history and culture of their states.

In addition to the delicious recipes that depict the flavor of the Big Sky region, this book introduces you to a wonderful variety of cookbooks from all across each state. Below each recipe is the name of its contributing cookbook. A special Catalog of Contributing Cookbooks Section (see page 259) shows each book's cover, along with a description and ordering information. This section is particularly popular with cookbook collectors.

We wish to extend a heartfelt thank you to everyone who contributed to this cookbook, especially those of you who so generously offered your favorite recipes. We appreciate the food editors and the bookstore and gift shop managers who guided us to their state's most popular cookbooks. Thanks also to each state's tourism department and many Chambers of Commerce for providing historic and informative data. To Tupper England, we thank you for bringing Montana and Wyoming to life with your inspiring illustrations. And to our assistant, Terresa Ray, we thank you for all your help in putting the parts of the puzzle together so efficiently.

We hope you find *Best of the Best from Big Sky Cookbook* as intriguing as we did. We invite you to partake of the cuisine of the wild west . . . Montana and Wyoming . . . with flavor as big as the sky.

Gwen McKee and Barbara Moseley

CONTRIBUTING COOKBOOKS

Amish Country Cooking
Best-of-Friends, Festive Occasions Cookbook
The Best of Rural Montana Cookbook
Bitterroot Favorites & Montana Memories
Breakfast and More
Brisbin Community Cookbook
Cent$ible Nutrition Cookbook
Cheyenne Frontier Days™ "Daddy of 'em All" Cookbook
Columbus Community Cookbook
Cooking with the Ladies
The Cool Mountain Cookbook
Cow Country Cookbook
Duck & Goose Cookery
Favorite Recipes
Favorite Recipes of Montana
Feeding the Herd
Festival of Nations Cookbook
The Fine Art of Cooking
The Fine Art of Cooking Volume 2
Fire Hall Cookbook
Fire Hall Cookbook #2
First Ladies' Cookbook
Food for the Soul
French Family Favorites
From the High Country of Wyoming
Game on the Grill
Get Your Buns in Here
The Great Entertainer Cookbook
The Great Ranch Cookbook
Heavenly Recipes and Burnt Offerings
Here's What's Cooking
The Hole Thing Volume II
Home at/on the Range with Wyoming BILS
Horse Prairie Favorites
Irene's Country Cooking

★ ★ ★ ★ ★ ★ ★ ★ ★ ★ ★ ★ ★ ★ ★ ★ ★ ★

CONTRIBUTING COOKBOOKS

Irma Flat Mothers' Club Cookbook
Jackson Hole à La Carte
The Kim Williams Cookbook and Commentary
Lewis and Clark Fare
Montana Bed & Breakfast Guide & Cookbook
Montana Celebrity Cookbook
Mountain Brook's Wacky Wonders of the Woods
Potluck
The Pure Food Club of Jackson Hole
Ranch Recipe Roundup IV
Rare Collection Recipes
Recipes from Big Sky Country
Recipes from the Heart
Recipes to Make You Purr
Salad Sampler from Quilting in the Country
Sharing Our Best
Simac Family Favorites
Soup's On at Quilting in the Country
Souvenirs
Story, Wyoming's Centennial Community Cookbook
A Taste of Jackson Hole II
A Taste of Montana
Tastes & Tours of Wyoming
Truly Montana Cookbook
What's Cooking, Flo?
What's This Green Stuff, Flo?
Wheat Montana Cookbook
Wild, Wild West Cowboy Cookies
With Lots of Love
Wolf Point, Montana 75th Jubilee Cookbook
Wonderful Wyoming Facts and Foods
Wyoming Cook Book
Yaak Cookbook
You're Hot Stuff, Flo!

BEVERAGES & APPETIZERS

PHOTO © JOHN REDDY PHOTOGRAPHY, INC.

Established in 1910 as the country's 10th national park, Glacier National Park in northwest Montana preserves over 1,000,000 acres of forests, alpine meadows, and lakes. The landscape is a hiker's dream with some 700 miles of maintained trails.

Coffee Banana Smoothie

2 small bananas, peeled,
  cut up and frozen
1½ cups skim milk
1 (8-ounce) container low-fat
  coffee yogurt

¼ teaspoon ground cinnamon
Dash of ground nutmeg
Fresh bananas and
  chocolate-covered coffee
  beans for garnish

In a blender combine frozen bananas, milk, yogurt, cinnamon, and nutmeg. Cover and blend until smooth. To serve, pour into glasses. Garnish with fresh bananas and chocolate-covered coffee beans. Makes 2 (1½-cup) servings.

Recipe from Candlewycke Inn B&B, Bigfork, Montana
Recipes from Big Sky Country

Joe's Breakfast Shake

1 banana
1 cup raspberries
1 cup vanilla-flavored yogurt
1 teaspoon vanilla

½ cup orange juice
8 ice cubes (about 1 cup)
Mint garnish (optional)

In the order listed above, place all ingredients except mint in the blender. Blend thoroughly. Serves 2 in stem goblets with mint garnish.

Recipe from The Sanders: Helena's Bed & Breakfast, Helena, Montana
A Taste of Montana

Established on March 1, 1872, Yellowstone National Park is the first and oldest national park in the world. Found within its 3,472 square miles is the world's most extensive area of geyser activity. There are more than 10,000 thermal features including geysers, hot springs, mudpots and fumaroles (a hole in a volcanic area from which hot smoke and gases escape). Yellowstone National Park is located 96% in Wyoming, 3% in Montana and 1% in Idaho.

Cranberry Cheesecake Shake

1 (3-ounce) package cream
   cheese
½ cup milk
2 cups vanilla ice cream

1 (8-ounce) can jellied
   cranberry sauce
1 cup fresh cranberries

Soften cream cheese. Place all ingredients in blender container and blend until well combined. Serve immediately.

Recipe from MacKenzie Highland Ranch, Dubois, Wyoming
Tastes & Tours of Wyoming

Strawberry Daiquiri

1 (10-ounce) package frozen
   strawberries
1 small can frozen lemonade

¼–⅓ cup sugar (optional)
Ice

Place strawberries and lemonade in blender and blend on low speed. Add sugar. Slowly add ice while blender is running. Blend until slushy.

Brisbin Community Cookbook

Graduation Punch

1 (46-ounce) can unsweetened pineapple juice
1 (46-ounce) can apricot nectar
2 (12-ounce) cans frozen concentrated lemonade

2 (12-ounce) cans cold water
2 (32-ounce) bottles 7-Up
Ice cubes
Lemon slices

Mix all together and float lemon slices on top of punch. Makes about 50 (6-ounce) punch cups.

Cooking with the Ladies

Wassail

1 quart hot tea
1 cup sugar
1 (32-ounce) bottle cranberry juice
1 (32-ounce) bottle apple juice

3 cups orange juice
¾ cup lemon juice
2 cinnamon sticks
12 whole cloves

Combine all ingredients in a large kettle. Bring to a boil and boil for 2 minutes. Reduce heat; simmer 20 minutes. Delicious hot or cold. Serves about 25.

Recipe from Prairie Breeze Bed & Breakfast, Laramie, Wyoming
Tastes & Tours of Wyoming

White Bean Dip

4 cloves garlic
2 (15-ounce) cans white kidney
  beans, rinsed, drained
¼ cup fresh lemon juice
½ cup virgin olive oil
1 tablespoon ground cumin
1 teaspoon cayenne, or to taste
Salt and white pepper to taste
¼ cup cilantro leaves
Chopped cilantro (optional)

Place garlic in food processor container. Process until finely minced. Add kidney beans and lemon juice; process until smooth. Add olive oil, cumin, cayenne, salt and pepper; process until well mixed. Add cilantro leaves; process for 30 seconds with on-off pulses. Transfer dip to bowl. Refrigerate, covered, until chilled or overnight. Sprinkle with chopped cilantro. Serve with tortilla chips or as a dip for crudités. Yields 8–12 servings.

Cheyenne Frontier Days "Daddy of 'em All" Cookbook

Black Bean Salsa

2 (15-ounce) cans black beans,
  drained
½ cup diced sweet red pepper
½ cup diced yellow pepper
¼ cup diced purple onion
¼ cup diced cucumber
2 tablespoons diced celery
2 tablespoons tomato juice
2 tablespoons red wine vinegar
1 tablespoon fresh lemon juice
1½ tablespoons chopped fresh
  thyme
½ teaspoon ground cumin
2 tablespoons chopped cilantro

Combine all ingredients. Refrigerate. Makes 1 quart.

Columbus Community Cookbook

In 1861, George Armstrong Custer graduated from West Point at the bottom of his class. However, during the Civil War (1861-1865), his skills at war propelled him to the temporary rank of brigadier general. After the war, Custer was required to revert to his previous rank of captain in the small regular army, but was always respectfully referred to as "General Custer." In 1866 he was appointed lieutenant colonel of the newly authorized 7th Cavalry. His army career ended June 25, 1876, at The Battle of Little Big Horn in Montana, which resulted in his death and a total loss of his troops. He remains the youngest general in U.S. history.

★ ★

Shoe Peg Corn Dip

1 (15-ounce) can shoe peg corn, drained
1 tomato, peeled, seeded and diced
½ green bell pepper, diced
½ red pepper, diced
10–15 ripe olives, sliced
½ cup diced red onion
Juice of 1 lime
½ cucumber, chopped
3 green onions, chopped
1 jalapeño, chopped
2 tablespoons sour cream
1½ tablespoons chopped cilantro
Seasoned salt and pepper to taste

Combine all ingredients and mix well. Refrigerate until well chilled. Serve with crackers or chips. Best prepared a day ahead.

From the High Country of Wyoming

Veggie Dip

1¼ cups mayonnaise
¾ cup sour cream
½ cup chopped green onion
½ cup chopped green pepper
1 teaspoon salt
¼ teaspoon pepper
½ teaspoon Tabasco sauce
¼ teaspoon garlic powder

Mix all ingredients together and let stand overnight. Very good with all raw vegetables.

Fire Hall Cookbook

Chicken Nugget Dip

¼ cup red pepper jelly (Chugwater Chili brand)
1 tablespoon Dijonnaise (mustard/mayonnaise blend)

Blend above ingredients. Serve as a dip with chicken or beef nuggets.

Here's What's Cooking

Gazpacho Dip

½ cup vegetable oil
3 tablespoons vinegar
1 teaspoon salt
1 teaspoon garlic powder
½ teaspoon pepper
4 or 5 green onions, thinly
   sliced
2 or 3 tomatoes, chopped

1 teaspoon coriander
1 (4-ounce) can chopped black
   olives, undrained
1 (4-ounce) can chopped green
   chiles, undrained
1 teaspoon chopped parsley
2 ripe avocados, chopped

Combine vegetable oil and vinegar in bowl; blend well. Add salt, garlic powder, and pepper; mix well. Add green onions, tomatoes, coriander, black olives, green chiles, and parsley; mix well. Chill. Fold in avocados just before serving. Serve with Doritos. Yields 10 servings.

Cheyenne Frontier Days "Daddy of 'em All" Cookbook

Artichoke Heaven

MMMmmmmm! Delicious!

6 small jars marinated
   artichoke hearts, drained
   and chopped into bite-size
   pieces
3–4 cups low-fat (or not)
   mayonnaise

8 cloves garlic, chopped
1 cup grated low-fat mozzarella
   cheese
½ cup grated Parmesan
   cheese, divided

Combine artichoke hearts, mayonnaise, garlic, mozzarella, and ¼ cup of Parmesan in a bowl. Place in lidded ceramic casserole, sprinkling with remaining Parmesan cheese. Cover and bake at 350° for 40 minutes. Uncover and continue to bake for 10–15 additional minutes, or until lightly browned. Serve hot with favorite crackers (Triscuits are highly recommended) or sliced baguettes.

Potluck

Major Grey's Delightful Dip

Sweet and smoky, a cocktail hour hit!

1 pound cream cheese, softened
2 cups shredded Cheddar
cheese
2 teaspoons curry powder
2 tablespoons plus 2 teaspoons
dry sherry

1 cup peach or mango chutney
1 pound bacon, cooked crisp
and crumbled
6 scallions, chopped

Blend cheeses with curry powder and sherry until creamy. Spread in an even layer on the bottom of a 9-inch quiche dish or pie plate. Spread chutney on top of cheese mixture. Top with bacon, then scallions. Serve at room temperature with sturdy crackers. Makes 12 servings.

Jackson Hole à la Carte

Spicy Beef Dip

1 pound ground beef
½ garlic clove, minced
¾ cup chopped onion
½ cup chopped green pepper
1 (8-ounce) can tomato sauce
¼ cup ketchup
1 teaspoon sugar

¾ teaspoon ground oregano
1 teaspoon salt
¼ teaspoon pepper
1 (8-ounce) package cream
cheese, softened
⅓ cup grated Parmesan cheese
Crackers or tortilla chips

Place ground beef, garlic, onion, and green pepper in a skillet. Cook until meat is lightly browned and onion is tender; drain well. Stir in tomato sauce, ketchup, sugar, oregano, salt, and pepper. Cover; simmer gently for 10 minutes. Remove from heat. Add cream cheese and Parmesan cheese. Heat and stir until cream cheese is melted and well combined. Serve warm with crackers or tortilla chips. Yields 3 cups.

Ranch Recipe Roundup IV

Salmon Dip with Dill

1 (7-ounce) can salmon
1 cup sour cream
¼ cup chopped green onions
1 teaspoon Worcestershire
  sauce

½ teaspoon dried dill weed
¼ teaspoon salt
Dash of hot pepper sauce

Drain and flake salmon. Combine with remaining ingredients. Chill and serve with fresh vegetables or crackers.

Fire Hall Cookbook #2

Salmon Pâté

Easily combined in a food processor, the ingredients for this delectable pâté may also be blended with an electric mixer, if the Camembert is shredded first.

1 (7¾-ounce) can salmon
9 ounces Camembert cheese
⅓ cup butter, softened
2 tablespoons chopped parsley
1 medium clove garlic, minced
¼ cup chopped scallions,
  white part only

¼ teaspoon crumbled dried
  thyme
½ teaspoon crumbled dried
  basil
Salt and pepper to taste
Lemon slice and chopped
  parsley for garnish

Drain salmon. Remove skin and bones. Remove rind from Camembert and cut cheese into chunks. Place all ingredients, except garnish, in a food processor fitted with the steel knife. Process until smooth; scraping down sides of work bowl as needed.

Place pâté in a serving dish. Chill, covered, several hours to blend flavors. To garnish, cover ½ of the surface of a lemon slice with chopped parsley. Place on pâté. Serve with crackers, party rye or cut-up raw vegetables. Makes 8 servings.

Jackson Hole à la Carte

Fresh Fruit with Sour Cream Grand Marnier Dipping Sauce

Delightful for pre-brunch or pre-luncheon munching!

1 (8-ounce) carton sour cream
2 tablespoons orange juice
2 tablespoons Grand Marnier
  liqueur
1 teaspoon grated orange rind
½ cup confectioners' sugar,
  sifted
Fresh fruit for dipping

Combine sour cream with orange juice, Grand Marnier and orange rind. Stir in confectioners' sugar. Place sauce in a small serving bowl. Chill, covered, 1–2 hours to blend flavors.

To serve, place bowl of sauce in the center of a serving platter. Surround sauce with attractively arranged fresh fruit. Use toothpicks to spear fruit for dipping. Makes 1½ cups sauce.

Note: This may also be presented as a salad at luncheons. Amaretto may be substituted for the Grand Marnier.

Jackson Hole à la Carte

Lynn's Creamy Caramel Fruit Dip

1 (8-ounce) package cream
  cheese, softened
¾ cup packed brown sugar
1 (8-ounce) carton sour cream
2 teaspoons vanilla
2 teaspoons lemon juice
1 cup cold milk
1 (3-ounce) package vanilla
  instant pudding mix
Assorted fresh fruit

In a mixing bowl, beat cream cheese and brown sugar until smooth. Add sour cream, vanilla, lemon juice, milk, and pudding mix, beating well after each addition. Cover and chill for at least 1 hour. Serve as a dip for fruit. Yields 3½ cups.

Story, Wyoming's Centennial Community Cookbook

C D Cajun Mushrooms

This has always been one of the most often requested recipes at the Continental Divide. It's great as an appetizer, luncheon entrée or a midnight supper.

3 tablespoons butter, divided
3 cups quartered mushrooms
½ cup chopped sweet red pepper
½ cup chopped green onions
1 tablespoon thyme
1 tablespoon granulated garlic

1 tablespoon Worcestershire sauce
1 tablespoon Tabasco
Salt to taste
3 cups whipping cream
2 tablespoons chopped fresh parsley

In a hot sauté pan, add 1 tablespoon butter and cook the mushrooms. Set aside in a baking dish. Melt the rest of the butter and add the pepper, onions, thyme, and garlic. Sauté until slightly cooked and add the rest of the ingredients, except parsley. Cook for about 7 minutes on high heat until the cream is partially reduced. Salt to taste. Pour the mixture over the mushrooms and place in a hot oven until the cream mixture begins to thicken and bubble. Sprinkle the chopped parsley over the top and serve with crunchy French or Cuban bread to dip in the mixture. Serve with a crisp Sauvignon Blanc or very cold dry Champagne.

Recipe by Jay and Karen Bentley, Continental Divide, Ennis, Montana

Montana Celebrity Cookbook

Famous musicians, actors and TV personalities from Montana: Jeff Ament, bass guitarist for Pearl Jam; Dirk Benedict, TV actor; Gary Cooper, movie actor; Chet Huntley, TV newsman; Myrna Loy, movie actress; George Montgomery, movie actor; Martha Raye, singer.

Crab Stuffed Mushrooms

24 large fresh mushrooms
¼ cup salad oil
1 (6-ounce) can crabmeat
1 egg, lightly beaten
2 tablespoons mayonnaise
2 tablespoons chopped onion

1 teaspoon lemon juice
4 ounces cream cheese,
  softened
½ cup bread crumbs, divided
2 tablespoons margarine,
  melted

Rinse and pat dry mushrooms. Remove stems. Brush mushroom caps with oil. Place on greased baking sheet. Combine crabmeat, egg, mayonnaise, onion, lemon juice, cream cheese, and ¼ cup bread crumbs. Fill mushrooms. Combine remaining bread crumbs and melted margarine; sprinkle over crab mixture. Bake at 375° for 20 minutes.

Brisbin Community Cookbook

Charbroiled Oysters
with Lemon Butter

Oyster lovers will stand in line for these.

LEMON BUTTER:
4 garlic cloves, minced
½ cup butter
¼ cup dry white wine

Juice of ½ lemon
Dash of salt
Pinch of ground white pepper

Cook garlic and butter in small saucepan over low heat, 2–3 minutes. Whisk in the wine, lemon juice, salt, and pepper; remove from heat. Keep warm on the side of grill.

24 fresh oysters in the shell

Discard any oysters that are not firmly closed. Scrub shells of remaining oysters. Place on barbecue grill or charbroiler and cook until shells pop open. Remove top shell and spoon in hot Lemon Butter; serve immediately. Serves 6–8.

The Fine Art of Cooking Volume 2

Pinwheels

1 (8-ounce) package cream
cheese, softened
1 (8-ounce) carton sour cream
1 cup shredded Cheddar cheese

1 (4-ounce) can diced green
chiles
¼ cup diced onion
Flour tortillas

Mix cream cheese, sour cream, shredded cheese, green chiles, and onion. Spread mixture thinly on tortillas. Roll up and refrigerate for an hour. Slice and serve.

Brisbin Community Cookbook

Wyoming Beef Pinwheels

2 tablespoons chopped fresh
red bell pepper or pimientos
⅓ cup grated Parmesan cheese
2 tablespoons chopped fresh
parsley
2 tablespoons Dijon mustard
½ teaspoon black pepper

3 pounds flank steak (2 steaks)
Salt and coarse-ground black
pepper to taste
3 tablespoons oil
2 cloves garlic, minced
Chopped parsley for garnish

Mix together red bell pepper or pimientos, Parmesan cheese, parsley, mustard, and pepper to blend. Spread over one side of each steak, dividing evenly. Roll lengthwise, tightly, jelly-roll-style. Season with salt and pepper to taste. Place seam-side-down and cut into 1-inch-thick slices to yield 24.

Thread on bamboo skewers (previously soaked in water, so they do not burn). Mix together oil and garlic, and brush pinwheels. Grill or broil until done. Sprinkle with additional chopped parsley. Yields 24 appetizers.

Wonderful Wyoming Facts and Foods

Wyoming is the 9th largest state, with 97,914 square miles, but has the fewest people, with only 493,782 (2000 Census).

Cowboy Cheese Puffs

1 loaf firm, unsliced white
  bread
¼ pound sharp Cheddar
  cheese

1 pound Velveeta cheese
¼ pound butter
2 egg whites, stiffly beaten

Remove crust from bread and cut into 1-inch cubes. Melt and stir cheeses and butter in top of double boiler over hot water until smooth. Remove from heat. Fold in stiffly beaten egg whites. Dip bread cubes in cheese mixture until well coated. Place on a cookie sheet, cover, and refrigerate overnight.

Bake in 400° oven for 12–15 minutes or until puffy and brown. Yields 4 dozen.

Wyoming Cook Book

Apricot Chicken Wings

The wings can be made ahead of time and held over for those late-comer guests.

1 small jar apricot jam
1 (8-ounce) bottle Russian
  dressing

½ package dry onion soup mix
3–4 pounds chicken wings

Mix the jam, Russian dressing, and onion soup mix together and pour over the chicken wings in an oven-proof baking pan. (It is easiest if you microwave the jam first.)

Bake at 350° for 2 hours. If your guests are late, turn temperature down and continue baking. Can leave wings in oven for 2–3 hours for those very late guests.

Best-of-Friends, Festive Occasions Cookbook

Montana's population of 904,433 ranks 44th in the United States, translating to less than one percent of the nation's population. The largest city in Montana is Billings, with 89,847 inhabitants (2000 census).

Sesame Thins

1¾ cups all-purpose flour
½ cup cornmeal
2 tablespoons sugar
½ teaspoon baking soda
½ teaspoon salt

½ cup butter or margarine,
  divided
½ cup water
2 tablespoons vinegar
2 tablespoons sesame seeds

In large bowl, mix flour, cornmeal, sugar, soda, and salt; with pastry blender cut ¼ cup butter into flour mixture until it resembles coarse crumbs. Stir in water and vinegar. With hands knead until well blended. Preheat oven to 375°. Divide dough into 30 small balls. On lightly floured board with floured rolling pin, roll balls in 4½-inch paper thin circles (edges may be ragged).

Place circles 1 inch apart on ungreased cookie sheet. Melt remaining butter (¼ cup). With pastry brush, lightly brush each circle with butter. Sprinkle with sesame seeds and press seeds firmly with pancake turner. Bake 8–10 minutes until lightly browned. Remove to wire rack to cool. When thoroughly cooled, store in tightly covered container. Makes 30.

Feeding the Herd

Editors' Extra: These are superb just to pick up and eat! Also great as dippers, especially with salsa and pesto, and excellent to serve under or alongside a meat dish or in the bread basket.

Cheese Ball

A stand-by recipe that never fails to please.

1 (8½-ounce) can crushed
    pineapple, well drained
2 tablespoons well-chopped
    onion
¼ cup well-chopped green
    bell pepper

Dash of salt
2 cups chopped pecans or
    walnuts, divided
2 (8-ounce) packages cream
    cheese, softened

Combine pineapple, onion, green pepper, salt, and ½ of the pecans and add to the cream cheese. Chill thoroughly. Make a ball and roll in the remaining pecans. Serve with a variety of crisp crackers.

Recipes to Make You Purr

Cheese 'N Chile Bread

1 loaf French bread
1 cup mayonnaise
3 cups shredded Monterey
    Jack cheese

1 (4-ounce) can diced green
    chiles
1 (4-ounce) can diced jalapeños

Slice French bread in half the long way. Mix mayonnaise, cheese, green chiles and jalapeños together and spread on each half of the French bread. Bake at 350° for 15 minutes. Then broil until cheese starts to get a little brown. Cut into bite-size pieces.

Sharing Our Best

Tomato, Leek and Goat Cheese Bruschetta

A nice twist on the Italian classic, this appetizer is delicious and gar-licky. A perfect snack to nibble while sipping a good Chianti Riserva.

1 leek, white part only
8 Roma tomatoes, cored and
  chopped
4 tablespoons chopped fresh
  basil
2 teaspoons finely chopped
  garlic
1 teaspoon chopped fresh
  rosemary

2 tablespoons extra virgin olive
  oil
Kosher salt
Ground black pepper
16 slices crusty French
  baguette, cut on a bias
½ cup fresh goat cheese
¼ cup grated Parmesan

Preheat the broiler. Cut the leek in half lengthwise and run under cold water to remove any residual dirt. Pat dry and cut into long thin strips, about 2 inches long and ⅛ inch wide. Stir the tomatoes, leek strips, basil, garlic, rosemary, and olive oil together. Season with salt and pepper and set aside.

   Place the bread slices on a sheet pan and toast under pre-heated broiler until light golden brown. Turn broiler off and preheat oven to 400°. Spread a thin (or thick, if you prefer) layer of goat cheese on the freshly toasted bread. Top with a generous tablespoon of tomato-leek mixture, then a teaspoon of Parmesan. Place in a 400° oven and bake for 7–10 min-utes, or until Parmesan is melted. Serve warm. Makes 8 servings.

Recipe from Lone Mountain Ranch, Big Sky, Montana
The Cool Mountain Cookbook

Fifty-three of Montana's fifty-six counties are larger in area than the state of Rhode Island.

Roquefort Grapes

A sophisticated beginning! For those of us who possess a passion for Roquefort, this elegant appeteaser is indeed the greatest beginning to any special repast. What else can I say?

1 (10-ounce) package almonds, pecans or walnuts, toasted
1 (8-ounce) package lite cream cheese, softened
⅛ pound Roquefort cheese, softened
2 tablespoons whipping cream
1 pound seedless grapes, red or green, washed and dried

Preheat oven to 275°. To toast nuts, spread them on a baking sheet and bake just until lightly toasted. (Almonds should be a light golden brown color; pecans and walnuts should smell toasted but not burned.) Chop toasted nuts coarsely (or finely, if preferred) in food processor or by hand. Spread chopped nuts on a platter.

In bowl of electric mixer, mix the cream cheese, Roquefort cheese, and cream, beating until smooth. Drop clean, dry grapes into the cheese mixture and gently stir by hand to coat them. Roll the cheese-coated grapes in the toasted nuts and place on a waxed-paper lined tray. Chill finished grapes before serving.

Serve on a silver tray alongside a bunch of "plain" grapes. Alert your guests that the grapes are indeed for eating. They look so beautiful that your guests may think that they are just for decoration. Yields about 50 grapes.

Best-of-Friends, Festive Occasions Cookbook

BREAD & BREAKFAST

PHOTO © GILLETTE CONVENTION & VISITORS BUREAU

Theodore Roosevelt named Devils Tower near Gillette, Wyoming, as the nation's first National Monument in 1906. This 1,267 foot tall rock formation is a sacred site of worship for many American Indians. It was featured in the movie "Close Encounters of the Third Kind."

Sylvia Shaw's
Baking Powder Biscuits

3 cups flour
2 tablespoons sugar
4½ teaspoons baking powder
¾ teaspoon cream of tartar

¾ teaspoon salt
¾ cup shortening
1 egg
1 cup buttermilk

Mix dry ingredients, cut in shortening, then beat in egg and milk. Knead 15 times, roll out ¾ inch thick. Cut and bake (on greased cookie sheet) at 400° for 12 minutes.

Recipe from Stonehouse Inn, Virginia City, Montana
Montana Bed & Breakfast Guide & Cookbook

Kirsty's Oat Biscuits

An English-Scottish recipe.

4 ounces butter (1 stick)
½ cup sugar
1 egg
1 teaspoon vanilla

½ cup flour
¼ teaspoon salt
1 teaspoon baking powder
2 cups rolled oats

Melt butter; add sugar, egg, and vanilla. Add dry ingredients. Pat or roll out on floured board. Cut out biscuits with biscuit cutter. Bake at 350° for 20 minutes.

Festival of Nations Cookbook

Prairie Biscuits

2 cups flour (Natural White™)
½ cup lard
1 teaspoon salt

½ teaspoon baking soda
4 teaspoons baking powder
¾ cup buttermilk

In bowl of flour, make a "well." Mix in lard (crumble the lard and flour with your hands) and work in the salt, baking soda, and baking powder. Sprinkle buttermilk into dough. Form a ball, knead on a floured surface or in hands. Form dough into size of biscuits desired and bake in hot Dutch oven over coals, or on greased cookie sheet in a preheated 450° oven until tannish in color.

Wheat Montana Cookbook

★ ★

Out-of-this-World Rolls

2 packages yeast
¼ cup water
3 eggs, room temperature
½ cup sugar

½ cup margarine, softened
1 cup warm water
4½ cups flour
2 teaspoons salt

Dissolve yeast in ¼ cup water. Beat eggs; add sugar, shortening, and 1 cup warm water. Combine with yeast mixture. Add flour and salt gradually. Knead. Raise until doubled, about 1 hour. Mix down. Put in refrigerator overnight.

Take out 3 hours before baking. Roll dough thin (½–¾ inch). Spread with softened margarine. Roll like jellyroll. Slice ¾ inch thick. Place in greased muffin tins. Bake at 375° for 20–25 minutes. This may be doubled for more rolls.

Wolf Point, Montana 75th Jubilee Cookbook

No Knead Rolls

1 cup boiling water
¼ cup butter or margarine
2 tablespoons sugar
1 teaspoon salt

¼ cup warm water
1 package yeast
1 egg, beaten
3½ cups flour

Into boiling water stir in butter or margarine, sugar, and salt. Cool to lukewarm. Measure warm water into mixing bowl and stir in yeast. Add first mixture to yeast; then add egg and flour. Beat until smooth. Store in refrigerator and use as wanted. Spoon desired amount onto greased cookie sheet. Let rise till double. Bake at 375° for about 30 minutes.

Recipe by Mrs. John H. Pierce,
Wife of State Representative from Billings, Montana
First Ladies' Cookbook

There are more public road miles in Montana than interstate highway miles in the entire United States.

Opal's Double Butterscotch Crescent Rolls

1 package dry yeast	½ cup butter, melted
¼ cup warm water	2 eggs
1 (3-ounce) package	2 teaspoons salt
butterscotch pudding mix	4½–5½ cups flour
1½ cups milk	

Soften yeast in warm water. Prepare pudding mix using 1½ cups milk; when thickened, add melted butter. Blend unbeaten eggs, salt, and softened yeast into pudding. Gradually add flour to form a stiff dough, beating well after each addition. Cover and let rise in a warm place about 1½ hours.

FILLING:

¼ cup butter, melted	⅔ cup grated coconut
⅔ cup brown sugar	⅓ cup pecan pieces
2 tablespoons flour	

Combine melted butter, brown sugar, flour, coconut, and pecan pieces.

Divide dough into thirds and roll each part into a 15-inch circle; cut dough into 12 wedges, using a pastry wheel. Place rounded teaspoon of Filling onto each wedge and roll up, starting with the wide end. Place on cookie sheet in crescent form. Let rise in warm place about 1 hour. Bake at 375° for 12–15 minutes.

GLAZE:

½ cup brown sugar	2 tablespoons butter
2 tablespoons water	1 cup powdered sugar

Combine brown sugar, water, and butter in saucepan. Bring to boil and boil 1 minute. Stir in powdered sugar; thin with milk, if necessary. Glaze rolls while still warm. Makes 3 dozen rolls.

Recipe from Bessemer Bend Bed & Breakfast, Casper, Wyoming
Tastes & Tours of Wyoming

Bread in a Bag

2 cups all-purpose flour, divided	3 tablespoons sugar
1 package fast-acting yeast	1 teaspoon salt
3 tablespoons nonfat dry milk powder	1 cup hot water (125°–130°)
	3 tablespoons vegetable oil
	1 cup whole-wheat flour

Combine 1 cup of all-purpose flour, undissolved yeast, sugar, dry milk, and salt in a 1-gallon heavy-duty freezer bag with a zipper lock. Squeeze upper part of bag to force out air. Shake and work bag with fingers to blend ingredients.

Add hot water and oil to dry ingredients. Reseal bag. Mix by working bag with fingers. Add whole-wheat flour; reseal bag and mix thoroughly. Gradually add enough remaining all-purpose flour to make a stiff dough that pulls away from the bag.

Take bread from bag and place on a floured surface; knead dough 2–4 minutes, or until smooth and elastic. Cover dough and let it rest for 10 minutes. Roll out dough to a 7x12-inch rectangle. Roll up from narrow end. Pinch to seal. Place in a greased loaf pan and let rise 20 minutes or until double in size. Bake at 375° for 30–35 minutes or until brown.

Nutrition Facts: Per 1 slice serving: Cal 80; Cal from Fat 15; Total Fat 2g; Sat Fat 0g; Chol 0mg; Sod 95mg; Carbo 14g; Dietary Fiber 1g; Sugars 2g; Prot 3g; Vit A 0%; Vit C 0%; Cal 2%; Iron 4%.

Cent$ible Nutrition Cookbook

James Cash Penney opened his first store, The Golden Rule Store, in Kemmerer, Wyoming, on April 14, 1902. Five years later, Penney bought The Golden Rule Store chain; six years after that, in 1913, he changed its name to JCPenney. Stores now number more than 14,000 and are located throughout the United States.

★ ★

Perfect Bread Machine Recipe

1⅛ cups water
3 cups whole-wheat flour
  (Prairie Gold® or Bronze
  Chief®)
1½ tablespoons sugar

1¼ teaspoons salt
1½ tablespoons butter
1½ tablespoons dry milk
1 envelope active dry yeast

Pour water into the bread pan. Add flour, sugar, salt, butter, and dry milk. Hollow out the center of the dry ingredients and put in yeast. If yeast contacts the water before kneading, the bread may not rise well. All ingredients should be at room temperature (70°–80°). When room temperature is below 65°, use lukewarm water (about 100°). Activate your bread machine following its instructions.

Note: Variations to instructions may apply based on your bread machine model. Refer to your machine manual.

Wheat Montana Cookbook

Blackfoot Fried Yeast Bread

1 cup lukewarm water
1 (1¼-ounce) package active
  dry yeast
1 tablespoon sugar

1 teaspoon salt
2½-3 cups unbleached flour
Oil or shortening for
  deep-frying

Place water in mixing bowl. Sprinkle yeast over water and allow to sit for 5 minutes. Add butter, sugar, salt, and 2½ cups flour. Knead, adding enough flour to form a stiff dough. Allow to rise for 1 hour. Place oil in a deep saucepan and heat to 350°. Form dough into disks 4 inches in diameter and about ¼ inch thick, and deep-fry for about 1 minute per side, until golden brown. Makes 8–10 pieces.

Truly Montana Cookbook

Parmesan Puffs

Guests' favorite!

¼ cup milk
¼ cup water
½ stick unsalted butter (¼ cup)
¼ teaspoon salt

½ cup flour
2 large eggs
1 cup freshly grated Parmesan cheese
Pepper to taste

In a heavy saucepan combine milk, water, butter, and salt and bring to a boil over high heat. Reduce the heat to moderate, add flour all at once and beat mixture with a wooden spoon until it leaves the side of the pan and forms a ball. Transfer the mixture to a bowl and whisk in eggs, one at a time, whisking well after each addition. Stir in Parmesan cheese and pepper to taste. Drop the batter in 8 mounds on a buttered baking sheet. Bake the puffs in upper ⅓ of a preheated 400° oven for 20 minutes, until crisp.

Recipe from Paradise Gateway B&B, Emigrant, Montana
Recipes from Big Sky Country

Poppy Seed Bread with Orange Glaze

2 eggs
¾ cup vegetable oil
1½ cups sugar
2 cups all-purpose flour
1 teaspoon salt
1 teaspoon baking powder

1 cup milk
1 teaspoon butter extract
1 teaspoon almond extract
1 teaspoon vanilla extract
1 tablespoon poppy seeds
Orange Glaze

Preheat oven to 350°. Combine eggs, oil, and sugar in large bowl; mix well. Combine flour, salt, and baking powder in bowl. Add flour mixture to egg mixture alternately with milk, mixing well after each addition. Add butter extract, almond extract, vanilla, and poppy seeds; mix well. Pour into greased and floured 6x10-inch loaf pan. Bake for one hour. Remove from pan. Let cool on wire rack.

Brush Orange Glaze on top, sides and bottom of bread with pastry brush. Repeat frequently until all glaze is used. Wrap in waxed paper, then in foil to store. Freezes well. Yields 10–12 servings.

ORANGE GLAZE:
½ cup sugar
⅓ cup orange juice
½ teaspoon butter extract

½ teaspoon almond extract
½ teaspoon vanilla extract

Combine sugar, orange juice, butter extract, almond extract, and vanilla in bowl; mix well.

Cheyenne Frontier Days "Daddy of 'em All" Cookbook

In order to move heavy freight trains from Ogden, Utah, to Green River, Wyoming, the Union Pacific Railroad often had to use two steam locomotives. To remedy the situation, the railroad designed Big Boy, a locomotive that could pull a 3,500-ton train unassisted over the Wasatch Mountains of Utah. The Big Boy and tender (the vehicle attached behind the locomotive which carried fuel and water) weighed 1,200,000 pounds (600 tons) and had a total length of 133 feet. Big Boy Locomotive No. 4004 can be viewed in Holliday Park in Cheyenne, Wyoming.

Zucchini Bread

¾ cup shortening
½ cup sugar
1 cup brown sugar
2 eggs
2 teaspoons vanilla
3 cups flour
1½ teaspoons baking soda

1 teaspoon baking powder
1½ teaspoons salt
1 tablespoon cinnamon
1 teaspoon nutmeg
½ teaspoon ground cloves
2 cups grated zucchini
¾ cup raisins

Cream shortening, sugars, eggs, and vanilla together. Add dry ingredients, zucchini, and raisins; mix well. Place in greased and floured bread pan. Bake at 375° for 1 hour or until done.

Food for the Soul

Flatwillow Colony Zucchini Bread

The colony makes dozens and dozens of loaves of this bread and sells them at the Billings, Montana, Country Market.

6 eggs
2 cups oil
4 cups sugar (scant)
3 cups white flour
3 cups whole-wheat flour
2 teaspoons baking soda
1 teaspoon salt
1 teaspoon baking powder

1 teaspoon cinnamon
2 teaspoons mace
2 teaspoons nutmeg (or more)
½ teaspoon ground cloves
  (optional)
4 cups peeled, grated zucchini
6 teaspoons vanilla
1½ cups chopped nuts

Preheat oven to 350°. In your mixer, place the eggs, oil, and sugar and beat well. Add flours, soda, salt, baking powder, spices, zucchini, and vanilla; mix well. Add nuts. Pour batter into 4 greased loaf pans and bake at 350° for 45-50 minutes, or until center springs back.

Heavenly Recipes and Burnt Offerings

Oatmeal Sunflower Millet Bread

2¼ cups warm water
½ cup honey
2½ tablespoons yeast
6½ cups whole-wheat flour,
   divided

⅝ cup safflower oil
½ cup oatmeal
¼ cup sunflower seeds
¼ cup millet
1½ tablespoons salt

Into a large mixing bowl, measure the water, which needs to be quite warm. Stir in honey. Sprinkle in yeast and stir until dissolved. When yeast rises to the surface and starts to foam, add 3 cups of flour and the oil, and beat for 100 strokes. The batter will look smooth and glossy. Cover and let rest for 20 minutes.

Add oatmeal, sunflower seeds, millet, and salt. Stir down the spongy dough. Add 1 cup of the remaining flour and stir well. Gradually add the rest of the flour. When the dough becomes too stiff to stir, turn onto a lightly floured counter and knead for about 10 minutes. The amount of flour will vary from day to day, depending on the weather. The dough will be soft, but not sticky. Cover the dough and allow to rise until doubled.

Punch down the dough and knead lightly for about 5 minutes. Shape into loaves. Place in papered and lightly oiled pans and allow to rise until doubled. Preheat oven to 350° and bake for about 40 minutes. The loaves will be nicely browned and sound hollow when tapped. Cool on a wire rack. Makes 2 loaves.

Get Your Buns in Here

Rhubarb Bread

Wyoming gardens are often filled with rhubarb in the spring. You can freeze the sliced fresh rhubarb in 1¹/₂-cup batches and then make the bread whenever you choose. The bread freezes well, also.

½ cup butter, softened
1 cup sugar
2 eggs
½ teaspoon orange extract
1½ teaspoons dairy sour cream
2 cups sifted flour
1 teaspoon baking powder

½ teaspoon baking soda
½ teaspoon salt
½ teaspoon nutmeg
1½ cups sliced rhubarb (⅛- to
  ¼-inch pieces)
1 cup chopped nuts

Cream butter and sugar. Add eggs, one at a time, mixing well after each addition. Blend in orange extract and sour cream. Sift together the dry ingredients and combine with the butter mixture. Stir in rhubarb and nuts. Pour into 1 greased 9x5x3-inch loaf pan (or 2 small loaf pans). Bake at 325° for 1 hour and 20 minutes for the large pan, about 1 hour for smaller pans.

Wyoming Cook Book

Shortbread

A simple Scottish recipe.

1 pound butter (not margarine)   4½ cups flour
1 cup sugar

Mix with hands until flour is used up. Pat the dough into 2 circles about ¾ inch thick. Pinch the edges and prick all over with a fork. Bake on ungreased sheet at 300° for 1 hour. When done, shortbread should be golden but not browned at all. Cut in wedges while still warm.

Festival of Nations Cookbook

Sula Peak Date Nut Bread

¾ cup chopped walnuts
1 cup chopped, pitted dates
1½ teaspoons baking soda
½ teaspoon sea salt
¼ cup butter

¾ cup boiling water
2 eggs
½ teaspoon vanilla extract
1 cup sugar
1½ cups flour

Preheat oven to 350°. In large mixing bowl combine nuts, dates, baking soda, and sea salt. Place butter on top of mixture and pour boiling water over butter; let stand 15 minutes.

In a separate bowl beat eggs; stir in vanilla extract, sugar, and flour. Combine all ingredients together; pour mixture into greased and floured 8x14-inch loaf pan. Bake in preheated oven for 1 hour. To test bread for doneness, insert toothpick into center of loaf and remove; a clean toothpick means bread is done.

Bitterroot Favorites & Montana Memories

Huckleberry Bread

½ teaspoon baking soda
2 teaspoons baking powder
2 cups flour
¾ cup sugar
¾ teaspoon salt
1 tablespoon orange rind

¼ cup orange juice
¼ cup melted butter or oil
¾ cup milk
1 egg, beaten
1 cup huckleberries
½ cup chopped nuts

Mix dry ingredients together, then add remaining ingredients, except huckleberries and nuts. Dry huckleberries with paper towel. In a loaf pan, layer ⅓ batter, then huckleberries and nuts. Bake at 350° for 50–60 minutes. Frost with powdered sugar frosting; may flavor with orange juice. Can also make as a coffee cake.

Fire Hall Cookbook

Cinnamon Sunrise Bread

2 teaspoons bread machine
  yeast
1⅓ cups flour (Natural White™)
2 cups whole-wheat flour
  (Prairie Gold®)
1½ tablespoons dry milk

3 tablespoons brown sugar
1 teaspoon salt
4 tablespoons butter
2 teaspoons cinnamon
1⅓ cups water
1 cup raisins

Combine all ingredients, except raisins, in bread machine basket. Add raisins after the rest of the ingredients have mixed for a while. Follow instructions for baking in your bread machine. (I set my machine on whole-wheat and select the 5-hour setting.) Makes 1 loaf.

Wheat Montana Cookbook

Wyoming Breakfast Bread

Great accompaniment to all of your favorite breakfast dishes.

3 cups all-purpose flour
1 teaspoon salt
1 teaspoon baking soda
1 tablespoon cinnamon
2 cups sugar
3 eggs, beaten

1 cup salad oil
2 (10-ounce) packages frozen
  sliced strawberries, thawed
1 (10-ounce) package frozen
  blueberries, thawed
1 cup chopped walnuts

Combine flour, salt, baking soda, cinnamon, and sugar in a large bowl and mix well. Pour combined eggs and oil into dry mixture; stir until all ingredients are moist. Add strawberries, blueberries, and walnuts. Pour mixture into 2 (8x4-inch) greased loaf pans. Bake at 350° for 1 hour or until a toothpick inserted near center comes out clean.

Let loaves cool overnight. In the morning, slice the bread and serve at room temperature, or warmed, with your favorite jam.

Wyoming Cook Book

★ ★

Skillet Cornbread

1 egg, well beaten
1 cup milk
1/3 cup shortening, melted
1 1/2 cups sifted flour

3 1/2 teaspoons baking powder
3 tablespoons sugar
1 teaspoon salt
3/4 cup cornmeal

Combine egg, milk, and shortening. Add flour, baking powder, sugar, salt, and cornmeal. Blend well. Pour into hot, greased iron skillet. Bake at 400° for 25–30 minutes.

Heavenly Recipes and Burnt Offerings

Spicy Corn Muffins

1/2 cup butter or margarine,
  softened
1/2 cup sugar
5 eggs
1 cup buttermilk
1 (4-ounce) can chopped green
  chiles, drained
1 1/4 cups cornmeal

1 cup all-purpose flour
1/2 teaspoon salt
2 teaspoons baking powder
1 cup whole-kernel corn,
  drained
1 cup shredded Cheddar cheese
1 cup shredded Monterey Jack
  cheese

In large mixing bowl cream butter and sugar. Add eggs, one at a time, beating well after each addition. Beat in buttermilk and chiles; mix well. Combine dry ingredients; gradually add to creamed mixture. Fold in corn and cheeses. Fill well-greased, cast-iron-shaped muffin pan or regular muffin cups with about 1/3 cup batter. Bake at 375° for 20–25 minutes or until a toothpick comes out clean. Cool for 5 minutes before removing from pans to wire rack. Serve warm with butter.

Ranch Recipe Roundup IV

The name Montana comes from the Spanish word montaña, meaning "mountain," even though the eastern part of the state consists of gently rolling pastureland.

★ ★

Banana Crumb Muffins

DOUGH:

1½ cups flour
1 teaspoon baking powder
1 teaspoon baking soda
½ teaspoon salt

2 large ripe bananas, mashed
¾ cup sugar
1 egg, slightly beaten
⅓ cup butter, melted

Combine the dry ingredients in a large bowl. In another bowl, combine bananas, sugar, egg, and butter and mix thoroughly. Stir into dry ingredients until moistened. Fill greased or paper-lined muffin cups ¾ full.

TOPPING:

⅓ cup packed brown sugar
1 tablespoon flour
⅛ teaspoon ground cinnamon

1 tablespoon cold butter or
    margarine

Combine brown sugar, flour, and cinnamon; cut in butter until crumbly. Sprinkle over muffins. Bake at 375° for 18–20 minutes or until muffins test done. Cool in pan 10 minutes until removing to a wire rack. Makes 12 muffins.

Recipe from Collins Mansion, Great Falls, Montana
Montana Bed & Breakfast Guide & Cookbook

Trapper Peak Huckleberry Yogurt Muffins

2 cups baking mix (Bisquick)
2 tablespoons sugar
¼ teaspoon baking soda
¼ cup butter, melted

1 egg
1 (8-ounce) container plain
    yogurt
1 cup huckleberries, drained

In large mixing bowl combine baking mix, sugar, and baking soda, and mix well with wooden spoon. Add butter, egg, and yogurt. Mix until moist. Mix in huckleberries. Fill muffin cake tins ½ full. Bake in preheated 400° oven 15–20 minutes until golden brown. Remove from oven and place on cooling rack. Makes 12 muffins.

Bitterroot Favorites & Montana Memories

Lemon Huckleberry Scones

Huckleberries are not available commercially but are very similar to the widely available blueberry.

2 cups flour
⅓ cup plus 2 tablespoons
  sugar, divided
2½ teaspoons baking powder
¼ teaspoon kosher salt
⅛ teaspoon ground nutmeg
½ cup (1 stick) cold butter,
  cut into chunks

1 egg
½ cup milk
2 teaspoons grated lemon zest
¾ cup fresh or frozen
  blueberries
1 tablespoon melted butter

Preheat oven to 400°. Stir together flour, ⅓ cup sugar, baking powder, salt, and nutmeg. Cut in the butter with pastry blender or by hand until mixture resembles coarse crumbs. Beat the egg with milk and lemon zest. Pour egg mixture over flour mixture and stir once or twice, then add the blueberries and stir just until moist.

Gather dough into a ball and place on greased baking sheet. Pat dough into a 9-inch circle, about ¾ inch thick. With a sharp knife, and without cutting all the way through, score the dough into 8 wedges. Do not separate the dough. Brush the tops with melted butter and sprinkle with remaining 2 tablespoons sugar. Bake until golden brown, about 20–30 minutes. Remove from oven and cool 2 minutes. Separate the scones into 8 pieces and serve. Makes 8 scones.

Recipe from Triple Creek Ranch, Darby, Montana
The Cool Mountain Cookbook

More pronghorn can be found in Wyoming than anywhere else in the world. As a matter of fact, with 416,000 pronghorn, Wyoming has 70% of the world's population. Often called "antelope," the pronghorn is actually a relative of the African gazelle. Capable of reaching speeds up to 70 miles per hour, the pronghorn is North America's fastest land animal.

Cranberry Walnut Scones

6 tablespoons butter
2 cups flour
1/4 teaspoon cinnamon
2 tablespoons sugar
3 teaspoons baking powder

1/2 cup milk
1/2 cup maple syrup
1/2 cup cranberries
1/2 cup chopped walnuts
1 egg, beaten

Cut butter into flour until coarse in texture. To this mixture, stir in cinnamon, sugar, and baking powder. Add milk and maple syrup. Stir until just blended. Add cranberries and nuts. Blend until distributed. If needed, add more liquid or flour to form a nice biscuit dough. Divide into 2 balls. Pat each half into a circle about 3/4–1 inch thick. Cut each circle into 8 wedges, as if cutting a pie. Brush with egg glaze. Bake on ungreased cookie sheet at 425° for 15 minutes or until golden. Makes 16 scones.

Breakfast and More

★ ★

Almond Apple Coffeecake

⅓ plus ¾ cup sugar, divided
½ cup sliced almonds
  (optional)
2 teaspoons cinnamon
½ cup butter or margarine
2 eggs
1 teaspoon vanilla

2 cups flour
1 teaspoon baking powder
1 teaspoon baking soda
½ teaspoon salt
1 cup sour cream
1 medium apple, pared, cored,
  and sliced

Mix together ⅓ cup sugar, almonds, and cinnamon, and set aside. Cream butter and gradually add ¾ cup sugar; beat until fluffy. Add eggs and vanilla. Sift together flour, baking powder, baking soda, and salt. Add to butter mixture. At low speed, add butter/flour mixture alternately with sour cream, beating well after each addition. Spread ½ of batter in greased and floured Bundt or tube pan. Top with apple slices, and sprinkle with ½ of almond mixture. Pour in remaining batter, and top with remaining almond mixture. Bake at 375° for about 45 minutes. Cool 30 minutes in pan.

Note: Can be baked, then wrapped in foil and frozen—reheated in foil at 350° for 50 minutes. Open foil last 10 minutes. (Can use apples which are no longer good eating, but haven't turned brown.)

With Lots of Love

Easy Sour Cream/Cinnamon Coffee Cake

CAKE BATTER:
1 box yellow cake mix
1 large box vanilla instant
  pudding mix
1 cup sour cream

½ cup milk
½ cup vegetable oil (scant)
4 eggs, beaten

TOPPING:
1 cup sugar
1 tablespoon cinnamon

1 cup finely chopped pecans

Preheat oven to 350°. In large bowl mix Cake Batter ingredients together well. Put half of Cake Batter in an oiled angel food cake pan. Pour half of Topping mix over batter and swirl with a knife. Place remaining Batter on top. Sprinkle with remaining Topping and lightly swirl with knife. Bake for 1 hour or until toothpick inserted in center comes out clean. Makes 10–12 servings.

Recipe from Creston Country Inn, Kalispell, Montana
A Taste of Montana

Overnight Coffee Cake

¾ cup butter
1 cup sugar
2 eggs
1 cup sour cream
2 cups unbleached flour
1 teaspoon baking powder

1 teaspoon salt
1 teaspoon nutmeg
¾ cup brown sugar
½ cup nuts
1 teaspoon cinnamon

The night before, combine butter, sugar, eggs, sour cream, flour, baking powder, salt, and nutmeg. Mix well and pour into greased 9x13-inch cake pan. Combine brown sugar, nuts, and cinnamon and sprinkle over this mixture. Cover and refrigerate. The next morning, preheat oven to 350°. Bake 35–40 minutes.

Breakfast and More

★ ★

Raspberry Cream French Toast

Simply delicious!

½ cup powdered sugar
2 teaspoons vanilla extract
½ cup milk
1 cup heavy cream
2 cups raspberries, fresh or
   frozen
6 eggs, beaten

12 slices day-old French bread
   (1 inch thick)
Vegetable oil as needed
Sifted powdered sugar
   (optional)
Fresh raspberries (optional)

Preheat oven to 400°. Place powdered sugar, vanilla, milk, heavy cream, and raspberries in a blender and blend until smooth. Pour mixture into a large bowl and whisk in beaten eggs. Place bread slices in a large shallow pan. Pour egg mixture over the bread and turn to coat both sides. Let sit 5 minutes.

Meanwhile, heat a nonstick skillet or griddle over medium-low heat. When hot, add 1 tablespoon of oil and heat for 1 minute. Add several soaked bread slices and cook for 5–6 minutes, until golden brown, then flip and cook on the other side until golden brown, 4–5 minutes more. Remove bread from skillet and place on a baking sheet in the preheated oven for 3–5 minutes, or until crisp.

While the first batch is crisping in the oven, cook the next batch of bread in the same manner, 5–6 minutes on the first side and 4 or more minutes on the other side. Finish in the oven for an additional 3–5 minutes. Sprinkle with powdered sugar and fresh raspberries, if desired. Serve with warm maple syrup. Makes 4–5 servings.

Recipe from Rusty Parrot Lodge, Jackson, Wyoming
The Cool Mountain Cookbook

French Toast Breakfast Bars

½ cup margarine or butter
1 cup brown sugar
1 teaspoon cinnamon
Bread slices (sandwich bread
  works best)

6 eggs
1½ cups milk
Dash salt

Melt margarine and pour in 9x13-inch pan. Add sugar and cinnamon. Cover with 2 layers of bread. Beat eggs, milk, and salt, and pour over bread; let stand in refrigerator overnight.

Bake at 300° for 40 minutes. Should not be soggy. Invert onto plate. May use extra syrup. Try raisin and cinnamon bread for a special treat.

The Best of Rural Montana Cookbook

Orange-Pineapple-Pecan French Toast

TOAST:
2 tablespoons butter
1 loaf French bread, cut
  into 1-inch slices
4 eggs
½ cup orange juice
¾ cup half-and-half

1 (8-ounce) can crushed
  pineapple
¼ cup sugar
1 tablespoon grated orange zest
½ teaspoon vanilla
¼ teaspoon nutmeg

TOPPING:
¼ cup butter, softened
½ cup firmly packed brown
  sugar

1 tablespoon light corn syrup
½ cup chopped pecans

The night before, melt butter in 9x13-inch pan and place bread. Combine and mix eggs, juice, half-and-half, pineapple, sugar, orange zest, vanilla, and nutmeg. Pour over bread. Combine Topping ingredients, except for nuts. Spread Topping over bread and sprinkle with nuts. Cover and refrigerate. The next morning, preheat oven to 350° and bake 40 minutes or until golden. Serves 6.

Breakfast and More

Apple Cinnamon French Toast

5 tablespoons butter
2 whole baking apples, peeled,
  cored, and sliced
1 cup firmly packed brown
  sugar
2 tablespoons corn syrup

1 teaspoon cinnamon
9 pieces French bread, sliced
  1 inch thick
3 large eggs
1 cup milk
1 teaspoon vanilla extract

Day before serving: In skillet, melt butter at medium heat. Add apple slices and cook until tender. Add brown sugar, corn syrup, and cinnamon. Cook, stirring until brown sugar dissolves. Pour into greased 9x13-inch pan and spread evenly. Arrange bread in one layer on top of apples. Mix eggs, milk, and vanilla. Pour over bread. Cover and refrigerate overnight.

Bake at 375° for 30–35 minutes. Mixture should be firm and bread golden. Cool in pan for 5 minutes. Invert a tray over French toast and carefully turn both over to unmold so apple layer is on top. Spoon any remaining sauce and/or apples over French toast. Serve immediately topped with sweetened whipped cream. Makes 6 servings.

Recipe from Fox Hollow Bed & Breakfast, Bozeman, Montana
A Taste of Montana

Sinfully Chocolate Waffles

My craving for chocolate brings this absolutely fabulous recipe to my best of friends (and probably a few "unfriendlies," too). When I received the recipe from a friend, I thought chocolate waffles were going a bit far . . . wrong—they are the BEST waffles I have ever had the privilege to savor. Need I tell you more!!!?

2 cups all-purpose flour	**2 eggs, separated**
4 teaspoons baking powder	**1½ cups low-fat milk**
1 teaspoon salt	**1 teaspoon maple flavoring**
3 tablespoons sugar	**4 tablespoons vegetable oil**
3 teaspoons cocoa	

In a large mixing bowl, add the dry ingredients and stir to mix well. Add egg yolks, milk, maple flavoring, and oil. Mix well. Beat egg whites until soft peaks form; add to batter mixture. Bake in waffle iron as you would any other waffle.

Serve with Mapeline Syrup or syrup of your choice. I spoon fresh fruit on top, then a little Mapeline Syrup on top of the fruit. Yields 6–8 waffles.

MAPELINE SYRUP:

2 cups granulated sugar	**½ teaspoon maple flavoring**
1 cup water	

Mix together and bring to boil. Serve warm with waffles.

Best-of-Friends, Festive Occasions Cookbook

Montana is home to seven Indian reservations: Blackfeet, Crow, Flathead, Ft. Belknap, Ft. Peck, Northern Cheyenne, and Rocky Boy. Together they make up about six percent of Montana's population.

★ ★

Old-Fashioned Potato Pancakes

We serve these with a heap of rustic bacon, grilled tart apples, and a fruity syrup, sometimes our own homemade chokecherry compote.

4 cups peeled, diced, raw
  baking potatoes, divided
2 tablespoons all-purpose flour
½ teaspoon baking powder
¼ teaspoon baking soda

½ teaspoon salt
2 eggs
2 tablespoons Butter Flavor
  Crisco

Using blender or food processor, liquefy 3½ cups of potatoes. Blend in the dry ingredients and eggs. Add the remaining ½ cup potatoes, blending or processing until chunks are quite small. Cook in Crisco on 375° griddle until crispy outside, tender inside, turning once. Serves 6 big appetites.

Recipe from Charley Montana Bed & Breakfast, Glendive, Montana
A Taste of Montana

Homemade Maple Syrup

1 cup brown sugar
1 cup white sugar
1 cup light corn syrup
1 cup water

Few grains salt
½ teaspoon maple flavoring,
  or to taste

Combine all ingredients except flavoring. Boil 1–2 minutes. Remove from heat; stir in flavoring. This will not sugar. Store in refrigerator.

Favorite Recipes of Montana

The famous Going-to-the-Sun Road is the only route through Glacier National Park in Montana that directly links the east and west sides, and is one of the park's most popular attractions. The road took eleven years to complete. The name was taken from nearby Going-to-the-Sun Mountain. The park superintendent at that time, J.R. Eakin, liked the name because "it gives the impression that in driving this road, autoists will ascend to extreme heights and view sublime panoramas."

★ ★

Flour Tortillas

2 cups flour
¼ teaspoon salt
½ teaspoon baking powder

4 tablespoons shortening
¾ cup cold water

Sift dry ingredients together and cut in shortening. Add water to make dry (stiff) dough. Knead on lightly floured board about 5 minutes. Wrap dough in waxed paper and let rest for a half hour (very important). Form into 2-inch balls. Roll out very thin, cook on dry griddle on both sides until lightly browned.

Fire Hall Cookbook #2

Sunrise Enchiladas

8 whole green chiles
  (about 2 [4-ounce] cans)
8 (7-inch) flour tortillas
2 cups cooked sausage,
  crumbled, or chopped ham
  or bacon
½ cup sliced green onions
½ cup finely chopped green
  bell pepper
2½ cups shredded Cheddar,
  divided

4 eggs
2 cups light cream
1 tablespoon flour
¼ teaspoon salt
1 clove garlic, minced
Tabasco
Avocado slices (optional)
Salsa for garnish
Sour cream for garnish
Cilantro for garnish

Place opened green chile on one end of tortilla. Combine meat, green onions, pepper, and ⅓ cup plus 3 tablespoons cheese. Spoon over green chile. Roll up and arrange in greased casserole dish, seam-side-down. Combine eggs, cream, flour, salt, garlic, and Tabasco, and pour over tortillas. Cover and refrigerate overnight. Uncover, and bake in 350° oven for 45–50 minutes. Sprinkle with remaining cheese and bake 3 minutes. Serve with avocado, salsa, sour cream, and cilantro. Makes 8 enchiladas.

Breakfast and More

Copper King
Cheese and Bacon Quiche

CRUST:

2 cups flour
½ teaspoon salt

⅓ cup margarine
4–5 tablespoons water

In medium bowl, sift flour and salt; cut in margarine until crumbly. Gather into ball using water to make crumbly dough stick together. Roll between 2 squares of waxed paper to a round that will line a pie pan completely, or line a spring form pan within ½ inch of edge.

FILLING:

1 pound bacon, fried and
    crumbled
1 pound shredded Swiss cheese
⅓ cup finely chopped onion
4 eggs

2 cups whipping cream
¾ teaspoon salt
¼ teaspoon pepper
½ teaspoon ground red pepper

Combine bacon, cheese, and onion; place in pastry-lined pie pan or spring form pan. Beat eggs lightly and add remaining ingredients. Beat until well blended. Pour egg mixture over other contents. Bake at 350° for 1 hour; test. If quiche is still soft in middle, add 15 minutes baking time, or bake until tester comes out clean. Let stand for 10 minutes and cut into wedges. Serve with fruit.

Recipe from Copper King Mansion, Butte, Montana
Montana Bed & Breakfast Guide & Cookbook

As telephone, telegraph and electrical wire was strewn throughout the country at the end of the 19th century, huge copper mines in the area around Anaconda, Montana, (near Butte) provided the necessary materials to build these lines. Marcus Daly, founder of Anaconda, built his own copper smelter just outside of town, which attracted thousands of workers from around the world. The Anaconda Stack, over 585 feet high and 75 feet interior diameter, is one of the tallest freestanding brick structures in the world and the only remnant of the huge copper smelting plant. The site is listed in the National Register of Historic Places.

Ham and Cheese Oven Omelet

8 eggs
1 cup milk
½ teaspoon salt
¼ teaspoon pepper
1 (4-ounce) package sliced ham,
  diced

3 tablespoons finely chopped
  onion
1 cup shredded cheese

Beat eggs, milk, salt, and pepper. Stir in remaining ingredients. Pour into greased 8x8x2-inch baking dish. Cook uncovered in 325° oven for 40–45 minutes, until omelet is set and top is golden brown.

Recipe can be prepared ahead of time and refrigerated. After pouring into baking dish, cover and refrigerate omelet no longer than 24 hours. Recipe can be doubled and baked in 9x13x2-inch pan for 40–45 minutes.

Cooking with the Ladies

Omelet in a Bag

This is a fun recipe for a crowd or just for one.

Chopped ham or bacon bits
Shredded Cheddar or Velveeta
  cheese
Chopped green pepper
Chopped onions

Chopped mushrooms
2 eggs (per person)
1 quart-size freezer baggie
  (per person)
Salt or pepper to taste

Put out bowls of chopped meats, cheese, and veggies. Each person puts 2 eggs and a spoonful (or as much as they want) of the fillings in a freezer bag. Put name on bag with pen. Squish the ingredients. Place in a pan of boiling water 12–15 minutes, until the omelet is done. You can take bag out of water and press on the bottom. If it is still soft and runny, put back in water till it is firm. When done, open bag and it will roll out.

Recipes from the Heart

Sunrise Sausage Casserole

1 pound bulk sausage, browned
  and drained
½ cup chopped onion
12 eggs
1½ cups milk
1 teaspoon salt
½ teaspoon pepper

1 teaspoon parsley
½ teaspoon thyme
¼ teaspoon dill weed
1 (16-ounce) package frozen
  hashbrown potatoes
1 cup shredded Cheddar cheese
½ cup chopped green pepper

Preheat oven to 350°. In skillet cook sausage and onion. Set aside. Beat eggs and milk in large bowl. Add salt, pepper, parsley, thyme, and dill. Stir in hashbrowns, cheese, green pepper, sausage and onions. Transfer to a greased 9x13-inch baking dish. Bake uncovered for 35–45 minutes or until a knife inserted near the center comes out clean. Makes 6–8 servings.

Recipe from Appleton Inn B&B, Helena, Montana
Recipes from Big Sky Country

Sausage Bread

1 loaf frozen bread dough,
  thawed
Garlic powder to taste
Pepper to taste
½–1 pound Italian sausage,
  casing removed
1 small onion, chopped

½ small red and green pepper,
  chopped
2 eggs, beaten, divided
Grated mozzarella cheese (8
  ounces)
Melted butter
Sesame seeds

Cut bread loaf in half; roll out each half into a square. Sprinkle with garlic powder and pepper. In a frying pan, crumble sausage and add onion and chopped peppers; sauté until done. Drain. Mix with ¼ of the beaten eggs. Put ½ of sausage mixture in middle of each square of bread. Put grated mozzarella cheese on top and fold bread up letter-style. Brush sides of bread with remaining egg mixture to seal edges. Baste top with butter and sprinkle with sesame seeds. Bake at 350° for 30 minutes or until brown.

Truly Montana Cookbook

Breakfast Strada

This feeds a large crowd. Serve with fruit and muffins for an easy breakfast.

8 slices white bread, toasted
  and cut in cubes
8–10 ounces grated sharp
  Cheddar cheese
8 eggs, beaten
4 cups milk

1 teaspoon dry mustard
½ teaspoon onion powder
Dash of pepper
½ pound bacon, cooked and
  crumbled

In a greased 9x13-inch pan place bread cubes. Sprinkle cheese over toast. Slightly but evenly, beat eggs and add milk, dry mustard, onion powder, and pepper. Mix and pour over bread and cheese. Cover and chill overnight.

Next morning uncover and bake in a 350° oven for 1 hour. Sprinkle bacon on top during the last 10 minutes of cooking.

Rare Collection Recipes

Glacier Breakfast Bake

2 cups fully cooked diced ham
1 (12-ounce) package frozen
  hashbrown potatoes
½ cup sliced fresh mushrooms
1 cup chopped green bell
  peppers
1 tablespoon instant minced
  onion

2 cups shredded Cheddar
  cheese, divided
3 cups milk
1 cup baking mix (Bisquick)
½ teaspoon salt
4 eggs

Grease a 9x13-inch pan. Mix ham, potatoes, mushrooms, green peppers, onion, and 1 cup cheese. Spread in pan. Stir milk, baking mix, salt, and eggs together until blended. Pour over potato mixture. Sprinkle with remaining 1 cup cheese. Cover and refrigerate for at least 4 hours, but no longer than 24 hours. Preheat oven to 375°. Bake uncovered for 30–35 minutes. Let stand for 10 minutes before serving. Makes 10–12 servings.

Recipe from La Villa Montana, Whitefish, Montana
Recipes from Big Sky Country

Grit Soufflé with Ham Sauce

So good it will turn a grits hater into a grits lover!

GRITS:

8 cups boiling water
1 teaspoon salt
2 cups grits
1 roll garlic cheese (or ½ cup processed cheese spread and 2 garlic cloves, minced)

1 stick butter
2 tablespoons sherry
1 tablespoon Tabasco
2 tablespoons Worcestershire
2 eggs, well beaten

Preheat oven to 350°. Combine and stir water, salt, and grits. Cook according to directions on grits package. Remove from heat and add butter, cheese, sherry, Tabasco, Worcestershire, and eggs. Pour into 9x13-inch pan and bake for 1 hour.

SAUCE:

2 tablespoons butter
3 tablespoons flour
1 can broth, beef or vegetable
½ cup chopped mushrooms
½ cup slivered almonds
2 cups chopped ham

½ cup chopped stuffed green olives
½ cup sherry
1 tablespoon Worcestershire
Cayenne pepper to taste

Combine butter, flour and broth and cook until thickened. Add remaining ingredients; simmer 10 minutes and serve over grits.

Breakfast and More

Egg Blossoms

2 sheets filo pastry
Fresh Parmesan, grated
Fresh spinach leaves
Eggs
Minced green onion
Salt
Pepper
Hollandaise sauce

Preheat oven to 350°. Cut filo into 6- to 6½-inch squares. Using 3 squares, stack askew, brushing melted butter between each layer. Gently push into prepared (sprayed) custard cups. Place spoon of fresh Parmesan in each cup, then fresh spinach. Break egg in each cup; salt and pepper as desired and top with minced onion. Place custard cups on cookie sheet. Bake 25 minutes. Remove blossoms (if possible) from cups. Before serving, place dollop of hollandaise sauce on top of each blossom.

Variation: You may serve egg on top of a buttered and toasted English muffin instead of baked in the filo blossom.

Breakfast and More

Editors' Extra: Easy to buy packaged powdered mix for Hollandaise sauce if you're not inclinded to make your own.

Sunshine Baked Eggs

1 pound bacon
14 eggs, lightly beaten
1 (20-ounce) can crushed
  pineapple, drained
1⅓ cups cottage cheese
1 teaspoon vanilla
Fresh parsley, chopped

Fry bacon until crisp, drain on paper towels, and crumble. In a large bowl, combine the eggs, bacon, pineapple, cottage cheese, and vanilla. Pour mixture into a greased 11x7-inch baking pan or casserole dish. Bake uncovered at 350° for 45 minutes or until knife inserted near the center comes out clean. Let stand for 5 minutes before serving. Garnish with parsley and serve with toast, jelly, and everyone's favorite beverage. Makes 8 servings.

Wyoming Cook Book

Baked Apple-Oatmeal

Wonderful!

2 cups milk	1 cup rolled oats
3 tablespoons brown sugar	1 cup diced, peeled apple
1 tablespoon butter	½ cup raisins
¼ teaspoon salt	Milk or cream
¼ teaspoon ground cinnamon	

In a saucepan combine milk, brown sugar, butter, salt, and cinnamon; heat just to boiling. Stir in the oats, apple, and raisins; heat until bubbles appear at the edge of the pan. Spoon into a buttered 1½-quart casserole and cover. Bake in a 350° oven for 30 minutes. Cover loosely with foil and keep warm in a low oven until ready to serve. Serve hot with milk or cream. Makes 4 servings.

From the High Country of Wyoming

Deluxe Crockpot Oatmeal

Prepare this at night, then have a delicious, nutritious breakfast waiting for you in the morning.

2 cups milk	1 cup old-fashioned oats
¼ cup brown sugar	(Quaker Oats)
1 tablespoon butter, melted	1 cup chopped apples
¼ teaspoon salt	½ cup raisins
½ teaspoon cinnamon	½ cup chopped almonds

Grease or spray Pam inside of crockpot. Put above ingredients inside crockpot and mix well. Cover and turn on LOW heat. Cook overnight or 8–9 hours. Stir before serving. Yields 6–8 servings.

Sharing Our Best

SOUPS, CHILIES, & STEWS

The 23-acre World Museum of Mining was built to preserve the 1890s mining camp Hell Roarin' Gulch in Butte, Montana. Within the mine and camp areas are a number of exhibits, displays and archives dedicated to preserving mining, ethnic, and social history.

Turkey Wild Rice Soup

3 (10-ounce) cans condensed
  chicken broth
2 cups water
½ cup uncooked wild rice,
  rinsed
½ cup finely chopped green
  onions
¾ cup all-purpose flour
½ cup margarine or butter
½ teaspoon salt

¼ teaspoon poultry seasoning
⅛ teaspoon pepper
2 cups half-and-half
1½ cups cubed cooked turkey
  or chicken
8 slices bacon, crisp-fried,
  crumbled
1 tablespoon chopped pimento
2–3 tablespoons dry sherry

Combine chicken broth and water in large saucepan. Add wild rice and green onions. Bring to a boil. Reduce heat. Simmer, covered, for 35–40 minutes or until rice is tender.

Spoon flour lightly into measuring cup; level off. Melt margarine in medium saucepan. Stir in flour, salt, poultry seasoning, and pepper. Cook, stirring constantly, for one minute or until smooth and bubbly. Stir in half-and-half gradually. Cook until slightly thickened, stirring constantly. Add half-and-half mixture slowly into rice mixture, stirring constantly. Add turkey, bacon, pimento, and sherry. Heat gently, stirring frequently; do not boil.

Garnish each serving with additional sliced green onions and crumbled crisp-fried bacon. Yields 8 servings.

Note: Uncooked regular rice may be substituted for part or all of wild rice. Reduce simmering time to 20–30 minutes or until rice is tender.

Cheyenne Frontier Days "Daddy of 'em All" Cookbook

Laramie County Library System, located in Cheyenne, Wyoming, is the oldest continually operating county library system in the United States. It was established in 1886 when Wyoming was still a territory.

★ ★

Country Chicken and Barley Soup

4 chicken thighs, skinned
½ cup barley
5½ cups chicken stock
1 stalk celery, chopped
3 small carrots, diced
1 large tomato, peeled and
  chopped
2 cloves garlic, minced

1 tablespoon tamari or soy
  sauce
½ teaspoon basil
Dashes of oregano, thyme, and
  cayenne pepper
2 tablespoons minced fresh
  parsley

Place all ingredients, except parsley, in a large saucepan. Bring to a boil, then cover and reduce heat. Simmer for 1¼ hours, stirring occasionally. Remove thighs; when they have cooled slightly, remove meat from bones; cut into bite-size pieces and return the meat to the soup. Simmer for an additional 15–20 minutes; stir in the parsley and serve. Makes 4 servings.

Wolf Point, Montana 75th Jubilee Cookbook

Bass Lake Chicken Noodle Soup

4 cups chicken broth
1 cup cooked and chopped
  chicken
1 (14-ounce) can whole-kernel
  corn, drained
1 (14-ounce) can kidney beans,
  drained
1 (14-ounce) can green beans,
  drained

1 cup chopped celery
1 cup peeled and thinly sliced
  carrots
1 package rigatoni noodles
1 teaspoon ground pepper
2 tablespoons parsley
1 tablespoon rosemary

Combine all ingredients in large saucepan. Cook 30 minutes on medium heat until carrots are tender. Serve hot. Makes 8 servings.

Bitterroot Favorites & Montana Memories

Minestrone Soup

1 cup dried white beans	1 cup water
1 quart water	¼ cup red wine
4 cloves garlic, minced	1 tablespoon dried oregano
2 stalks celery, chopped	1 tablespoon dried basil
1 onion, chopped	Salt and pepper to taste
1 (10-ounce) can chopped	2 bay leaves
tomatoes and green chiles	1 red potato, peeled and diced
1 (14½-ounce) can whole	½ pound fresh green beans,
tomatoes, chopped	cut diagonally into thirds
3 (14½-ounce) cans chicken	2 carrots, peeled and diced
broth with ⅓ less salt	⅓ cup elbow macaroni

Soak white beans for 6 hours in 1 quart of water; pour beans with soaking liquid into a pot. Bring to a boil and add garlic, celery, and onion. Cook 1½ hours or until beans are tender. Add chopped tomatoes and green chiles, chopped tomatoes with juice, chicken broth, water, red wine, and seasonings. Heat to boiling; add potato, green beans, carrots, and macaroni. Reduce heat to simmer and cook 30–45 minutes or until vegetables are tender. Yields 6–8 servings.

Nutritional information per serving: Cal 190; Chol 2mg; Fat 2.2g; Percent of Cal from Fat 10.2.

Festival of Nations Cookbook

Wagon Master Soup

1 large or 2 small cloves of
  garlic
2 ounces Parmesan cheese,
  cut into 2 or 3 pieces
4 ounces lean beef, cut into
  1-inch cubes
4 ounces lean pork, cut into
  1-inch cubes
4 ounces lean turkey, cut into
  1-inch cubes

1½ slices white bread, broken
  into bite-size pieces
¾ cup sliced onion, divided
⅓ cup milk
1 cup sliced carrots
1 cup sliced zucchini
1 (46-ounce) can chicken broth
2 cups cheese-filled tortellini
1 tablespoon basil

Place garlic, Parmesan cheese, beef, pork, turkey, bread, ¼ cup onion, and milk in food processor container with food processor running. Process until evenly ground. Shape into 1-inch meatballs. Place in stockpot. Add ½ cup onion, carrots, zucchini, broth, tortellini, and basil. Bring to a boil. Reduce heat. Simmer slowly for 30–40 minutes or until vegetables are tender. Yields 10 servings.

Cheyenne Frontier Days "Daddy of 'em All" Cookbook

Dorothy's Taco Soup

If you're a taco lover, you'll love this soup!

2 pounds ground beef
1 onion, chopped
2 (15-ounce) cans kidney beans
  with liquid
2 (15-ounce) cans white kernel
  corn with liquid

2 (10½-ounce) cans tomatoes
  with green peppers and
  onions
2 (15-ounce) cans tomato sauce
1 package taco seasoning

Brown ground beef and onion. Add remaining ingredients; cook for 1 hour or so. Serve with corn chips, olives, sour cream, and grated cheese. If too thick, add canned beef broth.

Soup's On at Quilting in the Country

Spanish Rice and Beef Soup

1 pound beef cube steaks
2 tablespoons butter
1 clove garlic, minced, divided
1 (6.8-ounce) package Spanish
rice mix
5 cups water

1 (14½-ounce) can chili-
seasoned diced tomatoes,
undrained
Chopped fresh cilantro
(optional)

Stack beef steaks; cut lengthwise into 1-inch-wide strips, then crosswise into 1-inch pieces. Heat butter in Dutch oven over medium-high heat until melted. Add ½ of beef and ½ of garlic; stir-fry 2–3 minutes or until outside surface of beef is no longer pink. (Do not overcook.) Remove from Dutch oven. Repeat with remaining beef and garlic. Season with 2 teaspoons seasoning mixture from rice mix.

Combine rice mix, remaining seasoning mixture, water, and tomatoes in Dutch oven; bring to a boil. Reduce heat to medium-low; cover tightly and simmer 15–17 minutes or until rice is tender. Return beef to Dutch oven; heat through. Stir in cilantro, if desired. Serve immediately. Makes 4 servings.

Ranch Recipe Roundup IV

Hearty Hamburger Soup

2 tablespoons butter
1 pound hamburger
1 cup chopped onion
1 cup sliced carrots
2 cups tomato juice
1½ teaspoons salt

¼ teaspoon pepper
½ cup chopped bell pepper
1 cup diced potatoes
1 teaspoon seasoned salt
¼ cup flour
4 cups milk, divided

Melt butter in saucepan; brown meat, then add onion and cook until transparent. Stir in remaining ingredients, except flour and milk. Cover and cook over low heat until vegetables are tender, about 20–25 minutes. Combine flour with 1 cup milk. Stir into soup mixture. Boil. Add remaining milk. This makes quite a large amount.

Amish Country Cooking

Hearty Winter Soup

4 (14-ounce) cans beef broth
1 (28-ounce) can whole
   tomatoes, cut up
1 pound Polish sausage
   (peel off casing), cut in
   half and slice
1 medium onion, chopped
1 cup sliced carrots
1 cup chopped celery

2 potatoes, peeled and cubed
1 cup green noodles
1 clove garlic
Salt and pepper to taste
1 teaspoon brown sugar
3 cups cabbage, thinly sliced
1 tablespoon Parmesan cheese
   per serving for garnish

Bring broth and tomatoes to a boil. Then add all ingredients, except for the cabbage and garnish. Bring to a boil; lower heat, cover, and simmer 1 hour. Add cabbage and cook 30 more minutes. Serve with cheese sprinkled on top. Serves 8–10.

Soup's On at Quilting in the Country

★ ★

Red and Gold Split Pea Soup

It's lucky nasturtiums are in flower right into fall because no one wants to cook split pea soup in summer, and besides, the bright red and gold of the nasturtium blossoms fit so splendidly on a fall table. Nasturtium flowers contain Vitamin C, so you are feeding your health and your eyes at the same time.

Don't be surprised to find a pungent taste. Nasturtium is in the same general family as watercress. But the smooth richness of split pea soup asks for an exotic garnish.

If you are out of nasturtiums in your garden, you can use marigold petals. Marigolds are also edible and the colors are the same—red-orange, yellow-gold. If you are out of flowers entirely, a dash of paprika will do nicely.

2 tablespoons chopped onion
1 clove garlic, minced
2 tablespoons oil
1 cup dried split peas
4 cups water
1 teaspoon salt
1/4 cup chopped celery leaves
Pinch of summer savory
1 potato, diced

1/2 cup grated carrot
1 rib celery, chopped
1 tablespoon chopped sweet red
  pepper
1/4 cup chopped parsley
1 cup yogurt
1/4 cup nasturtium flowers
  (petals only)

Sauté the onion and garlic in oil in a large, heavy pot. Add washed split peas, water, salt, celery leaves, and summer savory. Bring to a boil; cover, then simmer 45 minutes or until the peas are tender.

Add potato, carrot, celery, red pepper, and parsley. Simmer 25 minutes. Serve hot with a dollop of yogurt and a sprinkling of nasturtium petals. Serves 4.

The Kim Williams Cookbook and Commentary

The Jackson Hole Ski Area in Wyoming has the longest continuous vertical rise of any ski area in the United States. From the valley floor to the top of Rendezvous Mountain is 4,139 feet.

Hot Apple Soup

4 Granny Smith apples
4 McIntosh apples
2½ cups water
2 tablespoons lemon juice
¼ teaspoon nutmeg

½ teaspoon cinnamon
1 cup light cream or
   half-and-half
Unsweetened whipped cream
   for garnish

Peel, core, and quarter apples. Combine all ingredients except creams in saucepan and bring to boil. Simmer 15 minutes till apples are soft. Purée; return to pan, add cream, and heat through, but don't boil. Garnish each serving with a dollop of whipped cream and sprinkle with cinnamon sugar. Serve with graham crackers. Serves 4.

Recipes from the Heart

Autumn Soup

1 pound ground beef
1 cup chopped onion
⅔ cup bouillon (or 1 cube)
1 (15-ounce) can whole
   tomatoes
1 (8-ounce) can tomato sauce
2 red potatoes, diced (leave
   skins on)

⅓ cup red wine
Ground pepper to taste
1 bay leaf
¼ teaspoon basil
⅛–¼ teaspoon thyme
Juice from ½ lemon
1 cup sliced celery and leaves

Brown ground beef; drain fat, add onion and cook until golden. Stir in bouillon, tomatoes, tomato sauce, red potatoes, red wine, ground pepper, bay leaf, basil, thyme, and juice of ½ lemon. Bring to a boil. Cover and simmer for 1 hour, or until potatoes are tender. Add sliced celery and leaves. Simmer 15 minutes more. Makes 4 generous servings.

Mountain Brook's Wacky Wonders of the Woods

Cheesy Potato Soup

4–6 strips bacon
4 potatoes, cubed
Water
½ teaspoon garlic powder
(optional)
Salt and pepper to taste
1 tablespoon chopped onion
(or more)

1 (10½-ounce) can cream of
chicken soup or broth
2 tablespoons cornstarch
3 cups milk
1 cup shredded American or
Velveeta cheese

Fry bacon crisp; crumble and set aside. Cook potatoes in small amount of water (to cover potatoes). Add seasonings and onion. Add bacon. Cook until potatoes are done. Add soup or broth. Dissolve cornstarch in a little water. Add milk and cornstarch to potatoes. Stir in cheese. Heat until cheese is melted.

Note: Ham can be used instead of bacon. May omit cheese.

Simac Family Favorites

Tomato Soup

TOMATO SAUCE:
½ cup chopped onion   1 (14½-ounce) can tomatoes

Brown onion in small amount of oil. Add tomatoes; heat and set aside.

WHITE SAUCE:
2 tablespoons butter
2 tablespoons flour

2 cups milk
Parsley (optional)

Melt butter; add flour and continue to cook. This is a roux. Add milk, then bring to a boil. Cook a few minutes. Add hot tomatoes to the White Sauce. Can add parsley, if desired. Will not curdle if you remember to add the tomatoes to the milk. Serves 4.

Note: Remember this little rhyme to prevent curdle: Red, White and Blue—add Red tomatoes to White sauce or you'll be Blue.

French Family Favorites

Fresh Cream of Tomato Soup

2 medium-size onions, thinly
 sliced
4 tablespoons butter, divided
5 (14½-ounce) cans diced
 tomatoes, or comparable
 amount of fresh, diced,
 divided
1 bay leaf
4 whole allspice
3 sprigs parsley
1 teaspoon sugar
1 teaspoon salt
¼ teaspoon black pepper
½ teaspoon baking soda
3 cups half-and-half
½ cup flour
1 cup milk

Sauté onions in 2 tablespoons butter for 3–4 minutes. Add 3 cans of the tomatoes, bay leaf, allspice, parsley, sugar, salt, and pepper. Simmer for 8–10 minutes. Put into blender or processor and purée; return to pan. Add soda and half-and-half to the purée.

In a stockpot, melt 2 tablespoons butter. Blend in flour and cook over low heat until smooth and bubbly. Stir in milk; bring to a simmer, stirring constantly. Stir in purée and the remaining 2 cans tomatoes. This gives a chunky consistency. Bring to a simmer. Serve hot.

From the High Country of Wyoming

The Vore Buffalo Jump, near Sundance, Wyoming, contains the bones of an estimated 20,000 buffalo. For over three hundred years, Plains Indian groups stampeded bison over the rim into the deep natural sink hole in order to kill them for food and clothing.

Butternut Squash and Chipotle Pepper Soup

An interesting flavor combination results through mixing the naturally sweet butternut squash and the smoky hot chipotle. Kathy, my tester, was so smitten with this soup she ate two bowlfuls! And she talked about it for days (and many recipes) afterward. The presentation is clever, too, consisting of dainty cream swirls and crunchy squash chips.

½ cup finely chopped celery
1 medium onion, finely
  chopped
1 teaspoon salt
¼ cup butter (½ stick)
1 apple (preferably Braeburn),
  peeled, cored and chopped
½ teaspoon white pepper
½ teaspoon cracked black
  pepper
1 cup dry white wine

1 cup chicken stock
2 medium butternut squash
  (2½–3 pounds)
Oil
2 chipotle peppers (canned in
  adobo sauce), chopped
Milk for thinning (optional)
Vegetable oil for frying squash
  chips
½ cup sour cream
1–3 tablespoons milk

In a large soup pot, cook celery, onion, and salt in butter over medium heat until tender. Add apple, white and black pepper, white wine, and chicken stock. Turn heat to low and cover. Meanwhile, peel squash. With a vegetable peeler, shave 15–20 squash peelings (no skin) and set aside. Chop the remaining squash and add to soup pot. Cook until very tender, 45–60 minutes. While soup is simmering, heat about 1 inch oil in a saucepan over medium heat. When oil is very hot, add shaved squash peelings and cook until crisp and lightly browned. Remove from oil, drain on paper towels, and season with salt and white pepper. Set aside.

When squash is tender, purée in batches in a blender or food processor. (Caution! Hot liquid in a blender can shoot the lid off. Hold the lid down tight.) Return soup to pan and stir in chopped chipotles. Add a splash of milk to thin, if necessary. Heat until hot enough to serve, but not boiling.

For a nice presentation, ladle 6–8 ounces soup in a decorative bowl. Mix sour cream and 1–3 tablespoons milk. Using a squeeze bottle or pastry bag with a small tip, zigzag lines across soup surface. Top with fried squash curl. Serves 8.

The Great Ranch Cookbook

★ ★

"Eat Your Carrots" Soup

Your mother will be glad that you ate your carrots, and just think how good it is for your eyes!

1 tablespoon margarine	½ teaspoon salt
1 large onion, chopped	Ground pepper to taste
2 stalks celery, chopped	Tabasco sauce to taste
2 pounds carrots, chopped	¼ cup fresh dill; reserve a few
6 cups chicken broth	sprigs for garnish

In stock pot, melt margarine. Lightly sauté onions and celery. Add carrots, broth, salt, pepper, Tabasco, and dill. Boil 40 minutes. Purée in food processor. Serve immediately. Garnish with fresh dill sprigs. Enjoy!

Soup's On at Quilting in the Country

Red Pepper Soup

4 large red peppers, quartered and seeds removed	½ cup butter
2 large leeks, trimmed of all the green	2 cans chicken broth, divided
3 medium garlic cloves	Salt and pepper to taste
	¾ cup cream

Peel quartered peppers. Slice leeks; rinse well. Crush garlic. Melt butter in pot and add peppers, leeks, and crushed garlic. Toss to coat with butter; cover and simmer about 5 minutes. Add broth, salt and pepper and cook about 30 minutes. Strain soup. Process solids in blender or processor, adding ¼ cup broth. Whisk purée into remaining stock. Stir in cream; heat.

Brisbin Community Cookbook

With nine championship courses, Flathead Valley in Glacier National Park in Montana was named one of the "50 Greatest Golf Destinations" by *Golf Digest Magazine.*

Chicken Gumbo

1/3 cup flour
2 teaspoons salt, divided
1/8 teaspoon pepper
1/8 teaspoon garlic powder
1 (3-pound) broiler-fryer, cut up
2 tablespoons salad oil
2 tablespoons butter or
  margarine
2 onions, thinly sliced
1 (4-ounce) can mushroom
  pieces, drained

1 teaspoon sugar
1 teaspoon basil
1 (28-ounce) can tomatoes
2 chicken bouillon cubes,
  crumbled
Dash of hot pepper sauce
1 (10-ounce) package frozen cut
  okra
Hot cooked rice

Combine flour, 1 teaspoon salt, pepper, and garlic powder in a plastic bag. Put chicken, 2 pieces at a time, into bag and shake until well coated; set aside. Use a Dutch oven or large skillet to heat the oil and butter or margarine over medium heat. Add chicken and brown until crispy on all sides. Remove chicken pieces to plate and set aside.

Add onion slices to drippings in skillet, along with the mushrooms, 1 teaspoon salt, sugar, and basil. Return skillet to heat and cook over medium heat for 3–5 minutes, stirring occasionally. Pour in remaining flour from bag and stir well. Stir in tomatoes, bouillon cubes, and hot pepper sauce. Return the chicken pieces to the skillet. Bring to a boil; reduce heat to low, cover, and simmer for 30 minutes, stirring occasionally. Add okra and continue cooking, covered, for 10–15 minutes. Serve over hot rice.

Yaak Cookbook

Shrimp Gumbo

4 quarts water
2 ounces (¼ cup) shrimp/crab
  boil
2½ pounds peeled and
  deveined shrimp
3 tablespoons each butter
  and bacon fat
1 cup each diced celery, onion,
  and green pepper
1 (28-ounce) can tomatoes
1 teaspoon dried thyme

1 clove garlic, minced
1 bay leaf
1 teaspoon Worcestershire
  sauce
1 tablespoon gumbo filé powder
1 teaspoon salt
½ teaspoon pepper
1 (10-ounce) package frozen
  cut okra, defrosted (optional)
¼ cup rice

Bring water to boil in a large pot. Put shrimp boil in cheese-cloth bag; add to the boiling water with the shrimp. Bring to a boil, then reduce heat and simmer 10 minutes. Turn off heat and let stand 10 minutes. Drain shrimp, reserving 2 cups stock.

Put butter and bacon fat in a Dutch oven; add celery, onion, and green pepper. Cook until tender; add 2 cups shrimp stock, tomatoes, thyme, garlic, bay leaf, Worcestershire sauce, filé powder, salt, and pepper. Simmer 45 minutes. Add shrimp, okra, and rice; simmer 30 minutes or until rice is tender. Makes 6–8 servings.

Truly Montana Cookbook

Norwegian Fish Chowder

3 pounds cod or haddock
12 whole peppercorns
1 tablespoon chopped parsley
1 bay leaf
Dill weed to taste
3–4 carrots, cut into 1-inch
  pieces
2–3 small onions, cut in half

1 small head cauliflower,
  broken into florets
1½ cups water
2½ cups milk
1 cup thin cream
Pinch of pepper
Salt to taste

In a large pan, set fish over fire with enough water to cover. Add whole peppercorns, parsley, bay leaf, and dill; let simmer until fish comes away from the bone easily. Take fish out of pot; flake in fairly large pieces. Boil down fish stock until it is reduced by half. In another pan, place cut-up carrots, onions, and cauliflower all together and cover with 1½ cups water. When cooked (but not too soft) add these vegetables (and water) to the reduced fish stock. Add heated milk and cream to this and a small pinch of pepper. Salt to taste. Add fish. Heat well. Use chopped dill for garnish. Serve with warm French bread.

Columbus Community Cookbook

Butte Clam Chowder

1 onion, chopped
¼ cup margarine or butter
3 cans cream of potato soup

3 cans minced clams and juice
1 large can clam chowder
1 quart half-and-half

Saute onion in margarine. Add soup, clams and juice, clam chowder, and half-and-half. Bake overnight in the oven at 150°.

Soup's On at Quilting in the Country

All American Clam Chowder

3 slices bacon
½ cup minced onions
1 (7½-ounce) can minced clams
  (save clam liquor)

1 cup cubed potatoes
1 can cream of celery soup
1½ cups milk
Dash of pepper

Cook bacon in frying pan until crisp. Remove and break into 1-inch pieces. Brown onion in bacon fat. Add clam liquor and potatoes. Cover and cook over low heat until potatoes are done, about 15 minutes. Blend in bacon pieces, minced clams, and other ingredients. Heat, but do not boil. Bacon may be used for garnish.

Recipe by Former First Lady Barbara Bush
First Ladies' Cookbook

Potato Bacon Chowder

8 slices bacon, cut up
1 cup chopped onion
4 cups cooked and cubed
  potatoes
1 cup water

1 can cream of chicken soup
1 cup sour cream
1¾ cups milk
½ teaspoon salt
Pepper

Fry bacon until crisp. Remove bacon and sauté onion in drippings. Remove onion and drain on paper towel. To cooked, cubed potatoes add water, soup, sour cream, milk, seasonings, and cooked onion and bacon, saving some bacon to crumble on top. Simmer, but do not boil.

The Best of Rural Montana Cookbook

Montana remained a territory for twenty-five years before it was admitted to the Union as the 41st state on November 8, 1889, by presidential proclamation of President Benjamin Harrison.

Corn Chowder

4 tablespoons butter
1½ cups finely chopped onion
4 cups peeled and diced
  potatoes
3 cups water (or just enough
  to cover potatoes)
2 (17-ounce) cans cream-style
  corn
2 (10-ounce) packages frozen
  corn kernels

1 (13-ounce) can evaporated
  milk
1 (13-ounce) can water
1 (13-ounce) can fresh milk
Salt to taste
Freshly ground pepper to taste
3 tablespoons chopped fresh
  parsley leaves

Melt the butter in a 7-quart pot. Cook the onion for 5 minutes over medium heat, stirring often. Add potatoes and 3 cups water and bring to a boil. Cook over medium to high heat for about 15 minutes, or until potatoes are tender. Add remaining ingredients, except the parsley, and bring to a boil. Lower heat and simmer for 5 minutes. Purée ½ the soup, a few cups at a time, in a blender and return to pot. Stir well. Garnish each bowl with a little parsley. Serves 16.

From the High Country of Wyoming

Chili Fresca

¼ cup oil, divided
1 pound breast meat, sliced
2 cups diced onions
8 cloves garlic, minced
1 teaspoon salt
1½ teaspoons ground cumin
1 teaspoon dried leaf oregano
1 teaspoon dried leaf marjoram
½ teaspoon chili powder
½ teaspoon red pepper flakes
¼ teaspoon cayenne pepper
2 (14½-ounce) cans whole
  peeled tomatoes
2 cups beef bouillon
2 (15-ounce) cans pinto beans
1 cup minced cucumber
2 tablespoons minced fresh
  cilantro
⅓ cup minced green onion
  (just the greens)

In a deep saucepan, heat 3 tablespoons oil over medium-high heat. Brown sliced meat in the oil, and remove from pan. Add the rest of the oil, then onions, garlic, salt, cumin, oregano, marjoram, chili powder, red pepper flakes, and cayenne, and lower the heat to medium. Sauté, stirring frequently, until the onions are soft, about 3–4 minutes. Return the meat to the onion mixture in the pot; add tomatoes, bouillon, and beans. Lower heat to a simmer; stir pot well. Then cover and let simmer 45 minutes, until meat is quite tender.

In a small bowl, combine the minced cucumber, cilantro, and green onion. Set aside, at room temperature, until ready to serve the chili. To serve, pour soup into individual bowls, top each serving with 2–3 tablespoons of the cucumber mixture, and eat immediately. Serves 2–4.

Duck & Goose Cookery

The only east-to-west mountain range in the United States is Wasatch Mountain Range located in Mountain View, Wyoming, near Fort Bridger.

Ellie's Vegetarian Chili

½ cup cracked wheat, bulgur
½ cup water
3 cups canned tomatoes (28 ounces), drained; reserve juice
3 tablespoons olive oil
3 cups chopped onion
3 garlic cloves, pressed or finely chopped
2 green bell peppers, chopped
2 tablespoons chili powder (Chugwater Chili Gourmet Blend)
1 teaspoon ground cumin
2 teaspoons salt, or to taste

2 cups corn, frozen or fresh, cooked
1½ cups cooked black beans, drained, or 1 (15-ounce) can with juice
1½ cups cooked red kidney beans, drained, or 1 (15-ounce) can with juice
1 tablespoon Tabasco or other hot sauce (optional)
Grated Cheddar or Monterey Jack cheese (optional)
Chopped fresh cilantro (optional)

Cook wheat in ½ cup water and ½ cup juice from tomatoes in saucepan. Cover and bring to boil on high heat, then lower heat and simmer gently for about 12 minutes. Do not over-cook!

In large pot, sauté in oil the onions, garlic, and green peppers until onions are translucent. Add Chugwater Chili Gourmet Blend, cumin, and salt. Chop tomatoes in can and stir into pot. Stir in corn and beans and heat on low heat. When wheat is cooked, but still chewy, add it to the pot, including liquid. Add additional water as needed. Add hot sauce, if desired. Cover and simmer for a few minutes to blend flavors. Serve plain or topped with cheese and cilantro.

Here's What's Cooking

When appointed justice of the peace for the South Pass District in Wyoming in 1870, Esther Hobart Morris became the world's first female justice of the peace.

★ ★

Drovers' Stew

2 tablespoons olive oil
4 boneless, skinless chicken
  breast halves (1 pound), cut
  into 1-inch pieces
1 cup chopped onion
½ medium green bell pepper,
  chopped
½ medium yellow bell pepper,
  chopped
1 teaspoon chopped garlic

2 (14½-ounce) cans stewed
  tomatoes
1 (15-ounce) can pinto beans,
  drained and rinsed
¾ cup picante sauce
1 tablespoon chili powder
1 tablespoon ground cumin
½ cup shredded Cheddar
  cheese
6 tablespoons sour cream

In large stockpot, heat olive oil over medium heat. Add chicken, onion, bell peppers, and garlic, and cook until chicken is no longer pink. Add tomatoes, beans, picante sauce, chili powder, and cumin. Reduce heat to low and simmer for 25 minutes or up to 2 hours. Place in individual serving bowls and top with cheese and sour cream.

From the High Country of Wyoming

Vegetable Chicken Stew

1 (3- to 4-pound) chicken
2 cups chopped onions
2 cups chopped celery
4 cloves garlic, chopped
1 tablespoon olive oil
4 cups sliced carrots
4 cups chicken broth
1 tablespoon parsley
½ teaspoon basil

3 chicken bouillon cubes
1 teaspoon Worcestershire
  sauce
¼ teaspoon thyme
Dash of pepper
1 (28-ounce) can diced or
  stewed tomatoes
½ teaspoon chili powder
1 (15-ounce) can white beans

Boil chicken in 4 cups water. Remove chicken; pour off grease and reserve broth. Remove chicken from bone and set aside. Saute onions, celery, and garlic in olive oil. In soup kettle or large saucepan, add sautéed vegetables to carrots, chicken broth, parsley, basil, bouillon cubes, Worcestershire sauce, thyme, pepper, tomatoes, chili powder, and beans. Bring to boil and simmer for 30 minutes. Add chicken and heat thoroughly.

Soup's On at Quilting in the Country

Spicy Lentil Stew

1½ cups uncooked lentils,
  rinsed
4 cups chicken broth
  (homemade, canned, or
  bouillon-based)
2 cloves garlic, finely chopped
1 cup chopped onion
1 cup large carrot pieces

1 cup chopped green pepper
  (optional)
1 (15-ounce) can diced
  tomatoes, with juice
1 medium sweet potato, peeled
  and cut into chunks
¼–½ teaspoon cayenne pepper
½ teaspoon ground cumin

Using a large pot with lid, combine lentils, chicken broth, and garlic. Bring to a boil; lower heat, cover, and simmer for 20 minutes. Turn off heat and let lentils sit for 1 hour.

In the meantime, prepare remaining ingredients. After 1 hour, reduce heat to medium. Add all remaining ingredients. Cook, uncovered, until carrots and sweet potato are tender, about 30 minutes. Makes 6 servings.

Variation: Serve over rice or other grain.

Nutrition Facts: Per 1½-cup serving: Cal 270; Cal from Fat 15; Total Fat 1.5g; Sat Fat 0g; Chol 0mg; Sod 660mg; Carb 44g; Dietary Fiber 18g; Sugars 11g; Prot 19g; Vit A 150%; Vit C 80%; Cal 8%; Iron 30%.

Cent$ible Nutrition Cookbook

Christmas Eve Beef Stew

1 (4-pound) beef brisket (or any sturdy beef cut)
Flour
3 tablespoons margarine or butter
3 tablespoons vegetable oil
3 garlic cloves, finely chopped
2 tablespoons chopped fresh parsley
2 (1-inch pieces) orange peel
1 bay leaf
2 cups warm Burgundy wine
¼ teaspoon nutmeg
4 carrots, sliced
6 ribs of celery (cut into strips)
12 small white onions
1 teaspoon each salt and pepper, or to taste
1 pound fresh mushrooms, quartered
1 (10-ounce) package frozen peas

Remove fat from brisket and cut into 2-inch cubes. Flour cubes (I throw flour and beef in paper bag and shake). Brown very well in a large heavy Dutch oven on stove in butter and oil. Add garlic, parsley, orange peel, bay leaf, wine, and nutmeg. (Add water if wine doesn't cover beef.) Bring to boil and reduce heat. Cover and simmer on low heat for 1½–2 hours, until meat is tender. Add carrots, celery, onions, salt, and pepper. Cook until meat is thoroughly tender. Add mushrooms and peas the last ½ hour. Serve over noodles or potatoes. Serves 4–6.

The Hole Thing Volume II

Old Faithful is the most recognized geyser in Yellowstone National Park, Wyoming. Old Faithful erupts 18 to 21 times a day, usually reaching its average height of 130 feet, but has gone as high as 184 feet in 15 to 20 seconds. On average, about 5,000 to 8,000 gallons of water are discharged during each eruption.

Buffalo Stew

Flavor improves if stew is kept a day in refrigerator.

6 pounds buffalo steaks, cut in 2-inch chunks	1 (12-ounce) can beer
10 tablespoons butter or margarine, divided	1 teaspoon chopped garlic
4 large onions, thinly sliced	1 tablespoon vinegar
½ cup flour	1 teaspoon sugar
1 (10½-ounce) can beef broth, undiluted	1 teaspoon thyme
	1 bay leaf
	Salt and pepper to taste

Brown buffalo on all sides in 4 tablespoons butter in a large, preferably cast-iron, casserole. It may be easier to do in 3 or 4 batches, since meat browns best in a single layer. Remove and sauté onions in 2 tablespoons butter until lightly browned. Set onions aside

Add remaining butter to the pan along with flour and mix to a paste. Add beer and broth gradually, beating with a whisk until sauce is thick and smooth. Add remaining ingredients and the meat and onions. Mix gently together. Bring to a boil. Cover and bake at 275° for 3–8 hours, until tender. Serves 6–8.

The Great Entertainer Cookbook

SALADS

PHOTO © CITY OF SHERIDAN, WYOMING CONVENTION & VISITORS BUREAU

Each July, for over 70 years, Sheridan, Wyoming, has hosted the largest single go-round PRCA (Professional Rodeo Cowboys Association) rodeo in the country. Rodeo is the official state sport of Wyoming.

Bar 94 Ranch Chicken Salad

1 head cabbage, chopped
3 or 4 cooked chicken breasts,
  boned and shredded
2 packages Ramen Chinese-style
  noodles, broken up (reserve
  flavor packet for Sauce)
4 tablespoons untoasted sesame
  seeds or hulled sunflower
  seeds
4 tablespoons chopped green
  onions
1 cup slivered or sliced almonds

Combine all ingredients; toss well. Toss with following Sauce; chill.

SAUCE:

4 tablespoons sugar
1 cup vegetable oil
6 tablespoons wine vinegar
2 teaspoons mixed salt and
  pepper
1 flavor packet from noodles

Combine and toss with salad.

Favorite Recipes of Montana

Mexicali Chicken Bean Salad

1 (16-ounce) can black beans
1 (16-ounce) can kidney beans
1 (16-ounce) can white beans
2 cups cubed, cooked chicken
1½ cups cubed Cheddar
  cheese
3 medium green peppers,
  chopped
2 cups chunky salsa, medium
½ cup chopped red onion
¼ cup chopped fresh cilantro
2 tablespoons lime juice

Rinse and drain beans. Add rest of ingredients and stir until well combined; refrigerate. Makes a great appetizer with chips or a side dish.

Recipe from The Horned Toad Bed & Breakfast, Ten Sleep, Wyoming
Tastes & Tours of Wyoming

The Bridger-Teton National Forest in Wyoming is the second largest national forest in the lower 48 states, encompassing 3.4 million acres.

More Than Chicken Salad

MARINADE:

2 tablespoons lemon juice
1 teaspoon prepared mustard
¼ cup oil
¼ teaspoon salt
¼ teaspoon pepper

¼ teaspoon tarragon
¼ teaspoon basil
¼ teaspoon thyme
¼ teaspoon marjoram

Combine ingredients in a cruet and shake.

SALAD:

2 cups cooked and diced chicken
1½ cups halved seedless green
   grapes
1 cup mayonnaise

½ cup chopped celery
½ cup slivered almonds,
   toasted
1 teaspoon lemon juice

Toss chicken with Marinade and refrigerate 2 hours. Add remaining ingredients and toss to blend. Serve on lettuce bed or with tomato slices. Serves 6.

The Great Entertainer Cookbook

Crunchy Turkey Salad

12 cups cubed, cooked turkey
   or chicken
4 cups sliced celery
3 jars watermelon pickles,
   drained and cut into
   quarters

1 medium onion, thinly sliced
3 cups mayonnaise
4 teaspoons salt
2 teaspoons curry powder
¼ teaspoon pepper
4 cups chow mein noodles

Divide turkey, celery, pickles, and onion between 2 bowls. Mix mayonnaise, salt, curry powder, and pepper. Toss half the mayonnaise mixture gently with each turkey mixture. Cover and refrigerate no longer than 12 hours. Just before serving, stir in half of noodles into each turkey mixture. Serves a bunch (18-20).

Favorite Recipes

Salmon Mousse Salad

1 envelope unflavored gelatin
1/4 cup water
1/2 cup chicken broth, boiling
2 tablespoons fresh dill, or
  1 tablespoon dried dill
1/2 cup mayonnaise
1 tablespoon lemon juice
1/2 teaspoon paprika

2 small green onions, finely
  chopped
1 teaspoon salt
2 cups finely flaked cooked
  salmon
1 cup heavy cream
Fresh parsley for garnish

Oil a 1½-quart mold (fish shape is nice). In a large bowl, sprinkle gelatin over water and let stand until softened. Add boiling chicken broth and stir until dissolved. Stir in chopped fresh dill and let cool for 10 minutes. Add mayonnaise, lemon juice, paprika, green onions, and salt. Whisk well and refrigerate 20–30 minutes, until mixture starts to thicken. Add flaked salmon; mix well and taste for seasoning.

In a separate bowl, beat heavy cream until stiff, and gently fold into the salmon mixture. Pour into the mold and refrigerate at least 2 hours (overnight is best), until firm. Serve on a large platter and surround the salmon with fresh parsley for garnish.

Salad Sampler from Quilting in the Country

Wild Rice Salad

1/2 pound raw wild rice
5½ cups stock or water
1/2 cup cashew pieces
1 cup yellow raisins
1/4 cup chopped mint

Grated rind of 1 orange
4 scallions, sliced
1/4 cup olive oil
1/3 cup orange juice
Ground black pepper

Rinse rice in cold water. Bring liquid to a boil. Add rice and simmer, covered, about 45 minutes. Put towel in a colander and pour in rice to drain. Mix everything together and let it stand for a minimum of 2 hours. Serve at room temperature.

With Lots of Love

★ ★ ★ ★ ★ ★ ★ ★ ★ ★ ★ ★ ★ ★ ★ ★ ★ ★ ★ ★

Fettuccine Heaven Salad

This recipe is fantastic at the height of tomato season!

DRESSING:
½ cup extra virgin olive oil
1 medium garlic clove, minced
2 tablespoons balsamic vinegar
1 teaspoon salt
Freshly ground pepper to taste

Shake Dressing ingredients together.

SALAD:
1 pound fettuccine, fresh if
  available
1 medium red onion, diced
1 (3½-ounce) jar capers,
  drained
1 cup pitted and sliced Greek
  olives
1 bunch basil leaves, sliced
1 bunch fresh spinach, coarsely
  chopped (leaves only)
3 pounds ripe tomatoes, diced

Cook fettuccine al dente; drain and toss with Dressing. Add onion, capers, olives, and basil. Just before serving, toss with spinach and transfer to a serving bowl lined with extra spinach leaves. Top with tomatoes and serve at room temperature.

Salad Sampler from Quilting in the Country

Pete's Potato Salad

10 medium to large potatoes	1–2 tablespoons dry dill weed
6 large eggs	Salt and pepper to taste
3–4 ripe tomatoes	Juice from the dill pickles
5–6 Polish dill pickles	(secret ingredient)
1–2 cups mayonnaise to suit	

Boil potatoes in their skins and cool. Hard-boil the eggs and cool. Take a large bowl and an hour or so, and start your labor of love. Peel the potatoes and dice into bowl. Peel the eggs and dice over top. Dice the tomatoes and Polish dill pickles over top. Now add several wooden spoonfuls of mayonnaise to the 4 ingredients; add the dill weed, salt and pepper, and the secret ingredient and mix well with wooden spoon. Use mayonnaise and pickle juice by "feel" and with discretion and taste. The potato salad has to flow like good concrete, not too thick and not too watery.

If you want a professional opinion, ask your Italian friends to be the judge on the potato salad (and hope they don't say it tastes like concrete). Allow 1 potato per person; if you have leftovers, the kids will devour the stuff before they go to bed.

Fire Hall Cookbook #2

Sweet Potato Salad

4 or 5 sweet potatoes	4 eggs, boiled, chopped
Real butter	½ cup mayonnaise
4 green onions, chopped,	½ cup Durkee's Famous
tops and all	Dressing
1½ cups finely chopped celery	½ teaspoon salt

Cook sweet potatoes with skins on. While hot, peel and mash. Add a goodly amount of real butter. Prepare onions, celery, and eggs and add to potatoes. Mix mayonnaise, Durkee's (found near mayonnaise), and salt and stir into hot mixture. Cover and refrigerate overnight.

Lewis and Clark Fare

★ ★ ★ ★ ★ ★ ★ ★ ★ ★ ★ ★ ★ ★ ★ ★ ★ ★ ★ ★

Autumn Salad

SALAD:

2 heads butter lettuce
½ red onion, diced
1 (4-ounce) package blue cheese, crumbled

1 Granny Smith apple, diced
½ cup chopped pecans or walnuts
½ cup dried cranberries

RASPBERRY VINAIGRETTE:

⅓ cup raspberry jam
¼ cup olive or canola oil
4 teaspoons rice vinegar
4 teaspoons cider vinegar, or 8 ounces raspberry vinegar

1 teaspoon coarse-grind mustard, or ½ teaspoon dry mustard

Toss all Salad ingredients. Pour blended Raspberry Vinaigrette over salad.

Salad Sampler from Quilting in the Country

Greek Feta Salad

DRESSING:

1 cup heavy mayonnaise
1 tablespoon dried oregano leaves

1 teaspoon black pepper
¾ cup Italian salad dressing

Whisk Dressing ingredients together in a small bowl; set aside.

SALAD:

1 pound medium-size pasta shells
1 cup chopped celery
½ pound Greek feta cheese, crumbled

¾ cup sliced black olives
½ cup shredded Parmesan cheese
2 ripe tomatoes

Cook pasta in plenty of water, al dente. Drain, and rinse well with cold water. Toss Dressing with pasta and remaining ingredients (except tomatoes). Chop tomatoes coarsely, and gently fold them into the salad. Serves 8.

Salad Sampler from Quilting in the Country

Japanese Cabbage Salad

SALAD:

½ cup sliced or slivered
  almonds, toasted
2 tablespoons sesame seeds,
  toasted
½ medium cabbage, shredded
12 ounces fresh bean sprouts

2 cups sliced fresh mushrooms
2 green onions, chopped
½ cup sunflower seeds
Chicken-flavored instant
  noodles, broken up
1½ cups chow mein noodles

Put almonds and sesame seeds in single layer in pan. Toast in 350° oven for about 5 minutes (watch carefully as they can get too dark in no time), until golden. Remove from oven. Set aside.

Put shredded cabbage and bean sprouts into large bowl. Add mushrooms, onions, and sunflower seeds. Add toasted almonds and sesame seeds. Combine broken noodles and chow mein noodles in small bowl. Set aside.

DRESSING:

1 package seasoning from
  instant noodles
½ cup cooking oil
2–4 tablespoons soy sauce

3 tablespoons vinegar
1 tablespoon granulated sugar
1 tablespoon salt
½ tablespoon pepper

Empty seasoning packet from box of noodles into small bowl. Add cooking oil, lesser amount of soy sauce, vinegar, and sugar. Add more soy sauce to taste. (It will depend on quantity of cabbage.) You will probably need full amount. Stir in salt and pepper. Put into container with cover. Can be made ahead. Before serving, shake Dressing. Pour over cabbage mixture. Toss. Sprinkle dry noodles over top. Serves 10–12

Recipe by Mrs. Stan Stephens, wife of former Governor of Montana
First Ladies' Cookbook

In 1924, Mrs. Nellie Tayloe Ross was the first elected woman governor (Wyoming) to take office in the United States. In 1933, she became the first female director of the U.S. Mint.

Asparagus Salad

Salad might be a misnomer here, but because the asparagus spears are drizzled with a luscious, tangy-sweet vinaigrette, I've classified this as a salad. It could be an appetizer or a side dish, too.

VINAIGRETTE:

½ cup balsamic vinegar
⅓ cup honey
¼ cup dried cranberries
¼ cup chopped yellow onion

½ teaspoon kosher salt
½ teaspoon white pepper
½ cup olive oil

Place the first 7 ingredients in a blender and blend for 10 seconds. With the blender running, slowly pour in the olive oil. (The cranberries will still be a little chunky and that is okay.) Set aside.

ASPARAGUS:

1 bunch (about 30 spears)
   asparagus
3 Roma tomatoes, cut into thin
   strips, seeds removed

8 green leaf or other lettuce
   leaves (optional garnish)

Bring a large pot of salted water to boil. Prepare a large bowl of ice water. Trim the asparagus. (I take a spear and bend it in half. Where it snaps is where the tender part ends and the tough part begins. Discard the tough ends or save for a vegetable stock.) When the water comes to a boil, drop the trimmed asparagus in the water and boil for 1–2 minutes, depending upon the thickness of the asparagus. Immediately remove the asparagus from the boiling water and plunge into the ice water to stop the cooking process.

When the asparagus is cool (usually takes about 3 or 4 minutes), drain and pat dry. Toss the asparagus and tomato strips with about ¼ cup or more of the Vinaigrette. Line 4 plates with lettuce leaves (optional) and divide the asparagus among the 4 plates. Makes 4 servings.

The Cool Mountain Cookbook

Raspberry Vinaigrette

The color alone is enough to make you swoon. Try this on a number of salads . . . I promise you'll never want bottled dressing again.

1/4 cup fresh or frozen raspberries
1 tablespoon chopped red onion
1/4 teaspoon finely chopped garlic
1/4 teaspoon pink peppercorns (optional)

1/4 teaspoon minced fresh thyme leaves
2 tablespoons raspberry vinegar
2 tablespoons rice wine vinegar
2 tablespoons red wine vinegar
1/2 cup olive oil
1/4 cup honey

Blend raspberries, red onion, garlic, pink peppercorns (optional), thyme and all 3 vinegars in a blender. With the blender on medium speed, slowly drizzle in olive oil, then honey, blending until creamy. Strain through a small-holed sieve to trap raspberry seeds. Chill. Makes 1 cup.

The Cool Mountain Cookbook

Watercress Salad

Like a bear coming out of hibernation and making its first meal on wild greens, I start my eating year with a watercress salad. It's my spring tonic.

2 cups watercress (tips and leaves only)
1 cup celery, cut in short strips

1 avocado, peeled and sliced
4 tablespoons French Dressing

Wash watercress. (If using wild greens, soak for one hour in a water purifying solution of 8 drops household bleach to 1 gallon water.) Rinse well. Dry on a paper towel. Toss watercress, celery, and avocado with French Dressing. Serve on lettuce leaves.

FRENCH DRESSING:
1/4 cup vinegar
3/4 cup oil
1/4 teaspoon salt
1/4 teaspoon black pepper

1/4 teaspoon paprika
1/4 teaspoon dry mustard
1/4 teaspoon dried oregano

Place all ingredients in a jar and shake well. Store, covered, in a cool place. Makes one cup.

The Kim Williams Cookbook and Commentary

Spinach-Avocado-Orange Toss

DRESSING:

½ teaspoon grated orange peel
¼ cup orange juice
½ cup oil
2 tablespoons wine vinegar

¼ teaspoon salt
2 tablespoons sugar
1 tablespoon lemon juice

Combine ingredients in a jar and shake until thoroughly blended. Chill.

SALAD:

6 cups washed and torn fresh
  spinach
1 avocado, peeled and sliced
1 small cucumber, thinly sliced

2 tablespoons sliced green
  onions
1 (11-ounce) can mandarin
  oranges, drained

Mix Salad ingredients in bowl and chill. To serve, pour Dressing over Salad and toss lightly.

Cooking with the Ladies

Spinach Salad with Strawberries and Mandarin Oranges

Spinach, torn bite size
Strawberries, sliced

1 (11-ounce) can mandarin
  oranges, drained

Combine salad greens (lettuce may also be added), strawberries, and oranges in a large bowl.

DRESSING:

¼ cup oil
3 tablespoons tarragon vinegar
¼ cup sugar

½ teaspoon dry mustard
⅛ teaspoon salt
Pepper to taste

Mix all ingredients. Shake well and pour over salad just before serving.

Lewis and Clark Fare

Apple Salad

8 apples	½ cup raisins
2 bananas	½ cup peanuts
½ cup diced celery	½ cup chopped walnuts

Dice apple; do not peel. Place in weak salt water to prevent from turning dark while preparing other ingredients. Cut up bananas; drain and rinse apples. Combine all salad ingredients.

DRESSING:

| ¼ cup peanut butter | ¼–½ cup sugar |
| ⅛–¼ cup milk | ½ cup salad dressing |

Combine Dressing ingredients and blend well. Stir gently into fruit mixture.

Wolf Point, Montana 75th Jubilee Cookbook

Pineapple-Banana Salad

2 packages lemon Jell-O	½ cup sugar
4 cups boiling water	2 tablespoons flour
8 marshmallows, diced	2 whole eggs, beaten lightly
1 can crushed pineapple,	1 cup pineapple juice
drained	2 tablespoons butter
reserve juice	1 cup whipped cream
2 bananas, diced	½ cup crushed nuts
1 can of cherries, drained	

Dissolve Jell-O in water; while still hot, add diced marshmallows. Stir until completely dissolved. Cool. Add crushed pineapple, diced bananas, and cherries. Let set until solid.

In saucepan add sugar, flour, eggs, pineapple juice, and butter; cook and stir. When cool, fold in whipped cream. Spread on top of congealed salad and sprinkle with crushed nuts.

First Ladies' Cookbook

★ ★ ★ ★ ★ ★ ★ ★ ★ ★ ★ ★ ★ ★ ★ ★ ★ ★ ★ ★

Mandarin Orange Green Salad

1 tablespoon plus 1 teaspoon sugar

¼ cup sliced almonds

Melt sugar; add almonds when the sugar is just about melted. Do not allow the sugar to caramelize. Toss and set aside.

DRESSING:

¼ cup oil
2 tablespoons sugar
2 tablespoons vinegar
1 tablespoon parsley

½ teaspoon salt
½ teaspoon pepper
Dash of red pepper sauce

Combine all ingredients.

SALAD:

¼ head lettuce, chopped
¼ bunch romaine lettuce, chopped
2 sticks celery, chopped

2 green onions, chopped
1 (11-ounce) can mandarin oranges

Toss Salad ingredients; add coated almonds. Coat with Dressing and toss again just before serving.

Story, Wyoming's Centennial Community Cookbook

Grand Marnier Fresh Fruit Cup

¼ cup Grand Marnier liqueur
¼ cup sugar
2 pints blueberries
½ pound Bing cherries, halved and pitted

4 pounds peaches, peeled and sliced
1 pint fresh raspberries
Yogurt (optional)

Mix Grand Marnier and sugar, stirring to dissolve sugar. Prepare fruits and gently mix together. Add liqueur mixture to fruit. Refrigerate until ready to serve. Serve in individual cups with yogurt spooned over top, if desired.

Salad Sampler from Quilting in the Country

Make Ahead Fruit Salad

1 (15-ounce) can pineapple
  chunks
1 (15-ounce) can fruit cocktail
1 (11-ounce) can mandarin
  oranges
½ pound marshmallows

¼ cup fresh lemon juice
1 cup flaked coconut
½ cup chopped nuts (almonds,
  walnuts, pecans)
1 cup fresh or frozen berries
  (strawberries or raspberries)

Drain and reserve juice from pineapple, fruit cocktail, and mandarin oranges. Set juice aside. Combine fruits in bowl.

Melt marshmallows over gently boiling water until completely melted. Add 1 cup of fruit juice and ¼ cup lemon juice to marshmallows. Combine coconut, nuts, and berries, and add to fruit mixture. Fold marshmallow dressing into the combined mixture. Chill covered. May be chilled several hours or overnight. Serves 6–8.

Truly Montana Cookbook

Fresh Fruit Cups

½ cup sugar
1½ cups water
1 (6-ounce) can frozen
  lemonade
1 (6-ounce) can frozen orange
  juice
1 (20-ounce) can crushed
  pineapple, undrained

1 small box frozen strawberries,
  thawed
1 small jar cherries,
  undrained
3 large bananas, cubed small
Seedless grapes, to taste

Dissolve sugar in water, then add frozen lemonade, frozen orange juice, and crushed pineapple (with juice); mix well. Add strawberries, cherries, bananas, and grapes; again mix well. Put fruit mixture in cups and freeze. Approximately 30–45 minutes before serving, remove cups from freezer, let melt, and serve icy. The cups will be the consistency of slush.

Salad Sampler from Quilting in the Country

Six "S" Salad

Splendid, Summertime, Sports Season, Sunflower Seed salad.

2 (11-ounce) cans mandarin oranges, well drained
½–1 head bibb lettuce, or 1 head red leaf or combination
1 bunch or more spinach
Chinese pea pods, blanched (optional)
Broccoli florets, fresh, cut small
½ cup chopped fresh parsley
1 large red onion, or 1 bunch green onions, sliced thin
1 (7½-ounce) jar sunflower nut meats, dry-roasted
1 (6- to 8-ounce) carton frozen orange juice concentrate
½ cup+ mayonnaise
Seasoned cooked chicken strips, heated

Place mandarin oranges in bottom of large salad bowl; add torn lettuce, spinach, pea pods, broccoli, parsley, onions, and sunflower nuts. Cover. Chill.

Whisk orange juice concentrate and mayonnaise until smooth; adjust mayonnaise to keep tart taste. Pour dressing to coat, but not drench salad, just before serving. Toss. Serve remaining dressing on the side. Serve topped with 3–4 hot seasoned chicken strips for each serving.

Optional additions: May add one or more or substitute, hard-cooked eggs, sprouts/bamboo shoots, cauliflower florets, olives/water chestnuts, cherry tomatoes/radishes, jicama, sliced thin; bacon, shrimp, nuts.

Variation for Dressing: Pineapple chunks and pineapple juice with mayonnaise and orange juice concentrate.

Recipe submitted by Bob Wilson, President/General Manager,
Billings Mustangs
Montana Celebrity Cookbook

Famous sports figures from Montana: Evel Knievel, motorcycle daredevil; Brent Musberger, TV sports announcer; Scott Davis, figure skater; Eric Bergoust, aerial ski jumper with 13 World Cup victories, two U.S. Championships, the Olympic Gold medal from Nagano in 1998, and three of the highest scores ever awarded in aerial ski jumping.

Apricot Salad

2 (3-ounce) packages orange
  gelatin
2 cups boiling water
1 (20-ounce) can apricots
1 (20-ounce) can crushed
  pineapple

½ cup apricot juice
½ cup pineapple juice
10 large marshmallows, cut up

In medium bowl, dissolve gelatin in boiling water. Set aside. Drain juice from apricots and pineapple into 2-cup pitcher. Pour apricots into a large bowl. Mash with a potato masher. Stir in pineapple. Set fruits aside.

In large saucepan, heat half the juice to boiling (reserve remaining half for Topping). Stir in marshmallows until melted. Stir in gelatin and fruits. Pour into 9x13-inch pan. Chill until set.

TOPPING:
½ cup pineapple juice, from
  above
½ cup apricot juice, from above
½ cup sugar
2 heaping tablespoons flour

1 egg
1 tablespoon margarine
1 (12-ounce) carton whipped
  topping
½ cup grated Cheddar cheese

In medium saucepan, mix remaining juices, sugar, flour, egg, and margarine. Beat with a wire whip. Stir and cook until thick. Cool well. Fold in whipped topping. Spread over gelatin mixture in pan. Sprinkle grated cheese over top. Chill. Yields 20–24 servings.

Irene's Country Cooking

Lemon Jell-O Salad

1 (6-ounce) package lemon
  Jell-O
3 cups boiling water
1½ cups miniature
  marshmallows

1 cup crushed pineapple,
  drained (save juice)
4 bananas, sliced

Dissolve Jell-O in boiling water. Add marshmallows and let melt. Allow to cool, but not set. Add crushed pineapple and bananas. Let this set before adding Topping.

TOPPING:
Reserved pineapple juice
1½ cups sugar
2 tablespoons flour
2 tablespoons butter

2 eggs, beaten
1 cup Cool Whip
Sliced almonds

Cook pineapple juice, sugar, flour, butter, and eggs till thick. Let cool to room temperature; add Cool Whip. Spread on Jell-O; garnish with almonds.

Heavenly Recipes and Burnt Offerings

Huckleberry Salad

1 (3-ounce) package raspberry
  Jell-O
1½ cups water
1 cup frozen or fresh
  huckleberries

1 small can pineapple and
  juice, crushed
1 cup Cool Whip or whipped
  cream
Chopped nuts (optional)

Dissolve Jell-O in hot water; add berries, pineapple and juice. Chill until partially set; fold in whipped cream and nuts. Chill until ready to serve.

Fire Hall Cookbook

★ ★

Overnight Layered Fruit Salad

2 cups shredded lettuce
2 Golden Delicious apples
2 navel oranges
2 cups seedless grapes

⅓ cup mayonnaise
⅓ cup sour cream
1 cup shredded mild Cheddar
    cheese

Spread lettuce on bottom of a 2-quart dish. Core, quarter and thinly slice apples; spread over lettuce. Peel and section oranges; squeeze teaspoon or so of orange juice over apples, and arrange orange sections over top of apples. Layer grapes next. Combine mayonnaise and sour cream; spread over grapes. Sprinkle cheese over all of it. Cover tightly with plastic wrap and refrigerate overnight.

Fire Hall Cookbook #2

Try and Guess Salad

3 (3-ounce) packages raspberry
    gelatin
1¼ cups boiling water

3 (1-pound) cans stewed
    tomatoes
6 drops Tabasco sauce

Dissolve gelatin in boiling water. Stir in stewed tomatoes, breaking them up with a spoon. Add Tabasco sauce. Mix well and pour into slightly oiled 3-quart ring mold and chill until firm. Unmold on salad greens and fill center with Sour Cream Dressing.

SOUR CREAM DRESSING:
1 pint sour cream
1 tablespoon creamy
    horseradish

¼ teaspoon salt
½ teaspoon sugar

Combine ingredients and serve over congealed salad. Serves 12.

The Fine Art of Cooking

VEGETABLES

Makoshika (Ma-ko-shi-ka), meaning "bad land," is the largest State Park in Montana. Wind and water erosion constantly change the landscape, creating a wide range of odd-shaped sandstone knobs and caprocks. Fossils of ten different species have been found there.

Great Potatoes

2–3 pounds potatoes, washed
1 onion, chopped
½ cup butter or margarine
Seasoned salt to taste
1 pint sour cream

1 package ranch-style dressing
mix
½ pound grated Cheddar
cheese

Dice unpeeled potatoes into a 2-quart covered casserole. Add onion. Slice butter and place over potato-onion mixture, then sprinkle generously with seasoned salt. Cover and bake for 1 hour at 350°. Combine dressing mix and sour cream. Spread over hot potatoes. Top with grated cheese. Return to oven for a few minutes until heated through and cheese melts.

Favorite Recipes

Flathead Lake Monster Potatoes

2 pounds frozen hashbrown
potatoes
1 can cream of mushroom soup
2 cups grated Cheddar cheese
2 cups sour cream

½ cup chopped onion
½ stick butter, melted
1 cup cooked elk sausage or
summer sausage

Combine hashbrowns, soup, cheese, sour cream, onion, melted butter, and elk meat. Turn into greased 9x13-inch pan.

TOPPING:
2 cups crushed cornflakes   ¼ cup butter, melted

Stir Topping ingredients together. Sprinkle over potato mixture. Bake at 350° for 30 minutes. (May add ½ cup green or red bell pepper for added zest.) Makes 8 side dishes.

Recipe from Outlook Inn B&B, Somers, Montana
A Taste of Montana

Montana's Flathead Lake is one of the 300 largest natural lakes in the world, and is the largest natural freshwater lake in the western United States. It covers an area of 191.5 square miles.

★ ★

Powderhorn Potatoes

Wonderful served with wild game or beef.

8 large potatoes	2 cups sour cream
1 cup grated sharp Cheddar cheese	1 bunch green onions, chopped
	Salt and pepper to taste
½ cup milk	2 tablespoons poppy seeds

Boil potatoes; drain, cool, and grate. Mix remaining ingredients, except seeds, and add to potatoes. Place in an oiled casserole. Sprinkle with poppy seeds to give the "gunpowder" effect. Bake, covered, at 350° for 30 minutes, then brown lightly under broiler. Serves 8–10.

The Great Entertainer Cookbook

Sweet Potato Delightful

1 can apple pie filling	1 cup whole cranberry sauce
2 large or about 4 medium sweet potatoes, cooked, sliced	2 tablespoons orange marmalade
	2 tablespoons apricot preserves

In a lightly buttered 8-inch baking dish or casserole, layer apple pie filling, then sliced sweet potatoes. Mix cranberry sauce with marmalade and preserves. Spoon over potatoes. Bake at 350° for 20–25 minutes. Serves 4.

Ranch Recipe Roundup IV

★ ★

Chantilly Potatoes

4 medium potatoes	Salt
½ cup chopped onion	Pepper
½ cup heavy cream	Chopped parsley
3 tablespoons butter	½ cup grated sharp cheese

Peel and cut potatoes into strips as for French fries. Place in the center of a large piece of heavy-duty foil. Add onions and mix. Pour over the cream, dot with butter, and sprinkle with seasonings, parsley, and cheese. Bring foil up over potatoes and seal all the edges together. Place in shallow pan and bake in a hot 425° oven for 40 minutes. Can add ham, if you wish. Serves 4.

From the High Country of Wyoming

Potato Croquettes

1 pint mashed potatoes	1 tablespoon chopped parsley
1 tablespoon butter	¼ tablespoon onion juice
1 tablespoon salt	1 egg, separated
¼ tablespoon pepper	Bread crumbs

Boil and mash potatoes. Add butter and seasonings. When cool enough to handle, add egg yolk. Roll into a ball and then into a cylinder. Roll in bread crumbs, then in white of egg, slightly beaten. Then roll in bread crumbs again. Fry in deep fat. Drain on brown paper.

The Pure Food Club of Jackson Hole

The Wyoming State Flag was adopted on January 31, 1917. The Great Seal of Wyoming is the heart of the flag. The bison is branded with the state seal representing the custom of branding. The colors of the State Flag are the same as those of the National Flag. The red border represents the Indian, and also the blood of the pioneers who gave their lives reclaiming the soil. White is the emblem of purity and uprightness over Wyoming. Blue, the color of the sky and mountains, is symbolic of fidelity, justice and virility.

Oven-Roasted Rosemary Potatoes

¼ cup olive oil, divided
2 tablespoons minced garlic
1 teaspoon dried rosemary
½ teaspoon salt

½ teaspoon pepper
6 large russet potatoes, cubed
  to ½ inch

Preheat oven to 425°. Line large baking sheet with aluminum foil and brush with 1 teaspoon olive oil. Mix all ingredients except potatoes. Add potatoes and toss. Evenly distribute potatoes on baking sheet. Roast 30 minutes on one side, then turn over and roast 30 minutes until crisp and brown on outside and soft inside.

Recipe from Skylodge Bed & Breakfast, White Sulphur Springs, Montana
Montana Bed & Breakfast Guide & Cookbook

Russian Scalloped Potatoes

2 small onions, chopped
4 tablespoons butter or
  margarine, divided
1 tablespoon flour
½ cup consommé
1 teaspoon Worcestershire
  sauce

½ cup sour cream
2 drops Tabasco sauce
1 (16-ounce) can white potatoes
2 cups ham, cut into thin strips
2 small dill pickles
Grated Parmesan cheese

Simmer onions in ½ the butter until soft, but not brown. Add flour; cook 5 minutes, then add consommé, Worcestershire sauce, sour cream, and Tabasco sauce. Continue cooking 10 minutes longer over low heat. Slice potatoes thin and sauté in remaining butter about 5 minutes.

Trim fat from ham and cut ham into strips about 1x½ inch. Peel the pickles and slice very thin. Mix potatoes, ham and pickles with onion mixture carefully, using a fork. Place in a greased 9x9-inch baking dish. Sprinkle with Parmesan cheese and bake at 350° for about 20–30 minutes. Good with cucumber salad and pumpernickle bread.

Truly Montana Cookbook

Caramelized Onion Tarts with Gorgonzola Sauce

ONION FILLING:

6 Vidalia or other sweet yellow onions
½ cup butter (1 stick)

2 tablespoons fresh thyme
Salt and pepper

Thinly slice the onions. In a large sauté pan, melt the butter and cook the onions until caramelized (deep golden brown color), about 25–35 minutes. Stir in fresh thyme and season with salt and pepper.

TART SHELLS:

1 sheet puff pastry, or 6 puff pastry circles

½ cup water
1 egg

I bought the package of puff pastry circles. There were 6 to a box and they were 3 inches in diameter, which is what you need for this recipe. If you buy the sheet, cut out 6 circles with a 3-inch cookie cutter. Mix water and egg together to make a wash. Brush circles with the egg wash and place on a lightly greased sheet pan. Bake until golden brown, about 20–25 minutes. Cool and then hollow a 2-inch circle out of the center. Set aside.

GORGONZOLA SAUCE:

1½ cups heavy cream
1 cup crumbled Gorgonzola cheese (blue cheese)

1 tablespoon chopped fresh thyme
Salt and pepper

Bring cream to a boil. Reduce heat and add cheese. Add thyme and season with salt and pepper. Cook another 2–4 minutes, until the consistency is thick enough to coat the back of a spoon.

Putting it all together: Place a puff pastry shell on a plate. Place about ¼ cup of caramelized onions on the inside and spread a few around the outside of the shell. Drizzle 2–3 tablespoons of sauce all over plate making sure a good portion is on the tart shell. Garnish with a sprig of fresh thyme. Makes 6 servings.

Recipe from Crescent H Ranch, Wilson, Wyoming
The Great Ranch Cookbook

Cherokee Wild Onions

Amid the underbrush on the creek banks in eastern Oklahoma grow the Cherokee wild onions. Easy to pick in the soft loam, they resemble the scallion, but are smaller. You can come across them in Wyoming, north of Cody off the Belfry Highway. Here in the great Northwest, some people refer to them as sheep onions.

Wild onion bundles (about 12 per serving)
Oil or shortening (about 2 tablespoons per serving)

Eggs (1 per serving)
Tabasco to taste (optional)

Clean and dice the onions. Heat approximately 2 tablespoons oil in a skillet. Add the diced onion and stir approximately 1 minute. Add 1 egg and continue stirring until well scrambled. Turn onto a plate and add a little Tabasco, if desired.

Recipes to Make You Purr

Honeyed Onions

6 medium onions
2 tablespoons chili sauce
1/2 teaspoon salt
2 tablespoons butter or margarine, melted

2 tablespoons honey
1/8 teaspoon pepper
1 teaspoon paprika

Peel onions and cut in half crosswise. Place them in 8x12x2-inch baking dish, cut-side-up. In small bowl, stir together other ingredients and brush over onion halves. Bake covered for an hour at 350°, or until fork-tender.

Wolf Point, Montana 75th Jubilee Cookbook

Montana has more than one nickname. Besides being called "Big Sky Country," it is also known as "Land of Shining Mountains," "Mountain State," and "Bonanza State."

Danish Tomato Moons

4 medium-size firm ripe
  tomatoes
1 teaspoon sugar
1/2 teaspoon basil
1 cup soft bread crumbs

2 tablespoons melted butter
1/4 cup crumbled Roquefort
  cheese
1/4 cup chopped, stuffed green
  olives

Halve tomatoes crosswise. Sprinkle with sugar and basil. Pierce each with a fork and let sugar melt in. Place on rack in broiler pan. Broil 4–6 inches from heat for 3 minutes or just until bubbly.

Toss bread crumbs with melted butter in a small bowl; stir in Roquefort and olives. Spoon over hot tomatoes. Broil 2 minutes longer, or until topping is toasty brown. Serves 4 as a side dish or 8 as a garnish.

The Fine Art of Cooking

Beefy Cowboy Beans

1 1/2 pounds ground beef
1 red or green bell pepper,
  cut into 1/2-inch pieces
1 medium onion, chopped
1/2 teaspoon salt
1/8 teaspoon pepper
1 (15 1/2-ounce) can Great
  Northern beans, rinsed,
  drained

1 (16-ounce) can baked beans
1/4 cup ketchup
1/4 cup prepared steak sauce
1 tablespoon packed brown
  sugar
2 teaspoons Worcestershire
  sauce

Brown ground beef with bell pepper and onion in large non-stick skillet over medium heat 8–10 minutes or until beef is not pink, breaking beef up into 1-inch crumbles. Pour off drippings; season with salt and pepper. Stir in remaining ingredients; bring to a boil. Reduce heat; cover and simmer 10 minutes, stirring occasionally. Makes 4 servings.

Ranch Recipe Roundup IV

Firehole Beans

Firehole Beans was given its name by cowboys up in the northern range when the cook prepared the dark ones more or less in the Boston-baked manner. "Firehole" in this case was not related to pit roasting, although this method was sometimes used, but was a corruption of frijoles, the name for beans in Spanish.

1 quart black beans	⅔ cup blackstrap molasses
1 rounded tablespoon salt	1 teaspoon dry mustard
3 quarts water	1 can tomatoes
½ pound salt pork	

Using a galvanized pail, soak the beans overnight. Pour off the top water and with it any floaters, twigs, etc. Swirl the beans for a time. This will allow any rocks to go to the bottom just like nuggets in a miner's pan. Lift the beans using the fingers of the two hands as a strainer. Transfer to a heavy iron pot, or Dutch oven, equipped with a well-fitting lid. Add salt and cold water. Bring slowly to a boil and keep boiling for 3 hours, adding water if the level drops beyond what appears to be a safe point. Slice the salt pork into 1-inch-wide strips and cut crosswise, forming squares of fat attached to rind. Add the pork, molasses, mustard, and tomatoes. Cover and bake at 350° about 2 hours, checking water level periodically.

Cow Country Cookbook

Garlicky Green Beans with Mushrooms

1 pound fresh green beans
1 tablespoon margarine
1 cup quartered fresh
  mushrooms

2 cloves garlic, minced
1/4 tablespoon onion powder
1/4 tablespoon salt
1/8 teaspoon pepper

Wash beans, trim ends, and remove strings. Arrange in a vegetable steamer, and place over boiling water. Cover and steam 5 minutes. Drain and plunge into cold water; drain again. Melt margarine in a nonstick skillet coated with cooking spray. Add mushrooms and garlic; sauté 3 minutes or until mushrooms are tender. Add beans, onion powder, salt, and pepper. Stir well. Cook 3 minutes or until thoroughly heated.

Rare Collection Recipes

Ranch Beans

1 can pork and beans
1 can hot chili beans
1 can dark kidney beans
1 cup catsup
1 cup brown sugar

1 large onion, chopped
1 teaspoon mustard
2 pounds ground chuck,
  browned and drained

Mix all ingredients and cook in crockpot on LOW for 3–4 hours, or bake uncovered in oven at 400° for 1 hour.

Horse Prairie Favorites

A phenomena much like a gold rush occurred in central Wyoming in the 1930s and 1940s as the search for Wyoming jade became intense. Some 7,000 to 8,000 pounds of jade were collected during the summer of 1945 alone.

François Ratatouille

Excellent hot or cold, as a main dish or to accompany other main dishes such as leg of lamb. May also be used as a filling for omelets or crêpes.

2 medium onions, thinly sliced
6 tablespoons extra virgin
  olive oil, divided
3 garlic cloves, finely minced
2 green peppers, thinly sliced
2 or 3 zucchini, diced into
  ¾-inch squares
1 eggplant, diced into ¾-inch
  squares

4 firm, ripe tomatoes, peeled
  and chopped (or canned
  Italian plum tomatoes)
1 bouquet garni*
6 tablespoons
Salt and freshly ground pepper
  to taste

Sauté onion in 2 tablespoons oil until translucent. Add garlic; cook briefly. Remove onion and garlic to large bowl. Sauté green pepper in 1 tablespoon oil and remove to bowl. Sauté zucchini in 1 tablespoon oil and remove to bowl. Sauté eggplant in 2 tablespoons oil until lightly browned. Remove. Add tomatoes and juice along with the bouquet garni and bring to a boil. If the sauté pan is large enough, add the other vegetables and continue to cook, covered, over low heat at a simmer for 15–30 minutes. Do not overcook.

Bouquet garni: 1 bay leaf, 4–6 sprigs fresh thyme or 1 teaspoon dried, 4–6 sprigs parsley or a bunch of parsley stems, all tied together in a double thickness of cheesecloth.

Souvenirs

★ ★

Scalloped Spinach

2 (10-ounce) boxes frozen
  spinach
¾ cup milk
¾ cup shredded cheese,
  divided

3 eggs, beaten
3 tablespoons chopped onion
½ teaspoon salt and pepper
1 cup soft bread crumbs
1 tablespoon butter, melted

Cook spinach; drain well. Mix with milk, ½ cup cheese, eggs, onion, salt and pepper. Turn into greased 8x8-inch baking pan. Bake at 350° for 25 minutes. Combine crumbs and butter; sprinkle over spinach, then sprinkle with remaining cheese. Bake 10–15 minutes longer. Serves 6.

Yaak Cookbook

Spinach Casserole

2 (10-ounce) packages frozen
  chopped spinach
1 (16-ounce) carton cottage
  cheese
2½ cups grated sharp cheese
3 eggs, beaten

3 tablespoons flour
1 stick margarine, melted
¼ teaspoon garlic salt
¼ teaspoon pepper
¼ teaspoon onion salt

Defrost spinach; squeeze out water. Mix spinach with remaining ingredients and place in greased 9x13-inch pan. Bake uncovered for 1 hour at 325°. Can be made in advance and refrigerated prior to baking.

Cooking with the Ladies

Beartooth Highway, a National Forest Scenic Byway in Montana, has been described by the late CBS correspondent Charles Kuralt as "the most beautiful road in America." From its beginning at the border of the Custer National Forest to its terminus near the northeast entrance to Yellowstone National Park, this 69-mile stretch of paradise will take you to the top of the world at 12,000 feet, and through the Custer, Shoshone, and Gallatin National Forests. Glaciers are found on the north flank of nearly every mountain peak over 11,500 feet in these mountains.

Scalloped Corn

1 can cream-style corn
2 cans whole-kernel corn,
   drained
½ cup diced celery
½ large onion, diced
1 cup grated Cheddar cheese
2 eggs, slightly beaten

2 tablespoons melted butter
¼ teaspoon paprika
1½ cups milk
1 teaspoon salt (optional)
¼ box (1 column) saltine
   crackers, crushed

Mix all ingredients thoroughly. Pour into greased 4-quart casserole. Bake at 325° for 1 hour.

Cooking with the Ladies

Uncle Bill's Corn Pudding

2 cups cream-style corn
2 eggs, very well beaten
2 tablespoons sugar
1 tablespoon flour
1 cup whole milk

2 tablespoons melted butter
¼ teaspoon garlic salt
Freshly gound pepper to taste
Buttered bread crumbs

Preheat oven to 350°. Prepare 1-quart casserole with non-stick spray. Combine all ingredients, except bread crumbs; pour into casserole dish. Top with buttered bread crumbs. Bake 30–45 minutes. Makes 4 servings.

What's This Green Stuff, Flo?

Zucchini Relish

10 cups peeled, chopped
  zucchini
4 cups chopped onions

1 red pepper, chopped
1 green pepper, chopped
5 tablespoons salt

Peel and remove seeds from zucchini. Grind all vegetables in a blender. Add salt. Let sit 8 hours. Wash and drain to remove salt.

BRINE:

2¼ cups vinegar
4½ cups sugar
4 tablespoons celery seed

½ teaspoon black pepper
1 teaspoon turmeric
1 teaspoon dry mustard

Combine vinegar, sugar, celery seed, black pepper, turmeric, and dry mustard. Add drained vegetables to pickling brine. Simmer over low heat for 30 minutes. Pack in hot jars and seal. Yields 5 pints.

Horse Prairie Favorites

Cody Carrots

2½–3 pounds carrots, cut in
  strips
1½ cups chicken broth
1 teaspoon minced onion
2 tablespoons butter
1–2 tablespoons horseradish

½ cup mayonnaise
1 cup crushed saltine crackers
3 tablespoons butter
Pepper
Parsley

Steam carrots in broth until barely tender. Remove carrots and transfer to 9x13-inch baking dish. To broth, add onion, butter, horseradish, and mayonnaise. Blend with whisk until smooth; pour over carrots. Sprinkle crackers over carrots, dot with butter, and sprinkle with pepper and parsley. Bake at 350° for 20 minutes. Serves 6–8.

The Great Entertainer Cookbook

PASTA, RICE, ETC.

PHOTO © JOHN REDDY PHOTOGRAPHY, INC.

The Mammoth Terraces, in Yellowstone National Park in Wyoming, are constantly changing in shape and color. The changes occur when active springs in the Terraces go dry and resume activity later, causing alterations in thermal activity.

Oniony Oven Alfredo

1 (12-ounce) package fettuccini
1 stick butter or margarine
2 cups cottage cheese
2 cups sour cream
1 medium to large onion, chopped
6 good dashes Tabasco
1 teaspoon salt
1 teaspoon garlic salt
1/2 heaping cup grated fresh Parmesan cheese

Cook noodles in boiling salted water; slightly undercook. Drain. Toss noodles in butter until it melts. Add remaining ingredients. Stir gently until well combined. Recipe can be frozen or refrigerated overnight. Also can be halved. When ready to serve, bake in 350° oven for 45 minutes.

The Best of Rural Montana Cookbook

Packbox Pass
Chili Pepper Penne

1 (20-ounce) package penne pasta
1/4 cup extra light olive oil
2 cups thinly sliced, cooked, boneless chicken
1 cup thinly sliced yellow bell pepper
1 cup thinly sliced leeks
1 tablespoon crushed garlic
4 tablespoons chopped fresh cilantro
1 teaspoon chopped fresh oregano
1 teaspoon ground pepper
1 teaspoon chopped parsley
1 cup chicken broth
1/2 cup sour cream
1/2 cup grated Romano cheese

Cook penne pasta according to directions on package; drain and set aside. In large saucepan, heat olive oil. Add cooked chicken, yellow peppers, leeks, garlic, cilantro, oregano, pepper, and parsley. Sauté for 10 minutes. Add chicken broth and sour cream, and simmer 4 minutes. Mix with penne pasta and sprinkle Romano cheese on top when ready to serve. Makes 4 servings.

Bitterroot Favorites & Montana Memories

Thai Shrimp Linguini

Any vegetables can be substituted in this dish, and the amount of sauce and cilantro can be varied to your own taste. Spiciness of the dish can be controlled by the amount of sauce and ginger used.

2 tablespoons olive oil
1¼ pounds shrimp, peeled
  and deveined
3 tablespoons chopped garlic
2 tablespoons chopped fresh
  ginger
1½ whole red peppers, seeded,
  julienned

12 artichoke hearts, quartered
1 small bunch green onions,
  chopped
⅓ cup chopped fresh cilantro
1 cup Thai Sauce
4–6 cups linguine, cooked al
  dente

In skillet over medium-high heat, add olive oil; heat and add shrimp, garlic, ginger, red peppers, and artichoke hearts. Sauté until shrimp are turning white, but are still translucent in seam along back. Add green onions, fresh cilantro, and Thai Sauce. Toss together and serve over linguine. Serves 4.

THAI SAUCE:
½ (4-ounce) can Panang
  red curry paste
6 tablespoons fresh lime juice
  (about 4 limes)

3 tablespoons rice vinegar
½ cup soy sauce
½ cup sesame oil

In food processor or blender, combine curry paste, lime juice, rice vinegar, and soy sauce. Blend well. With machine running, add sesame oil.

Recipe from Blue Lion Restaurant
A Taste of Jackson Hole II

The Bitterroot River in Bitterroot Valley, Montana, is one of the few rivers on the continent that flows north.

Linguine with Tomatoes and Basil

This dish is a perfect summer meal when the tomatoes have miraculously ripened in Mountain Brook! Delicious and easy.

4 large ripe tomatoes, cut in
½-inch cubes
1 pound Brie cheese, rind
removed and torn into
irregular pieces
1 cup fresh basil leaves,
cleaned and cut into strips
3 garlic cloves, peeled and
finely minced

½ cup plus 1 tablespoon
best-quality olive oil, divided
4½ teaspoons salt, divided
½ teaspoon pepper (freshly
ground, if possible)
6 quarts water
1½ pounds linguine
Parmesan cheese

In large serving bowl combine tomatoes, cheese, basil leaves, garlic, ½ cup olive oil, 2½ teaspoons salt, and pepper. Cover bowl and set aside, at room temperature, for at least 2 hours before serving.

Bring water to boil in large pot; add 1 tablespoon olive oil, 2 teaspoons salt, and linguine. Boil until linguine is tender, but firm, about 8–10 minutes. Drain pasta and immediately toss with tomato mixture. Serve at once, passing the peppermill and plenty of grated Parmesan cheese. Sometimes we like to add crumbled cooked bacon as well. Of course you'll need hot French bread with this!

Mountain Brook's Wacky Wonders of the Woods

Brrr! The coldest temperature ever recorded in the lower 48 states occurred on January 20, 1954, at Roger's Pass, Montana, (about 25 miles northwest of Helena) where the temperature dropped to 70 degrees below zero (actual temperature, not wind chill).

Great Northern Pasta with Clam Sauce

2 (8-ounce) packages cream cheese, softened
1 stick butter, softened
¼ cup snipped parsley
3 tablespoons basil (fresh or in jar)
2 teaspoons garlic powder (or fresh pressed, to taste)
⅔ cup grated Parmesan cheese
4 (6½-ounce) cans chopped clams, drained (reserve juice)
1 cup fresh sliced mushrooms, sautéed
⅔ cup sour cream
Cooked pasta (linguine, fettuccine, or spaghetti)
Black olives, sliced
Almonds, slivered

In large saucepan, melt cream cheese and butter, being careful not to boil! Add spices, Parmesan, drained clams, and 1 cup of reserved clam juice. Heat on medium-low until hot. Add mushrooms to sauce.

Blend in sour cream just before serving. Toss the pasta and sauce; serve in large shallow bowl, and top with olives and almonds.

This makes a lot of sauce, usually enough for two or three dinners for four. I make enough pasta for the first meal, then refrigerate extra sauce, cooking just enough pasta the next time. Serves 8–10.

Souvenirs

★ ★

Papa T's Red Sauce

This universal red sauce tastes delicious over pasta and/or herb-baked chicken breasts.

2 (28-ounce) cans whole
   tomatoes
2 (6-ounce) cans tomato paste
1 medium yellow onion,
   chopped
½ green pepper, chopped
3–5 green onions, chopped
6–8 fresh mushrooms, chopped

2 cloves garlic, minced
Olive oil
1 teaspoon basil
1 teaspoon parsley
¼ teaspoon oregano
¼ cup white wine (Chablis)
¼ teaspoon fennel seed
   (optional)

In large saucepan or slow cooker, place canned tomatoes. Crush with your fingers. Add tomato paste and stir. Sauté onion, green pepper, green onions, mushrooms, and garlic in olive oil. Add remaining spices and wine.

Transfer these ingredients to saucepan and stir. After heating to boiling, reduce heat to low and simmer, stirring frequently. Cook at least 2 hours. (If cooking all day, add 6 ounces water.) Add fennel seed for variety of flavor, if desired.

Optional: Add pre-cooked hamburger or Italian sausage.

Souvenirs

★ ★

Cowman's Spaghetti

This is a "he-man recipe" that can be used with an elk roast as well as beef.

1 (2-pound) chuck roast	1 (8-ounce) can tomato sauce
¼ cup flour	1 small clove garlic
1 teaspoon salt	1½ teaspoons salt
½ teaspoon pepper	1 bay leaf
2 tablespoons oil	¼ teaspoon oregano
1 (14½-ounce) can tomatoes	Cooked spaghetti
1 (6-ounce) can tomato paste	

Wipe roast dry; dredge in flour, salt, and pepper combination. Heat oil in skillet or Dutch oven. Brown roast on both sides in hot oil. When roast is brown, pour off excess fat. Add the remaining ingredients, except oregano and spaghetti. Simmer about 3 hours.

Thirty minutes before sauce is done, add oregano. Remove the roast and bay leaf and serve the sauce over buttered spaghetti. You may cool the roast and slice it to eat with the spaghetti, or you can use it for sandwiches.

Recipe submitted by Fred Fellows, an award-winning Western artist
Montana Celebrity Cookbook

Grouse Spaghetti

3 or more grouse	2 (6-ounce) cans tomato paste
3 cloves garlic	2 (14½-ounce) cans tomatoes
1 onion, chopped	Salt and pepper
1 cup chopped celery	Cooked spaghetti
Oil	

Bake or boil grouse. Cool. Take meat off the bone and dice. Cook garlic, onion, and celery in oil until soft. Add tomato paste and tomatoes; season to taste. Simmer 2 hours. Add diced grouse. Serve over cooked spaghetti.

Yaak Cookbook

Pierogi Casserole

1 pound cooked lasagne
  noodles
10–12 potatoes, cooked
¾ pound Cheddar cheese,
  grated

2 onions, finely diced
2 sticks butter or margarine
Salt to taste

Cook noodles according to package directions. Mash potatoes; add cheese and beat with mixer. Sauté onions in butter until soft. Add ⅓ of onion and butter to potato mixture. Salt to taste.

Generously butter a 9x13-inch baking pan. Place layer of lasagne noodles in pan, then a layer of potato mixture. Repeat, ending with noodles. Pour remaining onions and butter over all. Cover with foil (optional). Bake at 350° until heated through, usually about 30–45 minutes.

Story, Wyoming's Centennial Community Cookbook

Quick 'n Easy Mexican Macaroni

1 pound ground beef or turkey
¼ cup diced onion (optional)
1 tablespoon cooking oil
1 cup water
1 (1¼-ounce) package taco
  seasoning mix

1 (7¼-ounce) package
  macaroni and cheese dinner
Sour cream (optional)
Guacamole (optional)

In a frying pan, brown meat and onion in oil. Drain, if necessary. Add water to meat and then add taco seasoning mix. Stir. Simmer 15 minutes, stirring several times. Prepare macaroni and cheese dinner as directed on package, decreasing or omitting the margarine. Mix macaroni and cheese with meat. Top with sour cream and/or guacamole, if desired. Makes 4–6 servings. Good with a green salad.

Recipes from the Heart

★ ★

Pizza on the Barbecue

1 (16-ounce) jar marinara
  sauce
2 cups mesquite wood chips
  (optional)
2 cups water
Olive oil
1 tablespoon cornmeal
1 (1-pound) loaf frozen
  white bread, thawed

½ pound mozzarella cheese,
  shredded
¼ pound jack cheese, shredded
Optional toppings: onion, bell
  pepper, olives, artichoke
  hearts, red peppers, etc)

Reduce marinara sauce over medium heat to about ¾ cup. Mix wood chips with water and soak for 30 minutes to 4 hours.

On firegrate, ignite briquets (50 for 23-inch diameter barbecue). When covered with ash, push coals in a circle just larger than pizza pan. (If you plan to cook more than one pizza, at this time add 10 more briquets.) Set grill 4–6 inches above coals. Heat until 400°–450° (set an oven thermometer in center of grill, not over coals.) Oil a 14-inch pizza pan and sprinkle with cornmeal.

Roll out bread dough into a 15- to 16-inch circle. Lift into pan. Pat firmly out to pan edge. Spread sauce over dough, leaving 1 inch uncovered at edge. Mix cheeses and spread over sauce. Top with your choice of onion, bell pepper, olives, artichoke hearts, red peppers, etc.

Drain wood chips and sprinkle over coals. Place pizza on grill within rim of coals; cover barbecue. Cook with drafts open until crust is well browned on bottom and cheese is melted, about 15 minutes. Check crust after 10 minutes. Remove from barbecue and serve.

Souvenirs

★ ★

Crustless Quiche

1¼ cups milk
½ cup biscuit mix
3 tablespoons butter
3 eggs
Dash salt and pepper
Dash garlic powder (optional)

Dash cayenne pepper
1 cup diced ham, bacon, or shrimp
2 green onions, chopped
4 ounces sliced mushrooms
1 cup grated sharp cheese

Preheat oven to 350°. Combine the first 7 ingredients in food processor and mix well. Turn into greased 9- or 10-inch deep-dish pie plate. Mix together meat, onions, mushrooms, and cheese. Sprinkle over egg mixture, poking the meat mixture down into the egg mixture with a knife. Bake until the top is golden, about 45 minutes. Let stand for 10 minutes before serving. Makes 8 servings.

Recipe from The Timbers B&B, Ronan, Montana
A Taste of Montana

Hash Brown Quiche

3 cups shredded hash browns, thawed
⅓ cup butter or margarine, melted
1 cup diced, fully cooked ham
1 cup shredded Cheddar cheese

¼ cup diced green pepper
2 eggs
½ cup milk
½ teaspoon salt
¼ teaspoon pepper

Press hash browns between paper towels to remove excess moisture. Press into the bottom and up sides of a greased 9-inch pie plate. Drizzle with butter. Bake at 425° for 25 minutes. Combine ham, cheese, and green pepper. Spoon over crust. In small bowl, beat eggs, milk, salt, and pepper. Pour over all. Reduce heat to 350° and bake for 25–30 minutes. Allow to stand 10 minutes before cutting. Serves 6.

Story, Wyoming's Centennial Community Cookbook

Company Casserole

6 ounces wild rice, cooked
1 (10-ounce) box frozen
   chopped broccoli, thawed
1½ cups cubed, cooked
   chicken
1 cup cubed, cooked ham
1 cup (4 ounces) shredded
   Cheddar cheese
1 (4-ounce) can sliced
   mushrooms, drained
1 cup mayonnaise
1 teaspoon prepared mustard
½ teaspoon curry powder
1 (10¾-ounce) can cream of
   mushroom soup
¼ cup grated Parmesan cheese

In a greased 2-quart casserole, layer first 6 ingredients in order listed. Combine mayonnaise, mustard, curry, and soup. Spread over casserole. Sprinkle with Parmesan cheese. Bake at 350° for 45–60 minutes, until top is golden brown. Serves 8.

Favorite Recipes of Montana

Baked Broccoli and Rice

8 ounces frozen broccoli
¼ cup margarine
1 medium onion, chopped
½ cup chopped celery
1 (8-ounce) jar cheese spread
1 (10¾-ounce) can cream of
   mushroom soup, undiluted
1½ cups cooked rice (white,
   brown, wild or combination)

Cook broccoli according to package directions; drain. In skillet, melt margarine. Sauté onion and celery until tender. Add cheese spread, soup, rice, and cooked broccoli. Pour into a greased 2-quart glass baking dish. Bake at 350° for 40–45 minutes or until lightly browned around edges. Yields 4 servings.

Irene's Country Cooking

The Montana state flag contains the state seal which shows some of the state's beautiful scenery—a sun rises over mountains, forests, and the Great Falls of the Missouri River. A pick, shovel, and plow in the foreground represent mining and farming, so important to pioneers. Near the bottom, a ribbon contains the state motto, "Gold and Silver."

Curried Rice Mold

1⅓ cups pre-cooked rice
  (Minute Rice)
3 tablespoons grated onion
1 teaspoon curry powder
2 tablespoons butter or
  margarine
1 teaspoon salt
1 tablespoon wine vinegar

⅓ cup chopped almonds
1 cup finely chopped celery
⅓ cup chopped raisins or
  currants
1 cup cooked peas
¼ cup mayonnaise
Peach halves, avocado rings,
  and parsley for garnish

Prepare rice according to directions on package. Cook onion with curry in butter until soft but not brown. Add to rice with remaining ingredients, mixing well. Pack into individual molds or one large mold. Chill at least 3 hours. Unmold onto platter and surround with drained peach halves, avocado rings, and sprigs of parsley. Serve with Bombay Platter (page 162) and rolls or French bread.

Home at/on the Range with Wyoming BILS

MEATS

PHOTO © THOMAS BÖTTGER

The old west is alive and well in both Montana and Wyoming, where traditional cattle drives are still commonplace. You can even vacation on a working cattle ranch and participate in a cattle drive just like the real cowboys.

Beef Tenderloin
with Pepper Jelly Sauce

1 (4-pound) center-cut beef
  tenderloin
1½ teaspoons salt
¾ teaspoon chili powder
½ teaspoon coarsely ground
  black pepper

¼ teaspoon ground cumin
¼ teaspoon dried oregano
  leaves
1½ cups beef stock
¾ cup balsamic wine vinegar
⅓ cup jalapeño pepper jelly

Preheat oven to 450°. Trim fat from tenderloin. Tie at equal intervals in 4 places around tenderloin. Combine salt, chili powder, pepper, cumin, and oregano in small bowl. Rub mixture over tenderloin. Place tenderloin on rack in roasting pan in middle of oven. Roast for 30 minutes or to 120° on meat thermometer. Transfer to heated platter. Let stand at room temperature for 10 minutes before serving.

Pour off fat. Add stock, vinegar, and jelly to pan. Cook for 5 minutes or until slightly thickened, stirring occasionally. Serve in 1-inch-thick slices with sauce spooned over each serving. Yields 8 servings.

Cheyenne Frontier Days "Daddy of 'em All" Cookbook

★ ★

Shorty's Succulent Salsa Steak

½ cup salsa (medium to hot)
½ cup fresh lime juice
2 tablespoons hoisin sauce
   (available in oriental section
   of your supermarket)

2–4 cloves garlic, minced
1 pound sirloin steak (or
   individual filets, if preferred)
Thinly sliced green onions for
   garnish

Combine salsa, lime juice, hoisin sauce, and garlic. Place steak in glass pan. Pour marinade over meat. Cover and refrigerate at least 6 hours (overnight is better). Turn occasionally. Drain steak, reserving marinade. Broil or grill, brushing often with marinade. Garnish with thinly sliced green onions. Makes 4 servings.

You're Hot Stuff, Flo!

Flank Steak Barbecue

Delicious hot or cold!

¼ cup soy sauce
3 tablespoons honey
2 tablespoons vinegar
1½ teaspoons garlic powder
1½ teaspoons ground ginger,
   or 1 tablespoon fresh ginger

¾ cup salad oil
1 green onion, sliced
1 flank steak (about 1½
   pounds)

Mix all ingredients, except steak. Place meat in glass or plastic dish (do not use metal). Pour marinade over meat. Allow to marinate at least 4 hours (overnight is best), turning occasionally.

Barbecue over glowing coals, about 5 minutes on each side for medium rare or until done to your taste; may be broiled in oven. Baste with marinade as meat cooks. Slice diagonally to serve. Makes 4 servings.

Favorite Recipes of Montana

My Favorite Beef Stroganoff

2 round steaks, cut into cubes
Flour
1 small onion, finely chopped
1¼ cups water, divided
¼ cup butter or margarine
2 beef bouillon cubes
1 (4-ounce) can mushrooms,
  undrained

1 (10¾-ounce) can mushroom
  soup
1 cup sour cream
1 (8-ounce) package noodles,
  cooked

In frying pan, brown floured cubes of beef. Add onion, ¼ cup water, butter or margarine, and bouillon cubes. Simmer until onion is tender. Remove from frying pan, removing all brown particles, too. Put meat and onion with juice in roasting pan, adding mushrooms, mushroom soup, and remaining 1 cup water. Simmer 1½ hours. Add sour cream and noodles, cooked according to package directions. Cook 10 minutes longer. Serve hot.

Horse Prairie Favorites

Editor's Extra: This can be done in one pot—a Dutch oven or large deep pan.

Oven B-B-Q Steak

2–3 pounds round steak,
  cut to serving size
Flour
½ onion, chopped
¾ cup ketchup
½ cup vinegar

¾ cup water
1 tablespoon prepared mustard
1 tablespoon Worcestershire
  sauce
½ teaspoon salt
½ teaspoon pepper

Pound steak well; roll in flour and brown in oil in oven-proof pan. Mix remaining ingredients and pour over steak. Bake 2 hours at 350°.

Irma Flat Mothers' Club Cookbook

Beef Pineapple Fantasy

1½ pounds top round steak
  (½ inch thick)
2 medium green peppers
1 medium white or yellow onion
1 (2½-ounce) jar sliced
  mushrooms, drained
1 (15½-ounce) can pineapple
  chunks, drained; reserve juice
2 tablespoons soy sauce

1½ tablespoons cornstarch
1 (6-ounce) box frozen pea pods
2 tablespoons cooking oil
¼ teaspoon salt
¼ teaspoon pepper
1 beef bouillon cube
1 cup boiling water
½ cup English walnuts,
  quartered

Trim excess fat from meat and slice in thin strips, 1–1½ inches long. Slice peppers and onions into 1½-inch strips and put aside. Drain mushrooms; put aside. Mix ½ cup pineapple juice, soy sauce, and cornstarch; put aside. Place frozen pea pods in boiling water for 1 minute to separate. Drain; put aside.

Heat oil in frying pan or Chinese wok over medium-high heat. Add meat and sprinkle with salt and pepper. Stir frequently while cooking. Drain excessive liquid from meat after it has cooked 5 minutes. Return to stove and continue cooking 10 minutes, until brown. Dissolve bouillon cube in boiling water; add to meat. Continue cooking for 5 additional minutes. Add peppers, onion, mushrooms, pineapple chunks, and pea pods; cook 5 minutes more, stirring frequently. Add cornstarch mixture and walnuts. Stir continually while cooking for 10 minutes. Turn heat to warm and serve. Serves 4–6.

The Fine Art of Cooking

Wyoming was admitted to the Union on July 10, 1890. The 44th state is also known as "Big Wyoming," "Equality State," and "Cowboy State." Wyoming is known as the "Equality State" because Wyoming women were the first in the nation to vote (bill enacted 1869 by territorial legislature), serve on juries (1870), and hold public office (1870).

Six-Shooter Steak

Some camp cooks cut tough steaks very thin and fried them quickly. A better method was to cut them thick and pound them. There were many preferences for pounding—a dull butcher knife, the back of a cleaver, a chain flail, even the side of a dish. But the favorite among old-time cooks was the six-shooter—the barrel fit the hand, and the butt ending in a wedge of steel was shaped to bruise the meat, to pulp and tenderize it, without punching holes all the way through.

1 teaspoon whole peppercorns   **1 cup lard**
1 cup flour   **Salt to taste**
2 full-cut round steaks

Pulverize the peppercorns. Don't grind them, just crush them on a slab of hardwood. Brush them into the flour; any fragments left will be picked up when the steak is pounded. Cut the round steaks into the desired sizes. Do not trim off the fat. Using the butt of a six-shooter, pound them while sprinkling them lightly with flour and pepper. Don't hammer. Merely lift the gun and let if fall. Its weight will be sufficient. Don't work them down too thin. They are best reduced to about ⅔ of their original thickness.

Heat a heavy iron skillet or griddle. Melt the lard, and when it is hot enough to smoke, fry the steaks a few at a time, browning on both sides and setting aside in a warm pan while they are still red in the middle. Salt them. Cover the pan and keep it hot but not sizzling. The redness will fade after 3 or 4 minutes, and your genuine, old-time six-shooter steaks will go to the table done through, tender and delicious.

Cow Country Cookbook

Editor's Extra: We suggest using an alternate method of tenderizing the steak rather than using a gun, but wanted to preserve this authentic recipe.

Finger Steaks

1½ pounds round steak or
  any other steak
1 cup milk
1 egg, beaten

1 cup+ flour, divided
2 teaspoons salt
2 pinches garlic powder
1 teaspoon cayenne pepper

Cut steak into 2½x1½-inch strips. In small bowl mix milk and egg. Mix 1 cup flour with salt, garlic powder, and cayenne pepper. Coat meat with small amount of unseasoned flour; dip into egg mixture, and finally in seasoned flour. Place on cookie sheet and freeze overnight. Deep-fry at 350° for 10–15 minutes. Meat is done when it floats. Serve hot.

Favorite Recipes of Montana

Steak and Dressing
Powder River

2 pounds round steak, sliced
  thin
4 cups bread crumbs
½ cup chopped celery
¼ cup minced onion
⅓ cup butter, softened

1 teaspoon salt
Hot water or broth
Dash pepper
Poultry seasoning and sage
Bacon strips

Pound steak very flat and cut into serving-size pieces. Combine bread crumbs, celery, onion, butter, and salt. Add water or broth to moisten, just until crumbs stick together well. Season to taste.

Spoon dressing onto steak pieces and roll like a jellyroll. Wrap with bacon and fasten with toothpicks. Place in a greased pan and bake, covered, at 350° for 60 minutes.

Recipe from Powder River Experience, Arvada, Wyoming
Tastes & Tours of Wyoming

Southwestern Beef Brisket

1 (3-pound) fresh beef brisket
1¼ teaspoons salt, divided
½ teaspoon pepper, divided
2 tablespoons cooking oil
1½ cups water
1 (8-ounce) can tomato sauce
1 small onion, chopped
2 tablespoons red wine vinegar

1 tablespoon chili powder
1 teaspoon dried oregano
¾ teaspoon ground cumin
½ teaspoon garlic powder
⅛ teaspoon ground red pepper
3 sweet red peppers, cut into
   strips
1½ cups sliced carrots

Season beef with 1 teaspoon salt and ¼ teaspoon pepper. In a Dutch oven, heat oil; brown the beef on both sides. Combine water, tomato sauce, onion, vinegar, chili powder, oregano, cumin, garlic powder, red pepper, and remaining salt and pepper. Pour over meat. Cover and bake at 325° for 2 hours. Add red peppers and carrots; bake 1 hour longer or until meat is tender. Remove meat; let stand 15 minutes before cutting. Thicken juices with a little flour, or cook over high heat to reduce and thicken.

Feeding the Herd

Vicki's Prime Rib

Salt and pepper
1 standing rib roast

4–6 garlic cloves, peeled

Salt and pepper to taste all sides of roast. With knife, make slits on both sides of roast and insert a garlic clove into each slit. Place roast fat-side-up on rack in baking dish. Insert meat thermometer in meat's thickest portion (without touching bone). Bake at 325° until thermometer registers degree specified for preferred doneness (25–30 minutes per pound as a rule).

Remove roast from oven; place on carving board or platter, covering with a tent of foil. Let stand 15–20 minutes before carving; internal temperature will rise 5–10 degrees. Rare 135°; medium-rare 140°; medium 150°; well-done 160° (never recommended). To carve meat, place roast on board or platter, large end down and ribs to your left. Insert fork between ribs. Cut across grain into ¼- to ½-inch slices. After slicing below first rib, cut bone off and set aside. Continue slicing meat and removing rib bones. Remove garlic cloves as they appear. Serve with Au Jus.

AU JUS:
Dripping from prime rib
1 (14½-ounce) can beef broth
Pepper to taste

Garlic powder to taste
Worcestershire sauce to taste

After removing the prime rib from baking dish, skim and discard fat from pan drippings. To drippings, add beef broth, pepper to taste, garlic powder to taste (few shakes) and Worcestershire sauce to taste (another few shakes). Bring to boil on top of stove. Let boil approximately 5–10 minutes until liquid is reduced. Serve on the side with prime rib. Truly a treat.

Rare Collection Recipes

Prime Rib Roast

Standing prime rib...any size. Let meat stand at room temperature for 1 hour before cooking. Preheat oven to 375°. Rub meat well with salt and sprinkle with pepper. Place meat, fat-side-up, in shallow roasting pan, uncovered. (Do not add water.) Cook for 1 hour. Turn off heat . . . DO NOT OPEN OVEN DOOR! Leave for minimum time of 5–6 hours. Before serving, turn oven on again to 375° and cook for the following times: 30 minutes for rare, 40 minutes for medium, 50 minutes for well done. Works every time!

Home at/on the Range with Wyoming BILS

French Dip

A new twist on an old recipe.

1 (3- to 4-pound) boneless rump roast	**1 cup chopped onion**
	1 cup chopped celery
1 cup chopped carrots	**1 or 2 packages au jus mix**

Place roast in large roaster with a tight fitting lid. Cover roast with chopped veggies. Add NO liquid. Bake covered at 350° for 3–4 hours. Remove from oven and place meat on carving board to cool. Transfer the cooked veggies to blender and blend until smooth. Prepare au jus in roaster adding the blended veggies. When beef has cooled, sliced into thin slices; add to au jus.

For serving, place slices of beef on French bun and spread au jus into small bowls or cups for dipping.

Note: Use as many packages of au jus as you want to have an adequate amount for however many persons you intend to feed. Also, add a little red wine to au jus—this is optional, of course. If you have an electric knife, it works great for slicing the beef.

Best-of-Friends, Festive Occasions Cookbook

Bistro Beef Steaks
with Wild Mushroom Sauce

1 medium onion, cut in half,
   divided
1¼ pounds ground beef
¾ teaspoon salt
Salt and pepper to taste
8 ounces sliced assorted
   fresh wild mushrooms,
   such as oyster, cremini and
   shiitake (about 3 cups)

1½ cups (12 ounces) beer,
   preferably honey lager, or
   non-alcoholic beer, divided
1 package brown gravy mix
2 teaspoons chopped fresh
   thyme, or ½ teaspoon dried
   thyme leaves, crushed,
   divided
Fresh thyme leaves or sprigs
   (optional)

Finely shred ½ onion. Thinly slice remaining ½ onion; set aside. Combine shredded onion, ground beef and ¾ teaspoon salt in large bowl, mixing lightly but thoroughly. Lightly shape into 4 (½-inch-thick) oval steaks. Sprinkle tops with salt and pepper, as desired. Heat large nonstick skillet over medium heat until hot. Place patties in skillet; cook 10–12 minutes to medium (160°) doneness, until not pink in center and juices show no pink color, turning once. Remove from skillet; keep warm.

Add sliced onion, mushrooms, and ¼ cup of the beer to same skillet; cook over medium-high heat 5 minutes or until vegetables are tender, stirring occasionally. Combine gravy mix with remaining beer in small bowl, mixing until smooth; stir into mushroom mixture in skillet. Add 1 teaspoon of the chopped thyme; simmer 1 minute or until thickened, stirring frequently. Spoon sauce over patties; sprinkle with remaining 1 teaspoon chopped thyme. Garnish with thyme sprigs, if desired. Makes 4 servings.

Ranch Recipe Roundup IV

Montana Pasty

The pasty was a favorite in Butte, a gift from the Cornish miners who were among the first of the European immigrants to arrive in the copper-mining city. It is still the cherished staple among the real people of Butte.

THE PASTY:

3 cups flour

1 teaspoon salt

½ pound Crisco (although the Cousin Jacks say lard is best)

2 eggs

1 cup water

THE STUFFING:

6 potatoes, diced

1 medium onion, chopped

½ stick margarine or butter, melted

1 teaspoon salt

1 teaspoon pepper

A good round steak or pork, diced

Mix flour, salt, and Crisco with egg beater until like cornmeal. Add 2 eggs and a cup of cold water. Put all this on a table, with a thin layer of flour; sprinkle water on slightly; and then knead into a roll. Put all this into the refrigerator to chill for awhile.

Take your pasty roll out of the refrigerator and make 10 round things with your rolling pin. Then fold them over with the Stuffing in the middle and make neat half-moon shapes, poking arty stab holes in them to let the steam out (pierce with a fork). Roll up the edges and press with the fork aesthetically. You can paint them with milk or egg white to make them brown, if you want. This enhances their natural beauty. Bake them in an oven for 1 hour at 425°. Serve with gravy or ketchup on a plate—or munch hand-held cold. A 10-pasty recipe.

Potluck

Green Chile Cheese Burgers by Denise

1 pound ground beef
½ cup finely sliced green
  onions
1 teaspoon Mrs. Dash
  Seasoning Blend
1 teaspoon minced fresh
  cilantro
2 cloves garlic, minced
2 teaspoons taco seasoning mix

1 (7-ounce) can chopped green
  chiles
Shredded lettuce
1 cup grated Monterey Jack
  cheese
1 cup finely chopped white
  onion
6 tablespoons salsa
Avocado slices for garnish

Combine beef, green onions, Mrs. Dash, cilantro, garlic, and taco seasoning. Shape into 6 patties and broil or grill. Heat green chiles. To serve, place meat patty on bed of shredded lettuce; mix heated chiles, cheese, and onion together and pour over meat, then top with salsa. Garnish with avocado slices. Makes 6 burgers.

You're Hot Stuff, Flo!

Summer Sausage

2 pounds hamburger
½ teaspoon garlic powder
⅛ teaspoon mustard seed
2½ teaspoons liquid smoke
1 cup water

¼ teaspoon onion powder
¼ teaspoon black pepper
2½ tablespoons Morton Tender
  Quick

Mix well; make into long rolls. Wrap in foil, shiny side in. Refrigerate 24 hours. Poke holes in bottom of foil. Place on rack of broiler pan with a little water in bottom of pan. Bake at 325° for 90 minutes. Unwrap to cool.

Fire Hall Cookbook

Shepherd's Pie

1 pound ground beef	2 cups cooked or canned peas
2 tablespoons fat	and carrots
1 cup chopped onion	2 cups seasoned hot mashed
1/2 cup diced green pepper	potatoes
1 (10 3/4-ounce) can cream of	Melted butter
mushroom soup	Parsley (optional)

Brown beef in hot fat; add onion and green pepper; cook until tender, but not brown. Stir in soup; place in greased 1 1/2-quart casserole; sprinkle peas and carrots over soup. Arrange mashed potatoes in ring on top; drizzle melted butter over top. Bake uncovered in a 350° oven for 25 minutes or until heated through. Serves 6.

Note: String beans may be substituted for peas and carrots.

Feeding the Herd

Quick Crescent Taco Pie

1 pound ground beef	1 (8-ounce) carton dairy sour
1 package taco seasoning mix	cream
1/2 cup water	6 slices American cheese
1/2 cup chunky salsa	Shredded lettuce
1 (8-ounce) can crescent	Sliced black olives
dinner rolls	Diced tomatoes
1 1/2 cups crushed corn chips,	
divided	

Brown meat in skillet; drain. Add seasoning mix, water, and salsa; simmer for 5 minutes. Spread crescent roll dough in 10-inch pie plate to form crust; press edges together at seams. Sprinkle 1 cup corn chips on crust bottom; keep remaining 1/2 cup. Spoon on meat mixture. Spread sour cream over meat. Cover with cheese slices; sprinkle on remaining 1/2 cup corn chips. Bake at 375° for 20 minutes, until crust is golden brown. Top with lettuce, olives, and tomatoes.

Wolf Point, Montana 75th Jubilee Cookbook

★ ★

Woody's Version of "Joe's Special"

1 tablespoon olive oil
2 pounds lean ground beef
2 medium white onions, chopped
4 cloves garlic, chopped
1/2 pound mushrooms, thickly sliced
1 package frozen chopped spinach, thawed and pressed dry

1 teaspoon garlic salt
Freshly ground pepper to taste
1/2 teaspoon oregano
1/2 teaspoon basil
Pinch of nutmeg (optional)
1/3 cup Parmesan cheese
4–6 eggs, lightly beaten
Additional Parmesan or Cheddar cheese, for garnish
Parsley for garnish

Heat oil in large skillet; brown beef. Add onions, garlic, and mushrooms. Cook until onions are soft, stirring occasionally. Add spinach, garlic salt, pepper, oregano, basil, nutmeg, and Parmesan cheese; continue cooking for at least 5 minutes. Add eggs; reduce heat to low and continue cooking until eggs are set. Do not stir too much. Garnish with additional cheese and parsley. Makes 6–8 servings.

What's Cooking, Flo?

Cowboy Joes

2 pounds lean hamburger
1 (10 1/2-ounce) can chicken gumbo soup
1 cup catsup
2 tablespoons prepared mustard

1 tablespoon chili powder (Chugwater Chili Gourmet Blend)
2 tablespoons brown sugar (optional)
1/4 cup chopped onion

Brown hamburger. Drain excess fat. Add soup and remaining ingredients and simmer for 15 minutes. Serve over hamburger buns or French bread.

Here's What's Cooking

Hobo Dinners

1 pound ground beef	2 large carrots
Worcestershire sauce	2 medium onions
Salt and pepper	1 (16-ounce) package frozen
4 medium potatoes	peas

Divide ground beef into 4 equal portions. Make patties and place each on an 18-inch piece of heavy-duty aluminum foil. Season each patty with Worcestershire sauce and salt and pepper to taste. Pull sides of foil up around patties to form a bowl.

Wash, but do not peel potatoes. Cut into ¼-inch rounds and place 1 slice on each patty. Slice carrots into ¼-inch rounds and add to each dinner. Slice onions and add to each. Top each with 4 ounces frozen peas. Seal each Hobo Dinner by crimping the foil as tightly as possible at the opening. Place on a cookie sheet and bake at 375° for 1 hour.

Cooking with the Ladies

Pizza Hot Dish

2 pounds hamburger	1 (8-ounce) can mushrooms
½ onion, chopped	¾ (1-pound) package noodles,
½ green pepper, chopped	cooked
(optional)	1 (8-ounce) package mozzarella
1 (10-ounce) can pizza sauce	cheese
½ cup catsup	1 (3½-ounce) package
2 (10¾-ounce) cans Cheddar	pepperoni slices
cheese soup	

Brown hamburger, onions, and green pepper, if desired. Then mix together with pizza sauce, catsup, soup, mushrooms, and cooked noodles. Pour mixture into a greased 10x13-inch casserole, or 2 or 3 smaller casseroles. Sprinkle with mozzarella cheese and arrange pepperoni slices on top. Bake at 350° for 1 hour. Can be frozen and baked as needed.

Wolf Point, Montana 75th Jubilee Cookbook

★ ★ ★ ★ ★ ★ ★ ★ ★ ★ ★ ★ ★ ★ ★ ★ ★ ★ ★ ★

Mrs. Annie Krug's Goulash

1–2 tablespoons Crisco or
   bacon grease
2½ pounds ground beef
3 teaspoons salt
1 teaspoon chili powder
5 small onions, chopped
1 red pepper, chopped
1 green pepper, chopped
2 large bunches celery, finely
   chopped

1 (28-ounce) can tomatoes
1 (10¾-ounce) can tomato soup
2 pimientos, chopped
¼ pound (1 stick) butter
2 (15-ounce) cans red kidney
   beans
3 tablespoons crushed,
   uncooked spaghetti
1 (4-ounce) can sliced
   mushrooms (optional)

Melt Crisco or bacon grease in large frying pan. Add meat and seasonings and cook 15 minutes, adding onions last 5 minutes. Add pepper to suit. Add celery, canned tomatoes, tomato soup, and pimientos. Add butter and cook slowly for 2½ hours. Last 20–30 minutes of cooking time, add red kidney beans and uncooked spaghetti. If desired, add mushrooms during the last 5–10 minutes. Serves 20.

Recipe from Charley Montana Bed and Breakfast, Glendive, Montana
Montana Bed & Breakfast Guide & Cookbook

Crockpot Pot Roast

1 onion, sliced
1 garlic clove, chopped
1 (4-pound) pot roast
2 teaspoons salt
½ teaspoon thyme

¼ teaspoon pepper
½ teaspoon rosemary
¾ cup red wine
3 tablespoons flour
¼ cup water

Put onion and garlic in bottom of crockpot. Lay roast on top. Sprinkle salt, thyme, pepper, and rosemary over roast. Pour red wine over all. Cook covered 12 hours on LOW, or 5–6 hours on HIGH. Use flour mixed to a paste with water to thicken juice for gravy.

Food for the Soul

Roger's Roaring Roast Beef Sandwich

RELISH:

2 tablespoons olive oil
2 tablespoons butter or
  margarine
2 tablespoons water
2 tablespoons prepared
  horseradish
1 (3-ounce) can chopped
  green chiles

2 teaspoons red wine vinegar
2 teaspoons chopped garlic
2 teaspoons Dijon mustard
1 large white onion, thinly
  sliced
Garlic salt to taste
Freshly ground pepper to taste

In a medium skillet heat olive oil and margarine; add water, horseradish, green chiles, vinegar, garlic, and mustard. Combine well and allow to bubble. Add onion slices and cover. Stir often, until onion is golden; add garlic salt and freshly ground pepper to taste.

4 Kaiser rolls, split
Dijon mustard

½ pound deli roast beef
8 slices Swiss cheese

Arrange rolls on cookie sheet; spread Dijon mustard on half of buns, then divide roast beef and place on bun bottoms. Place Relish on tops. Divide the cheese evenly between the bottoms and tops. Place in 350° oven until cheese starts to melt, then broil until cheese is golden. Serve with crisp dill pickles. Makes 4 servings.

You're Hot Stuff, Flo!

★ ★

Chili on a Stick

Summertime and the kitchen is hot—too hot to make chili. Unless you make chili on a stick! And use that randy old whitetail that doesn't taste very good, if that's all you have. The marinade will soothe all but the most gamy flavors.

2 pounds shoulder steaks	2 cloves garlic, minced
¾ cup red wine vinegar	½ teaspoon chili powder
½ cup apple juice	½ teaspoon salt
½ cup vegetable oil	1 teaspoon black pepper
¼ cup minced onion	½ cup mesquite wood chips
1 teaspoon dried leaf cilantro,	6 fresh, whole jalapeño peppers
or 1 tablespoon chopped	12 large-bulbed green onions
fresh cilantro	1 pound cherry tomatoes

Trim the steaks of all fat and sinewy material, then pat dry with paper towels. In a glass bowl or resealable plastic bag, combine the marinade ingredients: vinegar, apple juice, oil, onion, cilantro, garlic, chili powder, salt, and black pepper. Stir, then add the steaks. Place the marinating steaks in the refrigerator, covered or sealed, for 2–4 hours.

When the first hour is up, put the mesquite wood chips in a pail of water, and prepare the vegetables for the skewers. Wearing rubber gloves, cut off the tops of the jalapeños and core and seed them. Cut them in half lengthwise. Trim the tops and bottoms of the onions, leaving about 3 inches of green tops. Drain the meat, cut it up into 1- to 2-inch chunks, and alternate the meat, onion, jalapeños, and tomatoes on the skewers. Begin and end with the meat to secure the stringer.

For a propane barbecue: Drain the wood chips and place them in a wood box. Set it on one side of the coal grate. Preheat the unit for 10 minutes, then turn down to medium-high heat. For charcoal: Start 40 charcoal briquettes on one side of the grill, wait 25 minutes, then spread them out in a single layer, leaving room in the middle to nestle the wood box among the coals.

Place the kabobs over the hot coals, and not directly over the wood chips. Cover the grill and cook 8–10 minutes, basting often and turning once. Serve with lots of chips and Mexican beer in well-chilled glasses. Yields 6 servings.

Game on the Grill

★ ★

Veal Parmigiana

1 pound thin veal scallopini	¾ teaspoon salt
2 eggs, beaten	½ teaspoon dried oregano
1 cup seasoned bread crumbs	¼ teaspoon dried basil
¼ cup olive or salad oil	¼ teaspoon pepper
½ cup chopped onion	1 package sliced mozzarella
1 clove garlic, crushed	cheese, divided
1 cup tomatoes	¼ cup grated Parmesan
2 teaspoons sugar	cheese, divided

Preheat oven to 350°. Dip veal in eggs, then crumbs, coating lightly. In skillet, heat oil. Add veal and cook until brown; remove from skillet. Sauté onion in hot oil (add more if necessary); add garlic. Add tomatoes (smash tomatoes if using whole tomatoes). Add sugar and spices. Bring to boil, then reduce heat and simmer, covered, for 10 minutes. Place veal in baking dish. Add half sauce and half cheeses. Repeat layers, ending with Parmesan cheese. Cover with foil and bake 30 minutes. Serve over rice.

Sharing Our Best

Bourbon Pork Tenderloins

A winner for a dinner party.

2 pork tenderloins	½ cup bourbon
½ cup soy sauce	4 tablespoons brown sugar

Marinate tenderloins in remaining ingredients for up to 2 hours before baking. Bake 1–1½ hours at 325°; cool to room temperature.

MUSTARD SAUCE:

1 tablespoon dry mustard	2 tablespoons white wine
Dijon mustard to taste	vinegar
2 tablespoons sugar	4 egg yolks
½ teaspoon salt	1 cup heavy cream

Combine ingredients in top of double boiler and cook until thick. Serve at room temperature with sliced tenderloins.

Rare Collection Recipes

Schweineschnitzel

A German dish of pork cutlets with quick pan dressing.

2 pounds pork loins
1 egg
3 tablespoons water
½ teaspoon garlic salt
1 cup bread crumbs
4 tablespoons butter
1 apple, cored and chopped

½ onion, chopped fine
½ cup raisins
1 cup cubed dry white bread
½ teaspoon salt
⅓ cup white wine
Lemon wedges for garnish

Cut bone away from pork chops. Pound thin, to no more than ⅛ inch thick. Beat egg in water with garlic salt. Dip cutlets in egg, then in dry bread crumbs. Fry cutlets until crisp and light brown in butter. Set aside and keep warm.

In the same frying pan, add apple, onion, raisins, cubed bread, salt, and wine. Stir well. Cook and stir over low heat for 5–10 minutes. Spoon out stuffing and serve cutlets on top of the stuffing. Garnish with lemon wedges. Serves 2–3.

Festival of Nations Cookbook

★ ★

MEATS

Pat's Pork Chop Casserole

1 cup uncooked rice
3 tablespoons butter or
  margarine
2 Granny Smith apples
8 boneless pork chops
1 large white onion, sliced in
  thin rings

½ pound fresh mushrooms,
  sliced
1 (10¾-ounce) can cream of
  mushroom soup
1 (10¾-ounce) can cream of
  celery soup
Parsley for garnish

Cook rice according to package directions; place in 9x13-inch casserole which has been sprayed with nonstick spray. Dot top of rice with butter. Core apples and slice in ½-inch slices. Arrange the apples on top of the rice. Trim chops of all visible fat and place them on top of the apples. Place onion rings on top of the chops, then add the mushrooms. Finally, combine the 2 cans of cream soup and pour over all. Cover. Bake in 375° oven for 45 minutes; remove cover, and continue baking until top has started to brown, usually about 30 minutes. Garnish with parsley. Good served with baked tomatoes.

What's Cooking, Flo?

Pork Chop and Potato Bake

6 pork chops
Seasoned salt
Pepper
1 (10¾-ounce) can cream of
  celery soup
½ cup milk
½ cup sour cream
1 (24-ounce) package O'Brien or
  hash brown potatoes, thawed

1 (3-ounce) package cream
  cheese, softened
2 tablespoons chopped onions
1 cup shredded Cheddar
  cheese
1 (2.8-ounce) can French's
  French fried onions

Brown pork chops. Sprinkle with seasoned salt and pepper. Set aside. Combine soup, milk, and sour cream. Stir in potatoes, cream cheese, and onions. Spoon mixture into a 9x13-inch pan. Arrange pork chops over potatoes. Bake in 350° oven for 40 minutes. Top with cheese and French fried onions. Bake for 5 minutes more until cheese melts.

The Best of Rural Montana Cookbook

Pork Sauerkraut Platter

6–8 pork chops
Salt and pepper
2 (16-ounce) cans sauerkraut
1 medium onion, chopped
  (optional)
3 tablespoons brown sugar

1 ($10\frac{3}{4}$-ounce) can cream of
  mushroom soup
1 (4-ounce) can sliced
  mushrooms (optional)
4 cups hot mashed potatoes

Brown chops in heavy skillet, turning once. Remove chops from skillet and season with salt and pepper. Drain off part of fat from skillet. Empty drained sauerkraut in skillet; sprinkle with chopped onion and brown sugar. Heat about 5 minutes, stirring.

Empty sauerkraut into a large shallow greased baking dish and arrange chops on top. Spoon soup over chops. Sprinkle on mushrooms, if desired. Cover and bake in pre-heated 325° oven until chops are tender, about $1\frac{1}{4}$ hours. Remove from oven. Using a pastry tube or spoon, make a border of mashed potatoes. Brown under broiler. Makes 6 servings.

Wolf Point, Montana 75th Jubilee Cookbook

Western Barbecued Ribs

RIBS:

½ cup firmly packed brown
  sugar
¼ cup country-style Dijon
  mustard

3 cups apple juice
1 teaspoon hot pepper sauce
3 pounds beef, pork loin, or
  country-style ribs

In Dutch oven, stir together all ingredients, except ribs; add ribs. Cook over high heat until mixture comes to a full boil. Cover; reduce heat to low. Continue cooking, turning ribs occasionally, until ribs are fork-tender, 40–50 minutes. Prepare grill.

BARBECUE SAUCE:

¼ cup firmly packed brown
  sugar
¼ cup chopped onion
1 cup ketchup
½ cup Worcestershire sauce

¼ cup lemon juice
½ teaspoon coarsely ground
  pepper
¼ teaspoon salt
¼ teaspoon cayenne pepper

In 1-quart saucepan stir together all Barbecue Sauce ingredients. Place ribs on grill. Brush ribs with Barbecue Sauce. Grill, brushing with Sauce and turning occasionally, until ribs are done, 12–15 minutes. Cook remaining Barbecue Sauce over medium heat, stirring occasionally, until it just comes to a boil. Serve with ribs. Serves 4.

Favorite Recipes

★ ★

Jerry's Superb Short Ribs

4–5 pounds lean short ribs
1 teaspoon salt
¼ teaspoon sugar
⅛ teaspoon turmeric
⅛ teaspoon paprika
⅛ teaspoon celery salt
⅛ teaspoon black pepper
1 cup ketchup
¾ cup water
½ cup finely chopped onion
½ cup finely chopped green
   pepper

⅓ cup cider vinegar
¼ cup firmly packed brown
   sugar
1 tablespoon Worcestershire
   sauce
1½ teaspoons minced garlic
1 teaspoon dry mustard
½ teaspoon hot pepper sauce
½ teaspoon salt
¼ teaspoon basil
¼ teaspoon black pepper

Brown short ribs in oil (optional). Place in a roaster. Combine 1 teaspoon salt, sugar, turmeric, paprika, celery salt, and ⅛ teaspoon pepper; sprinkle over ribs. Bake, covered, for 1 hour at 350°. Drain off fat.

Meanwhile, combine the remaining ingredients and spoon over the ribs. Reduce heat to 275° and bake 2–3 hours, basting every 30 minutes, until the ribs are done and very tender. Serve with rice pilaf and tossed salad.

Simac Family Favorites

Leg of Lamb of the West

1 (5- to 6-pound) leg of lamb
1 cup dry red wine
1 cup red wine vinegar and oil
   dressing
2–3 cloves garlic, slivered and
   pierced into meat at intervals
Pepper to taste
2 onions, peeled and quartered

1 teaspoon Italian seasoning
1 teaspoon beef bouillon
   granules
2 tablespoons Worcestershire
   sauce
Dash Tabasco
¼ cup soy sauce
Dash paprika

Place leg of lamb and all other ingredients in roasting pan. Bake at 350° for 2½–3 hours, until meat is tender, basting frequently. (The secret is in the basting!) Skim off the accumulated fat and serve juices with meat. Serves 8–10.

Wonderful Wyoming Facts and Foods

Scrapple

1 pound or more meaty
   country pork spareribs
Water to cover
10 cups broth
2½ cups cold water
3 cups white cornmeal
1¼ cups flour
1 teaspoon Aècent (optional)

2–3 teaspoons salt
1 teaspoon garlic salt
1 teaspoon marjoram
1 teaspoon oregano
1 teaspoon thyme
1 teaspoon sage
½ teaspoon nutmeg

Cover meat with water. Cook until it falls off bones. Break meat into small pieces and remove excess fat. Bring broth and meat to a boil.

Mix together cold water, cornmeal, flour, Aècent, and salt; add garlic salt, marjoram, oregano, thyme, sage, and nutmeg. Add this to rapidly boiling broth and cook until very thick. Stir constantly. Pour into 2 greased loaf pans. When set, slice and fry to crisp. (Be careful, as the cornmeal pops.)

Irma Flat Mothers' Club Cookbook

Nordic Ham Loaf

1 pound ground ham
1 pound ground fresh pork
   (not sausage)
½ teaspoon salt

2 cups instant oatmeal
3 eggs
¼ teaspoon pepper

GLAZE:
2 tablespoons prepared
   mustard

½ cup brown sugar

Mix well the ham, pork, salt, oatmeal, eggs, and pepper. Spread into a greased 8-inch-square pan. Bake at 350° for 45 minutes. Combine Glaze ingredients and spread over cooked ham loaf. Return to oven for 10–15 minutes longer. Cut into squares.

French Family Favorites

Pan Fried Venison Steaks

1 pound steaks, ½ inch thick
¼ cup thick cream or
   evaporated milk

¼ cup flour
3 teaspoons butter
Salt and pepper to taste

Pound steaks thoroughly with sharp-edged meat pounder. Cut into serving pieces. Dip steaks into cream and dredge in flour. Brown one side in hot butter. Turn, salt and pepper to taste. Continue browning until second side is well browned.

Fire Hall Cookbook #2

Bou Bobs

Use caribou, mule deer, or whitetail, but use an adult animal—two years old or more. Mature animals have a more complex flavor and firmer texture to the meat, which the red wine vinegar and soy sauce complement. Make sure, however, that the meat you use is tender. Kabobs cook very fast, and there's no time for tenderizing.

1 pound tender caribou
¼ cup red wine vinegar
¼ cup soy sauce

¼ cup vegetable oil
1 teaspoon ground lemon peel
½ teaspoon pepper

Dry the caribou meat off with a paper towel, and cube it into 2-inch chunks. In a large bowl or resealable plastic bag, combine the red wine vinegar, soy sauce, oil, lemon peel, and pepper. Add the meat cubes, cover or seal, and marinate 24 hours in the refrigerator.

Start 40 briquettes, or preheat a propane barbecue and turn down to medium-high heat. Meanwhile, drain off and save the marinade. Pat the caribou chunks dry with paper towels, then place on skewers.

When the charcoals are white hot, and you can only hold your hand at cooking level for 4–5 seconds, lightly brush the meat chunks with the marinade and place on the grill. Cook about 5 minutes per side, then serve hot with risotto. Yields 4 servings.

Game on the Grill

Reuben Roll-Up

A treat for sauerkraut lovers!

DOUGH:

1 package hot roll mix
¾ cup warm water (105° -
   115°)

1 tablespoon caraway seeds
¼ teaspoon minced onion
1 egg

In large bowl, dissolve yeast from hot roll mix in warm water. Stir in caraway seeds, onion, and egg. Add flour from roll mix. Stir well. Cover and let rise in a warm place until doubled in size (45–60 minutes).

On a a well-floured surface, knead Dough until no longer sticky (2–3 minutes). Roll out Dough into a 12x15-inch rectangle.

FILLING:

¾ cup Thousand Island salad
   dressing
1 (12-ounce) can corned beef,
   shredded

1 (8-ounce) can sauerkraut,
   drained
1 cup shredded Swiss cheese

Preheat oven to 350°. Spread Dough with salad dressing to within 1 inch of the edge. Sprinkle with corned beef, then sauerkraut. Add cheese. Starting at long side, roll up tightly. Pinch bottom seam. Fold over and pinch ends. Place sealed-side-down on lightly greased cookie sheet. Let rise until not quite double in size (30–45 minutes). Bake for 40–45 minutes. Cool for about 10 minutes before serving. Serves 8–10.

The Hole Thing Volume II

Famous Wyomingites: Dick Cheney, Vice President of the United States of America; William F. "Buffalo Bill" Cody, scout; Esther Hobart Morris, first female justice of the peace; Nellie Tayloe Ross, first female governor; Curt Gowdy, Hall of Fame Sportscaster; Chris LeDoux, country music singer; J.C. Penney, businessman.

Master Meat Sauce

Master recipes save time and money. Many main dishes that could be family favorites can be made with the following Master Meat Sauce.

4 pounds lean ground meat	2 (15-ounce) cans tomato sauce
1 medium onion, minced	1 teaspoon garlic powder
1 (6-ounce) can tomato paste	1 teaspoon salt
1 (6-ounce) can water, or 1 can tomato soup	

Brown meat; drain fat. Add other ingredients. Simmer 20–30 minutes. Add water or tomato juice to thin, if necessary. Immediately place 1-cup portions in freezer-quality, plastic zip-top bags. Freeze.

Per ½ cup serving: Cal 160; Cal from Fat 100; Total Fat 11g; Sat Fat 4g; Chol 45mg; Sod 300mg; Carb 3g; Prot 14g; Dietary Fiber 1g; Sugars 0g; Vit A 6%; Vit C 0%; Calc 0%; Iron 8%.

Suggestions:

Spaghetti: Add 1½ teaspoons Italian seasoning or 1 package spaghetti sauce seasoning mix to 2 cups Master Meat Sauce. Heat. Mix with 4 cups hot cooked spaghetti.

Chili: Add 2–3 teaspoons chili powder to 2 (16-ounce) cans drained kidney beans and 2 cups Master Meat Sauce. Heat through.

Mini Pizzas: Add 1 teaspoon Italian seasoning and a dash of pepper to 1 cup Master Meat Sauce. Spoon 1–2 tablespoons over half a bagel, English muffin, or any other bread. Sprinkle with 1–2 tablespoons mozzarella cheese. Broil 2–3 minutes until cheese starts to brown.

Sloppy Joes: Add 1 tablespoon vinegar, 1 tablespoon brown sugar, and ¼ cup ketchup to 2 cups Master Meat Sauce. Heat. Serve on hamburger buns.

Pastafazool: Mix 1 (16-ounce) can chili beans and 2 cups cooked, drained macaroni with 1 cup Master Meat Sauce. Add ½ cup grated cheese. Serve with extra cheese at table.

Chimichangas and Burritos: Combine 1 cup Master Meat Sauce, 1 (16-ounce) can refried beans, 1 teaspoon cumin or 2 teaspoons chili powder, and ½ cup salsa. Heat through. Spoon on warm tortillas and roll.

Tacos: Add 1 teaspoon cumin or 2 teaspoons chili powder to 1 cup Master Meat Sauce. Heat through. Spoon 1–2 tablespoons meat into a taco shell. Add salsa, shredded lettuce, diced tomatoes, diced onions, and grated Cheddar or Monterey Jack cheese. Enjoy!

Cent$ible Nutrition Cookbook

Bass Peak Huckleberry Sauce

Tastes best on pork or beef.

½ cup butter
½ cup flour
2 cups warm water
1 cup huckleberries, drained

4 tablespoons sugar
1 teaspoon ground nutmeg
½ cup bourbon or rye whiskey

In large saucepan melt butter; add flour and water. Whisk over medium heat until smooth and bubbly. Add huckleberries, sugar, and nutmeg; boil until thick. Keep mixture hot. Add bourbon or rye whiskey just before serving. Makes 8 servings.

Bitterroot Favorites & Montana Memories

Wild Game Dip

This is an excellent accompaniment to all wild game dishes.

2 cups apricot preserves
¼ cup fresh lemon juice
½ cup white wine

2 tablespoons teriyaki sauce
¼ teaspoon cayenne pepper
Salt and pepper to taste

In saucepan, combine apricot preserves, lemon juice, wine, teriyaki sauce, cayenne pepper, salt and pepper. Stir until well blended. Cook and reduce to thicken. Yields 1½–2 cups.

Wonderful Wyoming Facts and Foods

POULTRY

Historic St. Mary's Mission in Stevensville, Montana, was established in 1841 by Father Pierre DeSmet, at the urging of local Indian tribes who wanted to learn from "blackrobes." Its furnishings are the handiwork of Montana's first medical doctor, Father Anthony Ravalli.

★ ★

Rosemary Ginger Roasted Chicken

The aroma of this chicken should be bottled and sold for perfume! It will make you swoon in sheer ecstasy. There is a subtle undertone of lemon and a peppery bite that's pleasantly surprising. The skin is crispy brown and the chicken just melts in your mouth. If there are any leftovers, make a flavorful chicken salad.

1 whole (2- to 2½-pound) chicken
5 tablespoons olive oil
3 tablespoons minced garlic
1 tablespoon black pepper
2 tablespoons chopped fresh rosemary
1 tablespoon each: chopped fresh parsley, sage, thyme

3 teaspoons salt
1 teaspoon cayenne
1 tablespoon chopped fresh thyme
1 teaspoon chopped fresh ginger
1 teaspoon grated lemon peel
Juice of ½ lemon

Discard any contents inside the chicken and rinse the bird thoroughly. Cut the backbone out; turn the bird over and break the ribs by pushing down hard with your palm. This makes the bird lay fairly flat.

Combine all other ingredients in a medium bowl. Pull the skin away from the bird and using your hands, rub the marinade into the meat, going all the way to the legs and thighs, as well as the breasts. Rub remaining marinade on the outside skin. Cover and refrigerate for 2 hours.

Preheat oven to 425°. Place chicken on a rack in a roasting pan. Fill the bottom of the pan with ¼ inch hot water. Roast for 40 minutes or until done. Let it rest for 5 minutes, then cut into quarters, or remove all the meat from the bones and transfer to a warm platter for serving. Serves 4.

Recipe by Craig Fellin's Big Hole River Outfitters, Wise River, Montana

The Great Ranch Cookbook

Chicken Pie

1 (4-pound) stewing or roasting fowl
Water, to barely cover
½ teaspoon salt
Shake of pepper
3 tablespoons butter
3 tablespoons flour
3 cups warm chicken broth (from stewing fowl)
1 cup cream
2 tablespoons chopped pimento
1 (4-ounce) jar button mushrooms, drained
Biscuits

Put fowl in large saucepan. Add water, salt, and pepper, and bring to a boil. Simmer until the meat falls from the bones (1½–2 hours). Cool. Discard skin. Remove meat from bones in large pieces. Place chicken pieces evenly in bottom of a 12-inch baking dish. In saucepan, melt butter; blend in flour; add broth gradually. Add cream. Beat all the while with a whisk. Add pimentos and mushrooms. Taste and adjust seasoning. Bring to boil before you pour over chicken. Top with uncooked biscuits (homemade, if possible). Preheat oven to 425°. Bake for 20–25 minutes.

Columbus Community Cookbook

Lander, Wyoming, claims to have held the first rodeo where cowboys were paid. Lander's first rodeo was held in 1893, and the annual "Pioneer Days Rodeo" has been held on the Fourth of July ever since.

Ginger Fried Chicken

Great for a picnic.

1 cup flour	2 teaspoons ground ginger
½ teaspoon cinnamon	1 chicken, cut up
(more if you wish)	½ cup margarine
¼ teaspoon pepper	½ cup soy sauce

Combine dry ingredients in a bag. Wash chicken. Coat chicken pieces with dry ingredients. Melt margarine in large oven-proof pan. Place chicken in pan meat-side-down. Cook 40 minutes in a 425° oven. Add soy sauce. Coat evenly; turn over chicken; cook 20–30 minutes more. Eat hot or cold.

The Fine Art of Cooking Volume 2

Bombay Platter

1 (3-pound) fryer, cut in	Flour, paprika, salt
serving pieces	Oil

Dip chicken in flour, paprika, and salt mixture. Fry in oil on both sides until lightly browned. Lay in 9x13-inch baking pan.

SAUCE:

½ cup dry wine	2 tablespoons oil
2 tablespoons brown sugar	½ teaspoon ginger
1 tablespoon soy sauce	1 tablespoon sesame seeds

Combine ingredients and pour over the chicken. Cover with aluminum foil and bake at 375° for 40–45 minutes. Serve with Curried Rice Mold (page 128), peach halves, and avocado rings.

Home at/on the Range with Wyoming BILS

Kentucky-Style Chicken

2 packages Italian salad
   dressing mix, divided
2 cups baking mix (Bisquick)
1 egg, beaten

⅔ cup club soda
1 (2- to 3-pound) chicken, cut
   into serving pieces

Mix 1 package dressing mix with baking mix. Mix the other package of dressing with egg and club soda. Dip chicken pieces into egg mixture, then into dry mixture. Set chicken pieces on a rack to drip. Fry for 3 minutes in deep 350° fat. Bake in oven for 30 minutes at 350°.

Sharing Our Best

Sweet and Sour Chicken

½ cup vinegar
¾ cup sugar
¼ cup water
½ teaspoon salt
3 tablespoons ketchup

2 tablespoons soy sauce
2 pounds drummettes
½ cup cornstarch
Crisco

Combine vinegar, sugar, water, salt, ketchup, and soy sauce and set aside. This makes enough sweet and sour sauce for 2 pounds of chicken drummettes.

Roll chicken drummettes in cornstarch. Brown in Crisco. Place in baking dish. Pour mixture over chicken. Bake at 350° for 20 minutes. Turn chicken and bake 15 minutes.

Horse Prairie Favorites

"The great registry of the desert," Independence Rock, is located on the Sweetwater River 50 miles southwest of Casper, Wyoming. It proudly displays the hand-scratched names of more than 5,000 pioneers who passed by on their way westward on the Oregon Trail.

★ ★

Dutch Oven Chicken Dinner

This recipe was a favorite of the crew and wranglers at Teton Trail Rides when the Rudds operated the concession in Grand Teton National Park from 1950 to 1993. It makes a hearty outdoor meal.

4 large boneless chicken
  breasts
1–1½ cups cubed potatoes
1–1½ cups cubed zucchini
1–1½ cups cubed carrots
1–1½ cups chopped cabbage
1 (16-ounce) can garbanzo
  beans

1 medium onion, chopped
¼ cup chopped green pepper
2–3 garlic cloves, chopped
1 (16-ounce) can chicken broth
1 (10½-ounce) can cream of
  chicken soup
Salt and pepper

On outdoor barbecue, grill chicken breasts until brown on both sides. Place cut-up potatoes, zucchini, carrots, and cabbage in bottom of a 12-inch Dutch oven. Mix in garbanzo beans (with juice), onion, green pepper, and garlic cloves. Place chicken breasts over top of vegetables. Pour chicken broth over meat and vegetables. Spoon out and spread cream of chicken soup over top of chicken. Season with salt and pepper as desired. Cover and cook on low to medium heat on outdoor grill for 1–1½ hours, until vegetables are tender.

The Pure Food Club of Jackson Hole

Saucy Chicken Cordon Bleu

4 skinless, boneless chicken
  breast halves
4 slices ham
4 slices Swiss cheese
1 cup flour
1 teaspoon salt
½ teaspoon pepper
½ teaspoon paprika
2 eggs, beaten
⅓ cup milk
1 cup dry bread crumbs
¼ cup vegetable oil

Preheat oven to 350°. Flatten chicken breasts without breaking through meat. Roll each ham slice in a cheese slice; then roll up in chicken breasts. In a shallow dish or bowl, season flour with salt, pepper, and paprika. In a separate dish or bowl, beat together eggs and milk. Dip chicken rolls in seasoned flour, then egg mixture, then bread crumbs. Heat oil in a large skillet and fry chicken until golden brown. Set aside.

MUSHROOM SAUCE:

1 (10¾-ounce) can cream of
  mushroom soup
½ pound fresh mushrooms,
  sliced
¼ teaspoon garlic powder
¼ cup milk
½ cup sour cream

In a large bowl combine soup, mushrooms, garlic powder, milk, and sour cream. Mix all together. Place chicken in a 9x13-inch baking dish and pour sauce over chicken. Bake for 20–25 minutes or until chicken is completely done. Serves 4.

Favorite Recipes

The paintbrush, the Wyoming state flower, is connected to the Native American legend of a young brave who tried to paint the sunset with his war paints. Discouraged that he could not match the brilliance of nature, he asked for help from the Great Spirit. The Great Spirit granted him paintbrushes rich in the colors he needed. With these, he painted his masterpiece and left the used brushes in fields, and these brushes sprouted the paintbrush flowers.

Chicken Enchiladas

6 boneless, skinless chicken
  breast halves (1½ pounds)
1 tablespoon butter
1 cup chopped onion
1 green bell pepper, cored,
  seeded, and chopped
1 red bell pepper, cored,
  seeded, and chopped
8 ounces grated Cheddar cheese
1 (4-ounce) can diced green
  chiles
1 cup purchased green chile
  salsa

½ cup chopped fresh cilantro
4 teaspoons ground cumin
Salt and freshly ground black
  pepper
12–15 (7-inch) flour tortillas
10 ounces Monterey Jack
  cheese, grated
1 cup whipping cream
½ cup chicken broth
Chopped avocado for garnish
Chopped tomatoes for garnish

Place chicken in pan of rapidly boiling water to cover, and simmer for 15–20 minutes till tender. Remove from heat; drain, cool and shred chicken. Preheat oven to 350°.

In medium skillet, melt butter over medium heat. Cook onion and bell peppers until just soft, 5–8 minutes. Transfer to large bowl. Add chicken, Cheddar cheese, green chiles, salsa, cilantro, and cumin. Season with salt and pepper to taste and mix well.

Grease a 10x15x2-inch baking pan or 2 smaller pans. In each flour tortilla, place ⅓ cup chicken mixture along an edge. Roll up from filling side and place seam-side-down in the pan. Sprinkle Monterey Jack cheese over enchiladas. Combine cream and chicken broth and pour over enchiladas. Cover pan with foil and bake for 30 minutes. Remove foil and continue baking for 10 minutes or until thoroughly heated. Garnish with avocado and tomatoes, if desired. Can serve tortilla soup with this dish.

From the High Country of Wyoming

Doris' Chicken Enchiladas

2 cups chopped cooked chicken
or turkey
1 cup chopped green bell
pepper
1 (8-ounce) package cream
cheese, cubed
1 (8-ounce) jar salsa, divided
6 (6-inch) flour tortillas
12 ounces Velveeta cheese,
cubed
¼ cup milk

Stir chicken, green pepper, cream cheese, and ½ cup of salsa in a medium saucepan on low heat until cream cheese is melted. Spoon approximately ½ cup of the chicken mixture down the center of each tortilla and roll them up. Place tortillas seam-side-down in lightly greased 8x12-inch baking dish. In a saucepan, combine and heat cheese and milk over low heat. Stir until smooth. Pour cheese sauce over tortillas, cover pan with foil and bake at 350° for 20 minutes or until thoroughly heated. Top with remaining salsa.

Wyoming Cook Book

Hunter's Chicken

1 pound boneless, skinless
chicken breasts, cut in strips
⅓ cup cornstarch
¼ cup margarine
½ teaspoon tarragon
½ teaspoon thyme
¼ teaspoon pepper
1 cup sliced green onions
2 cups chicken broth
¾ cup white wine
1 cup sliced mushrooms
3 tomatoes, cut in eights
3 or 4 cups cooked rice

Dredge chicken in cornstarch. Brown coated chicken in margarine. Stir in seasonings and onions. Cook a few minutes longer. Add broth and wine. Cover; simmer at least 10 minutes. Gently stir in mushrooms and tomatoes. Cover; simmer 5 minutes longer. Serve over rice. Serves 6.

The Fine Art of Cooking

★ ★

Blue Spruce Olive Chicken Mozzarella

4 chicken breasts
¼ cup flour
¼ teaspoon salt
¼ cup olive oil
1 clove garlic, crushed
1 medium onion, diced
1 (14-ounce) jar spaghetti sauce

1 (8-ounce) can sliced
   mushrooms
½ teaspoon oregano
½ cup sliced pimento-stuffed
   olives
1 (6-ounce) package sliced
   mozzarella

Skin and bone chicken breasts; cut into bite-size pieces. Combine flour and salt in a plastic bag and coat chicken. Heat oil in a skillet and brown chicken. Arrange chicken in shallow 2-quart baking dish, leaving the drippings in the skillet. Sauté garlic and onion in drippings until onion is tender. Stir in spaghetti sauce, mushrooms, oregano, and olives; pour over chicken. Cut cheese slices into strips and place on top of chicken. Bake at 350° until chicken is tender, about 30 minutes. Makes 6–8 servings.

Recipe from Blue Spruce Inn, Lander, Wyoming
Tastes & Tours of Wyoming

Chicken and Asparagus Casserole

1 pound fresh asparagus, or
  1 (15-ounce) can asparagus
1½ cups cooked cubed chicken
1 (10½-ounce) can cream of
  asparagus or cream of
  mushroom soup

⅓ cup milk
¾ cup Cheddar cheese,
  shredded
2 tablespoons butter or
  margarine, melted
5 tablespoons bread crumbs

In a shallow casserole dish, arrange asparagus on bottom. Spread chicken cubes over asparagus. Combine soup and milk. Pour over chicken. Sprinkle cheese over top. In small bowl melt margarine. Add bread crumbs and stir. Sprinkle over cheese. Bake at 450° for 15 minutes or until hot throughout and lightly browned. Yields 4 servings.

Irene's Country Cooking

Chicken Español

The following recipe is an attempt to bring together some of the major ingredients used in Spanish cooking.

Olive oil
4–6 chicken breasts
4–6 cloves garlic
3–4 red bell peppers

½ cup dry sherry
Fresh rosemary
Salt and pepper

Oil baking dish. Rub the skins of the chicken breasts with a little olive oil. Place a garlic clove under the skin of each breast. Slice the peppers into quarters. Arrange chicken breasts and sliced peppers in baking dish. Pour sherry over the chicken and lay rosemary on top. Sprinkle with salt and pepper. Bake at 350° until done, about 1 hour. Baste chicken a few times while baking.

Serve with fried potatoes, green salad, and crusty bread. A Spanish rioja wine will make the dinner more special.

Potluck

Chicken Supper

¾ cup chopped onion
½ cup chopped celery
1 tablespoon chopped green
   pepper
1 cup water or chicken broth
1 (10½-ounce) can cream of
   chicken soup or chicken
   broth
3 cups cubed chicken

1 (10½-ounce) can mushroom
   soup
1 teaspoon salt
⅛ teaspoon pepper
1 teaspoon Worcestershire
   sauce
1 cup cream
Biscuits

Simmer onion, celery, and green pepper in water or chicken broth until tender. Add chicken soup, cubed chicken, mushroom soup, salt, pepper, Worcestershire sauce, and cream. Mix well; pour into casserole dish. Cover top of casserole with uncooked biscuits. Bake at 350° for 40 minutes, or until biscuits are brown.

Variations: Good way to finish up the turkey. You can be creative with the vegetable amounts, meat, and liquids; the cream and Worcestershire sauce are a must. Can add peas, carrots, even leftover gravy, or a bit of dressing.

Mountain Brook's Wacky Wonders of the Woods

Garlic Lovers' Chicken

½ cup dry bread crumbs
⅓ cup grated Parmesan
   cheese
2 tablespoons minced parsley
½ teaspoon salt (optional)
⅛ teaspoon pepper
¼ cup milk

6 boneless, skinless chicken
   breast halves (1½ pounds)
¼ cup butter or margarine,
   melted
1–2 garlic cloves, minced
2 tablespoons lemon juice
Paprika

In a large resealable plastic bag, combine the first 5 ingredients. Place milk in a shallow bowl. Dip chicken in milk, then shake in the crumb mixture. Place in a greased 9x13x2-inch baking dish. Combine the butter, garlic, and lemon juice; drizzle over the chicken. Sprinkle with paprika. Bake, uncovered, at 350° for 25–35 minutes or until the juices run clear. Makes 6 servings.

Cooking with the Ladies

Turkey Rolls

1¼ pounds diced cooked
   chicken or turkey
1 (8-ounce) package cream
   cheese, softened
Lemon pepper to taste

1 (8-ounce) can refrigerated
   crescent rolls
1 (10¾-ounce) can cream of
   mushroom soup
½ soup can of milk

Mix together well the meat, cream cheese, and lemon pepper. Set aside. Spread out crescent rolls, and separate into triangles. To make larger rolls, dough can be rolled thinner with a floured rolling pin. Place a large spoonful of meat mixture in center of each roll. Wrap dough around meat mixture, sealing edges. Bake as directed on crescent roll package until rolls are lightly browned. Mix and heat mushroom soup with milk to make a gravy. Spoon over warm rolls. Baked rolls can be frozen and reheated later.

The Pure Food Club of Jackson Hole

Creamed Turkey

6 tablespoons butter or
  margarine
6 tablespoons flour
1 teaspoon salt
⅛ teaspoon pepper
1½ cups seasoned chicken
  broth

1 cup cream or milk
1 cup chopped cooked turkey
2 tablespoons sherry flavoring
  (optional)

Melt butter; add flour, salt, and pepper. Cook over low heat
until smooth and bubbly. Remove from heat; stir in chicken
broth and cream or milk. Bring to a boil and boil 1 minute,
stirring constantly. Stir the turkey in gently. Just before
serving, add sherry flavoring, if desired. Serve in pastry
shells or pastry cases or over biscuits, noodles or rice.

Recipes from the Heart

Smoked Turkey

BRINE:
2 gallons water
1 cup pickling salt
2 cups Morton Tender Quick

1 (3-ounce) bottle liquid smoke
Turkey

Mix all ingredients well and pour over turkey in plastic pail;
soak turkey for 24–36 hours, uncovered, in refrigerator (10
pound turkey for 24 hours). (Be sure turkey is completely
thawed before putting it to soak in the Brine.)

   Remove turkey from Brine; wash and dry. Brush turkey
skin with oil and place breast-side-down on rack in baking
pan. Bake in 350° oven for 1 hour. Turn oven down to 225°
and bake 1 hour for each pound of turkey (10 pounds for 10
hours).

Note: I soaked an 18-pound turkey for 29 hours and cooked 1 hour at
350° and 13 hours at 200°. It was smoked right and cooked just right!

Simac Family Favorites

Corn Bread Dressing, Country Style

Here's the dressing to try out posthaste. My family enjoys it as a side dish rather than "stuffed into a bird." It is especially yummy served with chicken gravy, country style.

1 cup chopped white onion
1 cup chopped celery with
  some of the leaves
¼ cup water
6 cups crumbled corn bread
6 slices toasted regular bread,
  torn into small pieces

5 eggs, beaten slightly
1 tablespoon ground sage
¼ teaspoon seasoned salt
1 cup cubed cooked turkey or
  chicken
2–2½ cups chicken broth,
  purchased or homemade

Cook the onion and celery in water for about 5 minutes; drain. Combine the corn bread, regular bread, cooked onion and celery, eggs, sage, salt, and cooked chicken or turkey. Stir in enough of the chicken broth to make the stuffing extra moist. Turn into a greased 8x8x2-inch baking dish.

Bake, covered, at 400° for 30 minutes. Uncover and bake another 5–10 minutes more, until dressing is heated through and the top is a little crusty. This dressing can be made early in the day. Cover and refrigerate until ready to bake.

Note: If you don't have any leftover chicken or turkey in your refrigerator, stop by the local deli and pick up just enough to add to this extra-special corn bread delight.

Best-of-Friends, Festive Occasions Cookbook

Bitterroot River Roast Duck

GLAZE:

1 (10-ounce) jar orange
  marmalade
½ cup frozen orange juice
  concentrate, thawed

1 tablespoon cider vinegar
1 tablespoon Worcestershire
  sauce
1 tablespoon brown sugar

Combine Glaze ingredients in saucepan; heat thoroughly and stir well.

2 ducks (split down back and
  butterflied)
1 teaspoon sea salt
1 teaspoon ground pepper

1 teaspoon poultry seasoning
1 cup plus 1 tablespoon water
1 tablespoon cornstarch

Preheat oven to 350°. Season ducks with sea salt, pepper, and poultry seasoning. Place split-side-down on rack in roasting pan. Prick duck in several places to let fat bake off. Roast for 20 minutes, uncovered.

Take duck out of oven and put in baking dish. Spoon Glaze over ducks and return to oven. Baste ducks every 10 minutes and continue baking for 40 minutes till duck is done. Remove ducks to serving dish. Deglaze pan by adding 1 tablespoon water to pan, scraping bottom. Dissolve cornstarch in 1 cup water; add to deglazed pan juices and heat to a boil. Serve sauce over ducks. Serves 4.

Bitterroot Favorites & Montana Memories

Native Americans used the roots of the bitterroot, the official Montana flower, for food by digging up the roots and drying them so they could be kept and used for months. The root was too bitter to eat unless it was cooked, and it was usually mixed with berries or meat. The bitterroot can be found growing near the mountains and boulders of western Montana in spring and summer.

Barbecued Goose
with Cumberland Sauce

1 whole goose (about 6 pounds)   **1 whole orange, peeled**

Preheat barbecue to 350° (for indirect cooking, see tip below.) Rinse the goose in cold water; pat dry with paper towels inside and out. Place the peeled orange inside the goose. Set the goose in an 8x12x1-inch disposable aluminum drip pan. Close the barbecue and cook until the meat thermometer reads 140°–150° (about 10 minutes per pound for about 6 pounds of bird in summer; longer on cool days). You'll get a slightly pink bird. Place the goose on a platter to cool. Remove the orange and save to make the sauce.

CUMBERLAND SAUCE:

2 tablespoons butter	**3 tablespoons dry red wine**
1 teaspoon Worcestershire sauce	**¼ cup red currant jelly**

In a small skillet, melt butter over medium heat. Trim the dark brown crust from the orange, and dice the rest, adding it to the melted butter. Sauté 2–3 minutes, until you smell the orange, then add Worcestershire, wine, and currant jelly. Once the jelly has melted, lower heat to simmer. Cook another 10 minutes, until the sauce thickens. Serve the goose hot with hot Cumberland Sauce. Or serve both chilled. Serves 4.

Tip: Used to be that barbecuing a duck or goose meant standing guard with fully loaded water pistols to prevent fat fires from ruining dinner. Best to use indirect cooking. If you have a propane barbecue, you need 2 burners, with only one lit. With a charcoal unit, simply build the fire on one side of the fire grate. Preheat both to 350°. Then place the goose on a cast-iron poultry grate over an aluminum drip pan, and place both on the side where the fire isn't. The goose drips into the pan, not the fire, so there's no flare-up.

Duck & Goose Cookery

Clay-Pot Goose
with Pineapple-Maple Sauce

If you cook a lot of birds, like them more than medium-rare, and don't like them dry, you really should try a clay pot. They infuse moisture into all wild birds—upland as well as waterfowl—and allow you to cook them to higher internal temperatures without losing as much moisture. A lot like a water smoker, but without the smoke, you're cooking indoors—an advantage during the holiday season.

1 snow goose, about 1½–2
  pounds
2 tablespoons unsweetened
  pineapple juice

2 tablespoons maple syrup
1 teaspoon spicy brown
  mustard

Do not preheat oven. Place the clay pot in a sink full of cold water to cover the top and bottom. Let soak for at least 15 minutes. Take one more look at the goose, trimming rough edges and pulling feathers you missed last fall. Dry inside and out with paper towels.

Combine pineapple juice, maple syrup, and mustard in a small bowl. Microwave 10–12 seconds on HIGH (700 watts) to liquefy the syrup. Stir the mixture well. Place the goose in the clay pot, breast up, and pour the juice mixture slowly over the breast, legs, and wings. Cover the pot and place in the center of a cold oven. For electric ovens, turn the oven to 300°; for gas ovens, turn the oven to 200° for 10 minutes; then 250° for 10 minutes, then 300°. Roast for 2 hours.

Remove the goose from the pot and carve as you would a Christmas goose. Serve with pan juices. (If you like lots of sauce, heat up some more of the pineapple, mustard, and maple syrup concoction in a saucepan just before the goose is done. Then combine that and the pan juices together to serve at the table.) Serves 3–4.

Duck & Goose Cookery

Mesquite-Smoked Pheasant Tacos

Two ways to do the smoke: Make a hot fire with chunks of mesquite, or make a fire with charcoal briquettes and add a generous handful of mesquite chips to the coals just before cooking.

Breasts of 2 pheasants
1 teaspoon ground cumin
1 teaspoon chili powder
½ teaspoon salt
½ teaspoon pepper
8 corn tortillas

1 tablespoon vegetable oil
4 Roma tomatoes, diced
2 cups sliced lettuce
4 ounces Monterey Jack cheese, grated
1 cup red salsa

Dry the breasts with paper towels and set aside. In a small bowl, combine the cumin, chili powder, salt, and pepper and stir to mix thoroughly. Rub this mixture on both sides of the breasts, cover, and place in the refrigerator 30–60 minutes.

Preheat a propane barbecue for 10 minutes, then turn down to medium-high heat. Or start 40 charcoal briquettes (or mesquite chunks) and wait 25 minutes. The fire is ready when you cannot hold your hand at cooking level more than 4–5 seconds. If you are using mesquite chips over the charcoal, set them to soak for 15–20 minutes while the fire is getting hot.

Brush the tortillas with a small amount of oil. Prepare the tomatoes, lettuce, cheese, and salsa.

Place the breasts on a lightly oiled grill directly over the fire and cook about 4–5 minutes to a side. As the pheasant cooks, lightly brown the tortillas over the fire, about 2–3 minutes each. Stack on a serving platter and cover to keep soft. When the pheasant is done, remove it from the fire and tear or slice the meat apart. Divide the pheasant, tomato, lettuce, cheese, and salsa among the tortillas, fold, and eat. Serves 4.

Game on the Grill

★ ★

Creamed Pheasant with Caramelized Onions

No matter what else I cook, this is what people remember. It harkens back to the classic pheasant fried in butter, then baked in cream sauce, but this is a lot easier. With the caramelized onions, I think it tastes a lot better, too.

2 tablespoons butter	2 tablespoons Dijon mustard
1/2 onion, thinly sliced	1/4 teaspoon white pepper
1/4 cup extra dry sherry	1 pheasant, cleaned
1/2 cup heavy cream	1 tablespoon flour

In a large skillet, melt the butter over medium heat, then add the onion slices and sauté until the onions are golden brown—caramelized. Turn the heat off and let onions sit.

Preheat a propane barbecue for 10 minutes, then turn down to medium-low heat. Or start 3 dozen charcoal briquettes on one side of the barbecue and wait 25 minutes. Optimum cooking temperature is 350° for both units.

While the barbecue heats up, combine the sherry, cream, mustard, and pepper in a small bowl. Mix thoroughly. Pat the pheasant down inside and out with paper towels and set it in a plastic oven bag that has been shaken with 1 tablespoon of flour. Pour the cream sauce and caramelized onions over the pheasant and close the bag. Make 6 small slits in the top of the bag, per package directions. Now place it on a clean drip pan for easy handling.

Place the pheasant in the barbecue, on the top shelf or over the unlit burner, and cook 60 minutes. Remove the pheasant from the bag, and serve with the cream sauce and mashed potatoes. Serves 4.

Game on the Grill

SEAFOOD

PHOTO © JOHN REDDY PHOTOGRAPHY, INC.

Known as "Old Misery" to early explorers and fur trappers who braved its raging currents, the Missouri River became a pathway for the expansion of the West. From the time of Lewis and Clark until the coming of the railroads, the Missouri (shown here at Mountain Palace) was the major water route to the Rocky Mountains.

Trout Hemingway, Barbour-Style

Ernest Hemingway was a great hunter and fisherman, so he knew and wrote of a good pan of fried trout. Simply speaking, there is nothing better than a freshly caught fried Rocky Mountain Trout; however, there are good ways and bad ways of preparing them. My version is perfect for cooking while camping out, or in the kitchen.

3 green onions with tops, finely chopped
1 tablespoon minced fresh parsley
Juice of 1 lemon
Salt and pepper to taste
6 freshly caught cut-throat or rainbow trout (about 8 ounces each)

6 strips of bacon
½ cup biscuit mix
¼ cup yellow cornmeal
1 teaspoon paprika
Lemon wedges for garnish

Combine green onions, parsley, lemon juice, salt and pepper, and spread in cavities of fish. In a large frying pan, over medium heat, cook bacon crisp. Remove from pan. Drain.

Combine biscuit mix, cornmeal, and paprika in a shallow pan. Carefully dredge both sides of trout in mixture. Cook fish in hot bacon grease until nicely browned, turning once. (For a 1-inch-thick fish, allow 10 minutes total or 5 minutes per side.) Top each trout with bacon slice and garnish with lemon wedge. Serve with tartar sauce, if desired. Serves 6.

Wonderful Wyoming Facts and Foods

★ ★ ★ ★ ★ ★ ★ ★ ★ ★ ★ ★ ★ ★ ★ ★ ★ ★ ★ ★

Trout in Foil

6 whole trout, cleaned
Lemon pepper seasoning
1 lemon, thinly sliced
3 slices bacon, halved
1 onion, thinly sliced

3 medium potatoes, scrubbed
  and thinly sliced
3 carrots, pared and thinly
  sliced

Preheat oven to 350°. You will need 6 sheets of heavy-duty foil (each 4 inches longer than the trout). Lay trout on sheet of foil. Sprinkle lemon pepper the length of the cavity and line with lemon slices. Close cavity and top trout with a half slice of bacon. Top with onion, potato, and carrot slices; seal foil securely. Put foil-wrapped trout on a baking sheet. Bake 15 minutes; turn and bake 10 minutes longer (small trout less time, large trout more time). Makes 6 servings.

Yaak Cookbook

Blodgett Lake Stuffed Trout

4 trout, cleaned—leave heads
  and tails on
2 tablespoons white wine
1 lemon, sliced thin
4 slices bacon, cooked and cut
  into 1-inch pieces
4 green scallion onions, sliced
  thin

2 mushooms, sliced
1 tablespoon butter
1 tablespoon lemon butter (½
  lemon juice and ½ melted
  butter)
1 teaspoon cumin
1 teaspoon ground red pepper

Preheat oven to 375°. Put trout in greased 9x13-inch baking dish; set aside. Melt butter in skillet and sauté bacon pieces, green onions, and mushrooms. Drain off fat. Stuff the trout with bacon mixture. Brush top of trout with lemon butter. Sprinkle cumin and red pepper on top of trout. Place lemon slices on top of trout and bake for 30 minutes. Serve hot with steamed rice. Makes 4 servings.

Bitterroot Favorites & Montana Memories

Montana Stuffed Baked Trout

The first stuffed baked trout I ever ate was a Christmas celebration in the Andes Mountains, on the border between Chile and Argentina. Mel and I were on a camping-fishing vacation. December is summer in South America. Mel caught the fish in a mountain lake, cleaned it, stuffed it with bread, onion, and herb stuffing, rolled it in wet newspapers (we didn't have aluminum foil in those days), and laid it on a bed of red-hot coals. We use the same recipe for Montana trout.

1 (2- to 3-pound) trout, cleaned
Salt and pepper
¾ cup tender celery, chopped
1 medium onion, chopped
1 tablespoon chopped green
 onion
2 tablespoons butter

4 or 5 slices medium dry bread,
 hand crumbled (about 2 cups)
2 tablespoons chopped parsley
¼ teaspoon black pepper
½ teaspoon sage
½ teaspoon basil

Wash trout and pat dry with a paper towel. Sprinkle with salt and pepper inside and out. Sauté celery and onion in butter for 5 minutes, then mix with other ingredients. Stuff the fish lightly with dressing. If there is leftover dressing, put it in a baking dish, add a few drops of water, cover, and bake along with the fish. (Fish dressing should be dry, as it absorbs moisture from the fish while baking, and will become pasty if water is added beforehand.)

Bake fish and dressing in preheated 350° oven for about 40 minutes. Serve with lemon wedges. Serves 4–6.

The Kim Williams Cookbook and Commentary

Fossil Butte National Monument is the preservation of a 50-million-year-old lake bed with fossils that spanned two million years recorded in its limestone. Species of fishes, insects, birds, and crocodiles are preserved there. The 8,198-acre park is located just 15 miles west of the town of Kemmerer in southwestern Wyoming.

Fillet of Salmon with Tomato Beurre Blanc

Beurre Blanc is French for white wine butter sauce. Many chefs today are adding additional ingredients to give the old classic a new twist. This Tomato Beurre Blanc is light and tangy and is a perfect accompaniment to the broiled salmon. You can grill the salmon, if you prefer.

²/₃ cup sour cream, divided
2 tablespoons Dijon-style
  mustard
2 (8-ounce) salmon fillets
2 teaspoons olive oil
1 pound (4 large) tomatoes,
  peeled, seeded and chopped
Salt and pepper to taste

⅛ teaspoon fresh thyme leaves
  (or ½ teaspoon dried)
1 tablespoon minced shallot
2 tablespoons white wine
2 tablespoons white wine
  vinegar
½ cup butter (1 stick), cut into
  8 pieces and very cold

Mix only ½ cup sour cream and mustard together, and coat salmon on both sides. Set aside.

Preheat broiler. Heat oil in a skillet over medium heat and add tomatoes, cooking for about 10–15 minutes, until juices are thick and somewhat reduced. Season with salt and pepper and stir in thyme. In a separate skillet over medium heat, combine shallot, white wine, and vinegar. Cook until the mixture is almost evaporated, with only about 1 tablespoon left. Whisk in remaining sour cream and heat through, about 2 minutes. Turn heat to the lowest setting.

While swirling pan, add butter, 1 piece at a time. When the piece is almost completely melted, add the next piece of butter and continue to swirl the pan. After 3 or 4 pieces have been added, remove pan from heat and continue to swirl and add butter. After the last piece has been added and melted, pour butter mixture into the warm tomato mixture. Season with more salt and pepper, if necessary. Keep warm while broiling the salmon, but watch the heat. Too much heat will "break" the sauce, and it will separate. Broil the salmon until opaque, about 3–5 minutes per side. Spoon 2–3 tablespoons sauce on a plate and top with salmon. Garnish with fresh thyme sprig and/or lemon wedge. Makes 2 servings.

Recipe from B Bar Guest Ranch, Emigrant, Montana
The Great Ranch Cookbook

Eggstraordinary Salmon-Cheddar Pie

3 large eggs
¼ cup milk
3 tablespoons parsley, divided
2 tablespoons butter, melted
2 tablespoons minced green onion
1 tablespoon plus 1 teaspoon lemon juice, divided
1 teaspoon Worcestershire sauce
½ teaspoon dry mustard

2 cups (8 ounces) shredded Cheddar cheese
1 (5½-ounce) can salmon, drained and deboned
1 (9-inch) pie shell, baked and cooled
¾ cup dairy sour cream
¾ cup finely chopped cucumber
1 teaspoon dill weed
⅛ teaspoon ground white pepper

Beat eggs in large mixing bowl. Add milk, 2 tablespoons of parsley, butter, green onion, 1 tablespoon lemon juice, Worcestershire sauce, and mustard. Fold in cheese and salmon; pour into cooled pie shell. Bake 25 minutes at 425° until crust is golden brown. After pie has cooled for at least 10 minutes, combine sour cream, cucumber, remaining 1 tablespoon of parsley, dill, and remaining 1 teaspoon lemon juice and pepper. Dollop each pie serving with sour cream mixture. Makes 6 servings.

The Best of Rural Montana Cookbook

★ ★

Crispy Cod Batter

⅔ cup cornstarch
⅓ cup flour
1 teaspoon vinegar
Water

1 tablespoon baking powder
Peanut-safflower oil
Cod or other white fish, cut in
   chunks

Combine cornstarch, flour, and vinegar. Add enough water to make a medium-thick batter, like for pancakes. Stir in baking powder. Heat oil in deep-fat fryer to 375°. Dip fish chunks in batter. Fry in fat until golden brown, about 3–4 minutes. Remove to drain on paper towel, then set in warm oven until ready to serve. The batter is crispy and delicious, and stays that way.

Mountain Brook's Wacky Wonders of the Woods

Scalloped Oysters

I often put a large pan of these out while I do the finishing touches on a holiday dinner—gets everyone out of the kitchen.

2 tablespoons minced green
  onion
2 tablespoons butter
½ cup fresh white bread
  crumbs

Salt and pepper to taste
6–8 oysters

Sauté onions in butter until golden. Add bread crumbs and brown lightly. Salt and pepper to taste. Spread half of the crumbs in the bottom of a small, greased baking dish, drained oysters next and the rest of the crumbs on top. Bake in 450° oven for 8–10 minutes until brown and bubbly. Serve at once.

Souvenirs

★ ★

Shrimp and Eggplant Jambalaya

Excellent as a side dish as well as a main dish.

1 medium eggplant	1 clove garlic, chopped
1 tablespoon cooking oil	2 (16-ounce) cans whole
½ cup chopped onion	tomatoes
½ cup chopped celery	1 cup rice
½ cup chopped green bell	Salt and pepper
pepper	1 pound shrimp, peeled

Peel and dice eggplant and fry in oil. When tender, add onion, celery, bell pepper, and garlic, and cook a few minutes. Add tomatoes and well-washed rice. Season to taste and let it all cook, covered, slowly for about 1 hour, adding water if needed. About 20 minutes before serving, add the cleaned shrimp, and cook until done. Serves 6.

The Fine Art of Cooking Volume 2

Grilled Caribbean Prawns

This is a super recipe which can be used to prepare shrimp as a party hors d'oeuvre, a first course, or grilled on skewers as a main entrée.

2 pounds large prawns, peeled and deveined

MARINADE:

¼ cup dark rum	¼ cup brown sugar
¼ cup fresh lime juice	1 teaspoon nutmeg
¼ cup soy sauce	½ teaspoon allspice
¼ cup extra virgin olive oil	½ teaspoon cinnamon
2 tablespoons minced fresh	
ginger	

In mixing bowl, blend rum, lime juice, soy sauce, olive oil, fresh ginger, sugar, nutmeg, allspice, and cinnamon.

Marinate prawns for 2 hours. Remove prawns from Marinade and grill until done. (Reserve Marinade and heat to serve as dipping sauce with prawns.) When the seam along the back has just changed from opaque to white, they are perfect. Serve warm.

Recipe from Off Broadway Grill
A Taste of Jackson Hole II

Seafood Paella

1½ quarts water
2 (8-ounce) cans tomato sauce
2 large onions, chopped
3 slices of swordfish
6 chicken broth cubes
¼ cup plus 1 tablespoon olive oil, divided
1½ pounds shrimp
Any other seafood (clams, scallops, etc.)
1 lobster tail, sliced
2 teaspoons minced garlic
½ red pepper, chopped
½ green pepper, chopped
2 cups converted rice
1 cup white wine
1 small jar pimiento strips
1 small can very young small early peas, drained
Fresh parsley
Lemon or lime wedges

Prepare a broth with water, tomato sauce, onions, swordfish, chicken broth cubes, and ¼ cup olive oil. Cook for at least 1 hour. Wash and peel the shrimp and all other seafood. Remove swordfish from broth and cut into chunks. Leave broth simmering.

Cover bottom of paella pan with 1 tablespoon olive oil and heat over medium heat. Add minced garlic and sauté, stirring so as not to burn the garlic, and add peppers and rice, continuing to stir. Start adding broth to rice, and when it starts boiling, gradually start adding the seafood and fish. Add white wine. Continue to add broth as needed. When rice is tender, sprinkle pimento strips and peas over top. Cover and allow to sit for about 15 minutes before serving. Garnish with parsley and lemon or lime wedges.

Story, Wyoming's Centennial Community Cookbook

Wyoming's Yellowstone Lake is the largest mountain lake in North America with more than 100 miles of shoreline.

★ ★ ★ ★ ★ ★ ★ ★ ★ ★ ★ ★ ★ ★ ★ ★ ★ ★ ★ ★

Seafood Giovanni

2 large onions, chopped
2 bell peppers, chopped
3 cups fresh mushrooms, sliced
Butter
3 cups canned tomatoes,
　drained and chopped

1 (8-ounce) package vermicelli
　pasta, cooked
3 cups flaked crabmeat, shrimp,
　or prawns (small)
2 cups sour cream
1 cup grated sharp cheese

Sauté onions, bell peppers, and mushrooms in butter. Add tomatoes, cooked vermicelli pasta, and crabmeat. Mix well. Add sour cream. Mix well again. Turn into greased 9x13-inch casserole. Sprinkle with grated cheese. Bake in moderate oven, 300°–350° for 30 minutes. Makes 12 servings.

Recipe from Time After Time B&B, Victor, Montana
Recipes from Big Sky Country

CAKES

PHOTO © JOHN REDDY PHOTOGRAPHY, INC.

At 308 feet, the Lower Falls of the Yellowstone River in Yellowstone National Park, Wyoming, is higher than Niagara Falls in New York. The volume of water flowing over the Lower Falls can vary from 5,000 gallons a second to 63,500 gallons a second at peak runoff.

Cranberry Cake
with Cream Sauce

3 tablespoons butter, softened
1 cup sugar
1 egg
2 cups all-purpose flour*
2 teaspoons baking powder

1 teaspoon nutmeg
1 cup milk
2 cups cranberries
2 tablespoons grated orange or
  lemon peel

In a mixing bowl, cream the butter and sugar. Beat in egg. In a separate bowl, combine flour (*for persons living in high altitude areas, ⅓ cup of additional flour should be added), baking powder, and nutmeg. Add dry mixture to the butter/sugar/egg mixture alternately with milk, starting with and ending with milk. Stir in cranberries and peel of your choice. Grease a 7x11-inch baking dish. Bake at 350° for 35–40 minutes, or until a toothpick inserted near the center comes out clean. Top with Cream Sauce.

CREAM SAUCE:
1⅓ cups sugar
1 cup heavy cream (unwhipped)

⅔ cup butter

While cake is baking, combine the sauce ingredients in a saucepan. Cook and stir over medium heat until heated through. Cut warm cake into squares; serve with the warm Cream Sauce.

Recipes to Make You Purr

Doris's Rhubarb Cake

5 cups diced rhubarb
1 cup sugar
1 (3-ounce) package raspberry
  Jell-O

1 white cake mix
Whipped cream

Spread rhubarb in greased 9x13-inch cake pan. Sprinkle sugar over the top. Sprinkle Jell-O next. Mix white cake mix as directed on package and pour over the rhubarb. Bake at 350° for 50–55 minutes. Turn out on a cookie sheet and serve with whipped cream.

Fire Hall Cookbook

Victorian Applesauce Cake

1½ cups sugar
2 cups flour
1½ teaspoons baking soda
1½ teaspoons salt
2 tablespoons cocoa
½ teaspoon ground cloves
½ teaspoon nutmeg
½ teaspoon cinnamon

½ teaspoon allspice
½ cup shortening
1½ cups applesauce, divided
2 eggs
¾ cup chopped dates
¾ cup raisins
¾ cup chopped nuts
¾ cup chopped cherries

Sift together all dry ingredients into mixing bowl. Cut in shortening. Add 1 cup applesauce and eggs; beat 2 minutes. Add remaining ½ cup applesauce. Beat 1 minute. Mix in dates, raisins, nuts, and cherries. Pour into greased 9x9-inch cake pan, sprinkle with topping, and bake in 350° oven for 50–55 minutes.

TOPPING:
¼ cup finely chopped nuts   2 tablespoons sugar

Sprinkle over top of cake before baking.

Lewis and Clark Fare

Huckleberry Crumb Cake

CAKE:

1¼ cups sugar
¼ cup shortening
2 eggs
2 cups sifted flour
½ teaspoon salt
1 teaspoon baking powder

¾ cup milk
1½ cups huckleberries
1½ teaspoons vanilla extract
1 tablespoon grated orange
    rind

Cream sugar and shortening. Beat in eggs. Add flour, salt, and baking powder alternately with milk. Fold in berries. Stir in vanilla and orange rind. Pour into 9-inch-square greased pan.

CRUMBLE TOPPING:

½ cup sugar
½ cup flour

¼ teaspoon cinnamon
¼ cup butter

Mix together all ingredients. Sprinkle Crumble Topping over batter. Bake at 350° for 45–50 minutes, until cake tests done.

Recipes from the Heart

Sheepwagon Carrot Cake

This is best when started in the evening before you head for bed, and finished in the morning. Sure makes the house smell wonderful.

1⅓ cups water
1⅓ cups sugar
2 cups grated carrots
1 cup raisins
1 teaspoon butter
1 teaspoon cinnamon

1 teaspoon ground cloves
1 teaspoon nutmeg
2⅓ cups flour
1 teaspoon salt
2 teaspoons baking powder
1 cup chopped nuts (optional)

In medium saucepan, mix together water, sugar, carrots, raisins, butter, and spices. Simmer over low heat for 5 minutes. Then cover and let rest 12 hours, or overnight.

Sift together flour, salt, and baking powder. Mix everything together well, including nuts, if desired, and bake in 2 oiled loaf pans or 1 tube pan at 300° for 50 minutes, or till cake tests done. Cool and wrap in foil. Freezes well.

With Lots of Love

Peanut Crunch Cake

1 package yellow cake mix	¼ cup vegetable oil
1 cup peanut butter	¾ cup chocolate chips, divided
½ cup brown sugar	¾ cup peanut butter chips,
1 cup water	divided
3 eggs	½ cup chopped peanuts

Beat cake mix, peanut butter, and brown sugar on low speed until crumbly. Set aside ½ cup for topping. Add water, eggs, and oil to the remaining crumb mixture. Blend on low until moistened. Beat on high 2 minutes. Stir in ¼ cup chocolate chips and ¼ cup peanut butter chips. Pour into greased 9x13-inch pan. Combine peanuts, remaining chips and reserved crumb mixture. Sprinkle over batter. Bake in 350° oven for 40–45 minutes or until toothpick inserted in the center comes out clean.

Ranch Recipe Roundup IV

Burnt Sugar Cake

2 cups sugar, divided	1 teaspoon vanilla
1½ cups water, divided	2½ cups flour, divided
Scant ½ cup butter	2 teaspoons baking powder
2 eggs, separated	

In heavy skillet brown ½ cup sugar. Then add ½ cup water and let boil to a syrup. Set aside. Beat together 1½ cups sugar, butter, egg yolks, 1 cup cold water, 1 teaspoon vanilla, and 2 cups flour.

Add ½ cup flour and 2 teaspoons baking powder to syrup. Add syrup mixture to batter mixture. Beat egg whites and fold in last. Bake in 2 greased layer pans or a greased 9x13-inch pan for 30–35 minutes at 350°.

Irma Flat Mothers' Club Cookbook

Stack Cake

Stack Cake was a traditional pioneer wedding cake put together at the wedding celebration. Each guest brought a layer of cake. The layers were put together with homemake applesauce, then stacked. The bride's popularity was measured by the number of stacks she had and by the number of layers in each stack.

The cakes were usually quite colorful and flavorful, as the guests proudly showed off their baking skills with many different types of cakes being brought to the bride.

Following is a typical 6-layer molasses cake, although you may choose to vary your layers.

1 cup butter	**Salt to taste**
1 cup sugar	**1 cup milk**
1 cup molasses	**1 quart applesauce**
3 eggs	**Whipped cream**
4 cups flour	**Pecans or walnuts, chopped**
1 teaspoon baking soda	

Cream together butter and sugar. Fold in molasses. Add eggs, one at a time, beating to incorporate. Mix together flour, baking soda, and salt. Add to creamed mixture alternately with milk, beating after each addition.

Grease and flour 3 (8-inch) round cake pans. Fill each with 1⅓ cups batter and refrigerate remainder for 3 more cakes. Bake at 375° for 15 minutes, or until done. Cool 5 minutes; remove from pans and cool on wire rack. Bake next 3 cakes.

When cool, spread applesauce between layers. Spread top with whipped cream and nuts. Serves 24.

Wonderful Wyoming Facts and Foods

The first interscholastic football game to be played under artificial light took place in Midwest, Wyoming, in 1925, between high school teams Midwest and Casper.

★ ★

Bear Creek Butter Cake

CAKE:

2 cups sugar
1 cup plus 1 tablespoon butter,
  softened, divided
4 eggs
3 cups flour

1 teaspoon baking powder
1 teaspoon sea salt
½ teaspoon baking soda
1 cup buttermilk
2 teaspoons vanilla extract

Cream together sugar and 1 cup butter, then add eggs, one at a time. In a large mixing bowl mix flour, baking powder, sea salt, and baking soda. In another bowl mix buttermilk and vanilla extract. Add to creamed mixture alternately with dry mixture. Rub 1 tablespoon butter over bottom of tube pan; pour mixture into pan and bake. Remove from oven and cool for 30 minutes.

1 cup sugar
¼ cup water

½ cup butter, softened
1 tablespoon vanilla extract

Cream together sugar, water, butter, and vanilla extract; pour mixture over top of cake.

Bitterroot Favorites & Montana Memories

Black Joe Cake

2 cups sugar
2 cups flour
2 eggs
¾ cup cocoa
½ cup oil
2 teaspoons baking powder

1 teaspoon baking soda
1 teaspoon vanilla
1 cup cold coffee
1 cup milk
1 teaspoon salt

Put all ingredients in a mixing bowl. Stir together. Batter will be thin. Bake in a greased 9x9-inch cake pan at 350° for 35 minutes.

Recipe from Red Lodge Cafe, Red Lodge, Montana
Festival of Nations Cookbook

★ ★

Twice the Guilt Cake

CAKE:

1 cup sugar	1 (13½-ounce) can crushed
1 teaspoon vanilla	pineapple, undrained
2 eggs	½ cup brown sugar
2 cups flour	½ cup coconut
1 teaspoon salt	½ cup chopped pecans
1 teaspoon baking soda	Whipped cream topping

Combine sugar, vanilla, and eggs. Beat 2 minutes at medium speed. At low speed add flour, salt, soda, and pineapple. Mix 1 minute. Pour into greased 9x13-inch pan. Sprinkle mixture of brown sugar, coconut, and pecans on top. Bake at 350° for 30–35 minutes. Just before Cake is done, prepare Sauce.

SAUCE:

½ cup butter	½ cup sugar
½ cup light cream	½ teaspoon vanilla

Heat ingredients together and pour mixture over warm cake. Cool and serve with whipped cream topping.

Recipe from Stoneheart Inn, St. Ignatius, Montana
Montana Bed & Breakfast Guide & Cookbook

Legend tells of an Indian chief whose son, known as "The Dreamer," refused to hunt buffalo the traditional way. He decided, instead, to stampede unsuspecting buffalo over cliffs to a rocky death below. Because of the sound the buffalo made as they fell, the Dreamer's buffalo trap was known as "water at the place where the buffalo chug." Therefore, the white settlers later took on the Indian name "Chugwater" for the little town of Chugwater, Wyoming.

Chocolate Cake

2 cups sugar
1¾ cups flour
¾ cup cocoa
1 teaspoon baking powder
2 teaspoons baking soda
1 teaspoon salt

2 eggs
1 cup strong coffee
1 cup buttermilk
½ cup vegetable oil
1 teaspoon vanilla

Preheat oven to 350°. Sift sugar, flour, cocoa, baking powder, soda, and salt into a large bowl. Add eggs, coffee, buttermilk, oil, and vanilla. Beat for 12 minutes. Butter a 9x13-inch or 12-inch round cake pan. Pour batter into pan. Bake 35–40 minutes, until done.

ICING:

12 ounces good semisweet
  chocolate
Sour cream

Vanilla or coffee liqueur
  (optional)

Melt semisweet chocolate in a double boiler. Turn off heat and stir in enough sour cream to produce a spreading consistency. Add a little vanilla or coffee liqueur if you want. Enjoy!

Potluck

Filled Fudge Cake

If you like chocolate, you'll love this cake.

2 cups sugar	2 teaspoons baking powder
1 cup canola oil	2 teaspoons baking soda
1½ teaspoons salt	¾ cup unsweetened cocoa
2 eggs	1 cup buttermilk
1 teaspoon vanilla	1 cup hot water
3 cups flour	1 cup chopped nuts (optional)

Cream sugar, oil, and salt. Add eggs and vanilla. Mix together flour, baking powder, soda, and cocoa. Add to creamed mixture alternately with buttermilk and hot water. Mix well. Add nuts, if desired. Grease well a large Bundt or angel food cake pan. Pour ½ of batter into pan.

FILLING:

¼ cup sugar	1 cup semisweet chocolate
1 teaspoon vanilla	chips
1 (8-ounce) package cream	½ cup coconut (optional)
cheese, softened	

Mix all Filling ingredients together well, and drop by spoonfuls on top of first layer of cake batter. Then cover with remaining batter. Bake at 350° for 1 hour. Do not turn out of pan until completely cool (3–4 hours). Turn out onto plate. Ice with thin chocolate glaze, if desired.

The Pure Food Club of Jackson Hole

Over 15 feature films have been made on location in Jackson Hole, Wyoming, including: "Shane," "Spencer's Mountain," "Any Which Way You Can," and "Rocky IV."

Whipped Cream Chocolate Cake

2 cups sour cream	4 tablespoons cocoa
4 eggs, well beaten	1 cup boiling water
2 cups sugar	2 teaspoons baking soda
3 cups flour	2 teaspoons vanilla
1 teaspoon salt	

Whip sour cream until stiff. Add eggs. Sift together sugar, flour, and salt; add to whipped mixture. Dissolve cocoa in boiling water; add soda, then add to above mixture. Add vanilla last and mix well. Bake at 350° for 40–45 minutes in a greased 9x13-inch baking pan.

BOILED FROSTING:

½ cup butter	1 teaspoon vanilla
1 cup brown sugar	Nuts and coconut as desired
¼ cup milk	

Place butter, brown sugar, and milk in saucepan and bring to a boil. Add vanilla and nuts and coconut, if desired. Spread over hot cake; place under broiler until golden brown. Be careful not to burn!

Feeding the Herd

★ ★

Black Forest Cake

Chocolate cake mix
1 large can cherry pie filling
3 cups whipping cream
¼ cup powdered sugar

1 tablespoon instant vanilla
  pudding
1 (4-ounce) chocolate bar (or
  chocolate chips)

Make cake according to package directions; bake in 3 (8-inch) round cake pans or in a spring form pan and cut into 3 layers.

Have cake layers ready and cooled. Transfer 1 layer to cake platter and spread with cherry pie filling. Beat whipping cream until thick; sift powdered sugar and instant pudding over cream and continue beating until cream makes stiff peaks. Put second layer of cake on top of cherries and spread with ⅓ of the whipped cream. Leave enough cream to frost remainder of cake. Top second layer with whipped cream, then add third layer and frost with remaining whipped cream. Use potato peeler to make curls on top of cake from chocolate bar. Or grate semisweet chocolate chips on top.

With Lots of Love

Easy Strawberry Cake

1 white cake mix
4 cups sliced strawberries

1 cup granulated sugar
1 pint whipping cream

Prepare batter for 2-layer size cake; mix according to package directions; turn into greased and floured 9x13-inch pan. Cover batter with strawberries; sprinkle strawberries with sugar. Pour whipping cream over ingredients in pan. Bake at 350° for 50–60 minutes or until cake springs back when touched lightly. Cream and strawberries sink to bottom, forming a lush custard layer.

Sharing Our Best

Sour Cherry Kuchen

Bursting with flavor, this is rather like a fruit quiche—and real men will love it!

CRUST:

½ cup cold butter, cut into 8 slices

2 cups flour

¼ cup sugar

¼ teaspoon baking powder

¼ teaspoon salt

Preheat oven to 400° (425° at 6,000 feet). For Crust, cut butter into dry ingredients until mixture resembles fine meal. Press onto bottom and up sides of an 11-inch tart pan with removable sides.

FILLING:

1 (1-pound) can tart red cherries packed in water, well drained

¾ cup sugar

1½ teaspoons ground cinnamon

1 egg, lightly beaten

1 cup whipping cream

Gently scatter cherries over top of Crust. Combine sugar with cinnamon and pour evenly over the cherries. Bake in the center of oven 15 minutes. Remove from oven. Blend egg and cream together. Pour carefully over cherry mixture. Bake 25 minutes longer, until golden brown. Cool to lukewarm on a rack before serving. Makes 8 servings.

Note: A 9x13x2-inch baking pan may be used in place of the tart pan. The Crust may be made in a food processor using frozen butter.

Jackson Hole à la Carte

Wyoming has the world's largest sodium carbonate (natrona) deposits and has the nation's second largest uranium deposits. Sodium Carbonate is a sodium salt of carbonic acid used especially in making soaps and chemicals, in water softening, in cleaning and bleaching, and in photography.

Mother's Best Angel Food Cake

2 cups egg whites (about 16)
1 teaspoon vanilla
½ teaspoon almond extract
½ teaspoon salt
2 teaspoons cream of tartar

2¼ cups sugar, divided
1½ cups flour
Raspberry or other flavor dry
  Jell-O (optional)

Beat egg whites, vanilla, almond extract, salt, and cream of tartar until soft peaks form. Add 1¼ cups sugar, 2 tablespoons at a time, and beat until stiff. Sift together and fold in flour and 1 cup sugar. Jell-O may be folded in for color and flavor at this time. Swirl for marbled effect. Bake 50–60 minutes in tube pan in moderate (350°) oven.

Amish Country Cooking

Orange Sauce for Angel Food Cake

1 cup sugar
4 tablespoons flour
Pinch of salt
2 cups hot water

Juice and rind of 1 orange
Juice of 1 lemon
2 or 3 eggs, separated
1 cup whipped cream

Cook sugar, flour, salt, water, juices and rind, and egg yolks. Cool. When cold, fold in beaten egg whites and whipped cream. Serve over angel food cake.

Lewis and Clark Fare

In their quest for an overland route to the Pacific Ocean, explorers in the Lewis and Clark expedition formed a camp with the Shoshoni Indians a few miles south of present-day Dillon, Montana, which they named "Camp Fortunate." Here, Sacagawea, the expedition's Indian guide and translator, learned that her brother, Cameahwait, was now chief of the Shoshoni tribe. (She had been kidnapped by plains Indians five years previously.) It was an emotional scene when brother and sister were reunited.

★ ★

Four-Day Make-Ahead Sour Cream Fudge Torte

FUDGE TORTE:

1 box devil's food cake mix   1 cup water
3 eggs   ½ cup oil

Heat oven to 350°. Grease and flour 2 (8-inch) cake pans. In large bowl, blend ingredients at low speed until moistened. Beat for 2 minutes at highest speed. Pour into pans. Bake for 30–40 minutes or until toothpick comes out clean. Cool cake in pans on cooling rack for 15 minutes. Remove from pans and cool completely. Split each layer in half, forming 4 layers. Fill and frost with Sour Cream Filling.

SOUR CREAM FILLING:

2 cups dairy sour cream   3 cups nondairy whipped
1 cup sugar   topping
3 cups flaked coconut

In large bowl, combine sour cream, sugar, and coconut. Gently fold in whipped topping. Use to fill between layers and to frost sides and top of Torte. Store covered in refrigerator.

Recipe from Big Horn B&B, Philipsburg, Montana
Recipes from Big Sky Country

Old-Fashioned Funnel Cake

2 cups milk	½ teaspoon salt
2 eggs, beaten	Oil
2 cups flour	Confectioners' sugar
1 teaspoon baking powder	Cinnamon

Mix milk and eggs together. Sift together flour, baking powder, and salt. Pour milk mixture into flour and mix thoroughly. Test consistency of batter to determine whether it will flow properly through funnel. If the batter is too thick, add milk to thin. If batter is too thin, add flour to thicken. Heat oil in deep fryer until hot enough to fry. Pour cake batter through funnel in deep fryer. Swirl funnel around to make decorative pattern by controlling outlet with finger. Fry until golden brown and floating. Drain and sprinkle with a mixture of confectioners' sugar and cinnamon while still hot. Serve hot!

Wonderful Wyoming Facts and Foods

Lemonade Cheese Cake

60 Ritz crackers	1 can pink lemonade, frozen
1 stick margarine	1 can condensed milk
½ cup powdered sugar	1 (8-ounce) container Cool Whip
1 (8-ounce) package cream cheese, softened	

Crush crackers and blend with margarine and powdered sugar. Press into 9x13-inch pan, reserving some for the top. Blend cheese, pink lemonade, and condensed milk. Fold in whipped topping and spread in pan. Top with remaining crumbs. Refrigerate for 2–3 hours.

The Best of Rural Montana Cookbook

Snow White Cheesecake

BASE:

1 package graham crackers (⅓ of box)

1 teaspoon ground ginger
2 ounces butter (½ stick)

Crush crackers finely; add ginger and melted butter. Press evenly over base of a greased 8-inch spring form pan. Refrigerate while preparing Topping.

TOPPING:

1 (8-ounce) carton cottage cheese
1 (8-ounce) package cream cheese, softened
1 cup cream
1/2 cup superfine sugar

1 teaspoon vanilla
1 package unflavored gelatin
⅓ cup water
2 egg whites
Fresh fruit for garnish

In a blender or food processor, blend cottage cheese; add cream cheese and enough cream to process smoothly. Add sugar, vanilla, and remaining cream. Dissolve gelatin in water over a pan of hot water. Cool and add to cheese mixture, running machine constantly. Pour into a large bowl. Beat egg whites until soft peaks form; fold into cheese mixture. Spread evenly over Base and refrigerate until firm. Decorate top with any fresh fruit.

The Fine Art of Cooking

West Yellowstone in Montana claims to be the Snowmobile Capital of the World. On average, more than 150 inches of snow falls there each year, accumulating on the more than 400 miles of snowmobile trails found there.

Chocolate Mousse Cheesecake

CRUST:

2½ cups crushed graham
  crackers

6 ounces butter or margarine,
  melted

Combine graham cracker crumbs and butter and press into a
9½x2½-inch spring form cake pan, lining sides and bottom.
Place in refrigerator to chill and set.

FILLING:

2 large tablespoons cream
  cheese, softened
1 teaspoon vanilla extract
1 egg, lightly beaten
4 tablespoons powdered sugar

1½ cups chocolate syrup
1 pint whipping cream
1 ounce unflavored gelatin
½ cup hot water

In a bowl, beat cream cheese until smooth with electric mixer.
Add vanilla, egg, and powdered sugar. Beat until smooth.
Add chocolate syrup and mix thoroughly. Place whipping
cream in a bowl and beat with electric mixer until soft peaks
form. Fold into the cream cheese mixture. Heat the gelatin
and ½ cup water in microwave for 30 seconds or until all of
the gelatin granules have dissolved. While slowly stirring the
cream cheese mixture, add the gelatin a little at a time. Pour
all into graham cracker crust. Chill until set (about 2½
hours). Serves 10.

Wyoming Cook Book

Amaretto Cheesecake

CRUST:

1½ cups chocolate wafer cookie crumbs

½ cup finely chopped toasted almonds

¼ cup butter, melted

2 tablespoons sugar

1 tablespoon amaretto

Place rack in middle of oven. Preheat oven to 375°. Grease a 9-inch spring form pan.

Mix all ingredients together in large bowl till well blended. Press into bottom of spring form pan; bake till brown, about 7 minutes, but no longer than 9 minutes. Cool on a rack. Decrease oven temperature to 350°.

FILLING:

3 (8-ounce) packages cream cheese, at room temperature

1 cup sugar

4 eggs

⅓ cup whipping cream

⅓ cup finely chopped almonds

¼ cup Bailey's Irish Cream

¼ cup amaretto

Using an electric mixer, slowly beat cream cheese and sugar till light and fluffy. Add eggs, one at a time, beating well after each addition. Add the remaining ingredients for the Filling and beat till well blended. Pour Filling into Crust. Bake until just set, about 1 hour. Turn off oven and let the cheesecake cool inside oven with oven door open, approximately 30 minutes. Center of cheesecake should be completely set by this time. Remove cake from pan. Preheat oven again to 350°.

TOPPING:

1½ cups sour cream

1 tablespoon sugar

½ teaspoon vanilla

Blend ingredients in small bowl till smooth. Spread this mixture over cake. Bake 10 minutes. Cover with plastic wrap and refrigerate overnight.

Home at/on the Range with Wyoming BILS

Pumpkin Walnut Cheesecake

CRUST:

⅛ cup sugar   Butter
1 cup graham cracker crumbs

Mix sugar and cracker crumbs together. Generously butter a 9x13-inch spring form pan and pat into bottom.

FILLING:

3 (8-ounce) packages cream   1 (16-ounce) can pumpkin
  cheese, softened   1 teaspoon cinnamon
¾ cup sugar   ½ teaspoon nutmeg
¾ cup brown sugar   ¼ teaspoon cloves
6 eggs (7 at high altitude)   ¼ cup heavy cream

Beat together cream cheese, sugars, eggs, pumpkin, spices, and cream. Pour into crust and bake at 325° for 1 hour and 35 minutes. Cheesecake is done when center is firm. Remove from oven, turn oven off, and close oven door.

TOPPING:

3 tablespoons butter, softened   ½ cup brown sugar
½ cup chopped walnuts

Mix together butter, nuts, and sugar. Spread on hot cheesecake; return to oven until completely cool. Cheesecake may be frozen. Serves 12–14.

The Hole Thing Volume II

COOKIES & CANDIES

PHOTO © JOHN REDDY PHOTOGRAPHY, INC.

Step back in time at the Four Winds Historic Village, near Ronan, Montana. The village represents the region as it was settled in the late 1800s, and includes the Jocko Indian Agency Building, a home and trading post, and an antique train and toy museum.

★ ★

Soft Ginger Cookies

1½ cups sugar
1 cup sour cream
½ cup shortening
2 teaspoons baking soda
Dash of salt
1 teaspoon ginger

1 teaspoon cinnamon
1 cup molasses
2 eggs
3½ cups flour
Additional sugar to sprinkle

Combine all ingredients except sugar to sprinkle. Roll out on a floured board. Sprinkle with sugar and cut out. Bake on lightly greased baking sheet for 10–12 minutes at 350°.

Food for the Soul

Gingersnaps

¾ cup butter
1 egg
1 cup sugar
¼ cup molasses
2½ cups flour

2 teaspoons baking soda
1 teaspoon cinnamon
1 teaspoon cloves
1 teaspoon ginger

Preheat oven to 350° (and be sure the heating element is off when you begin baking the cookies, or they will burn before cooking). Cream together butter, egg, sugar, and molasses. Sift in flour, baking soda, and spices. Mix well and cover. Put in refrigerator for about an hour (the dough must be cold, or your cookies will not cook properly). Roll into walnut-size balls, roll in granulated sugar, and bake on ungreased cookie sheet 8–10 minutes.

Note: Want an easy way to measure molasses? Fill your ¼ cup measure with oil. Pour oil back into its original container; this coats the inside of the measuring cup with oil. Fill with molasses and add to other ingredients. All the molasses will slide right out—pretty slick!

With Lots of Love

Glazed Fresh Apple Cookies

2 cups sifted all-purpose flour
1 teaspoon baking soda
½ cup soft butter or margarine
1½ cups packed brown sugar
½ teaspoon salt
1 teaspoon cinnamon
1 teaspoon ground cloves
½ teaspoon nutmeg

1 unbeaten egg
1 cup walnuts
1 cup finely chopped, unpared
 apples
1 cup raisins, chopped
¼ cup apple juice, milk or
 orange juice

Sift flour and soda together. Cream butter, sugar, salt, and spices. Add egg and mix thoroughly. Add ½ flour mixture, nuts, apples, raisins, and juice. Mix well. Add remainder of flour and mix again. Drop by rounded spoonsful on greased cookie sheet. Bake 11–14 minutes in a 400° oven. While warm, glaze with mixture below.

GLAZE:
1½ cups powdered sugar
2 tablespoons butter, softened

Enough orange juice to spread

Recipe by Mrs. Walter Myers, wife of Mayor, Virginia City, Montana
First Ladies' Cookbook

Pineapple Drop Cookies

1 cup brown sugar
1 cup white sugar
1 cup shortening
2 eggs, well beaten
2 teaspoons vanilla
½ teaspoon salt

½ teaspoon baking soda
2 teaspoons baking powder
4 cups flour
1 cup crushed pineapple
1 cup finely chopped walnuts

Mix sugars, shortening, eggs, and vanilla together. Add dry ingredients alternately with pineapple. Add chopped nuts. Drop by teaspoon onto greased baking sheet. Bake at 375° for about 12 minutes.

Recipes from the Heart

★ ★

Old-Fashioned Sour Cream Cookies

½ cup soft butter
1½ cups sugar
2 eggs
1 cup sour cream (non dairy)
1 teaspoon vanilla

½ teaspoon baking powder
2¾ cups flour
½ teaspoon soda
⅛ teaspoon salt

Mix together butter, sugar, and eggs. Add sour cream and vanilla. Sift together dry ingredients and add to first mixture. Chill at least 1 hour. Drop onto greased cookie sheet and bake 8–10 minutes at 425°. Do not overbake.

Horse Prairie Favorites

Perfect Raisin Cookies

2 cups raisins
1 cup water
1 cup chopped nuts
2 cups sugar
1 cup shortening
2 eggs

1 teaspoon vanilla
4 cups flour
1 teaspoon baking soda
1 teaspoon baking powder
½ teaspoon ground cloves
1 teaspoon cinnamon

Boil raisins and water for 5 minutes. Cool; add soda and nuts. Cream sugar, shortening, eggs, and vanilla. Combine flour, soda, baking powder, and spices. Add raisin mixture alternating with dry ingredients to creamed mixture. Drop by spoonful onto greased baking sheet and bake at 350° for 12–15 minutes. Cool and store with layers of waxed paper in covered buckets or crock.

Heavenly Recipes and Burnt Offerings

The first movie in which actor John Wayne had a speaking part, "The Big Trail," was filmed at Moran Junction, Wyoming, south of Jackson, in 1930.

★ ★

Million Dollar Cookies

½ cup butter, softened
½ cup white sugar
½ cup brown sugar
½ cup shortening
1 egg

1 teaspoon vanilla
2 cups flour
½ teaspoon baking soda
¼ teaspoon salt
½ cup chopped nuts

Cream butter, sugars, and shortening; add egg and vanilla. Sift flour, baking soda, and salt and add to creamed mixture. Fold in nuts. Roll into balls, place on ungreased cookie sheet and press flat with bottom of a glass dipped in white sugar. Bake at 350° for 10–12 minutes. Can be decorated as Christmas sugar cookies. Makes 4 dozen.

Mountain Brook's Wacky Wonders of the Woods

Macadamia Chip Cookies

I'm always looking for something new and different in the chocolate chip cookie world. This macadamia nut, chocolate chip combination is divinely decadent!

1 cup softened sweet butter
¾ cup granulated sugar
¾ cup firmly packed brown
  sugar
1 tablespoon vanilla extract
1 tablespoon Frangelico liqueur
  (optional)
1 tablespoon coffee liqueur
2 large eggs

2½ cups all-purpose flour
1 teaspoon baking soda
¼ teaspoon salt
2 (12-ounce) packages milk
  chocolate chips
1 cup chopped walnuts
½ cup chopped pecans
½ cup chopped macadamia
  nuts

Using large mixer bowl, cream first 6 ingredients until light and fluffy. Add eggs and beat well. Mix flour, baking soda, and salt in bowl. Stir into creamed mixture. Mix in chocolate chips and all chopped nuts by hand. Drop batter by ¼ cupfuls onto greased cookie sheets. Space cookies about 1 inch apart. Bake until cookies are light brown, about 15 minutes. Remove from oven, but be careful not to burn your mouth! Makes about 36 cookies.

Best-of-Friends, Festive Occasions Cookbook

Cream Filled Cookies

FILLING:

1 (8-ounce) package cream
  cheese, softened
¼ cup margarine, softened

3 cups powdered sugar
2 teaspoons vanilla

In medium bowl, combine cream cheese and margarine until creamy. Add powdered sugar and vanilla. Mix well.

COOKIES:

1 box devil's food cake mix
2 eggs

¾ cup shortening

Mix cake mix, eggs, and shortening well; form into balls and place on ungreased cookie sheet. Bake at 350° for 4 minutes on bottom rack and 4 minutes on top rack. Spread Filling in between 2 Cookies and sandwich together.

Favorite Recipes

Chrys' Devil Hermits

2 eggs
¼ cup milk
½ cup creamy peanut butter

1 family-size package fudge
  brownie mix
½ cup peanuts

Preheat oven to 350°. In mixing bowl, beat eggs until frothy. Add milk and peanut butter. Cream until smooth. Add brownie mix and peanuts. Drop by teaspoonfuls onto a greased baking sheet. Bake 8–10 minutes. Cool on a wire rack.

Recipes from the Heart

The nearly vertical monolith known as Devils Tower rises 1,267 feet above the meandering Belle Fourche River, Wyoming. Once hidden below the earth's surface, erosion has stripped away the softer rock layers revealing Devils Tower. The rolling hills of this 1,347-acre park are covered with pine forests, deciduous woodlands, and prairie grasslands.

Slice and Bake Chocolate Chip Cookies

Make ahead and keep in freezer until needed.

2 cups butter, softened
1⅓ cups sugar
1⅔ cups brown sugar
1 tablespoon vanilla
4 eggs

5½ cups flour
2 teaspoons salt
2 teaspoons baking soda
2 cups semisweet chocolate bits
1 cup chopped nuts

In a large bowl, cream butter and sugars. Beat in vanilla and eggs until light and fluffy. Add flour, salt, and baking soda; stir until blended. Stir in chocolate bits and nuts. Divide dough into 4 equal parts and shape each into an 9- to 10-inch roll. Wrap each roll in a 12x14-inch piece of waxed paper or plastic wrap. Place wrapped rolls in a plastic freezer container with a tight-fitting lid or wrap in heavy-duty foil. Can be stored in freezer for up to 6 months.

To bake, cut frozen dough into 1-inch slices and cut each slice into 4 equal pieces. Place on ungreased baking sheet about 1½ inches apart. Bake at 350° for 10 minutes or until lightly browned around the edges. Each roll makes about 3 dozen cookies.

Recipe from Trapper's Rest Bed & Breakfast, Shell, Wyoming

Tastes & Tours of Wyoming

★ ★

Cowboy Cookie Dough

Celebrating the West and the cowboy way of life, these elaborately deco-rated western Cowboy Cookies keep well, or at least until little bucka-roos get the munchies! At last, a sugar cookie that is delicious and does not break easily. Perfect for decorating.

Use a heavy-duty mixer or food processor for this large batch. The recipe is easily cut in half for a small electric mixer or for hand mixing.

8 cups flour
½ teaspoon cream of tartar
½ teaspoon salt
2 teaspoons baking soda
2½ cups sugar
¾ cup butter
¾ cup butter-flavored
  vegetable shortening

Rind of 1 large lemon, grated
4 medium eggs
2 teaspoons vanilla (Mexican
  preferred)
1 cup evaporated milk (or
  whipping cream)
Extra flour for rolling out
  dough

Sift flour and measure into a large bowl. With a wire whisk, thoroughly mix together the flour, cream of tartar, salt, and soda. Set aside.

Cream together the sugar, butter, and vegetable shorten-ing until light and flufffy. Add the lemon rind and eggs, and continue mixing. Stir vanilla into the evaporated milk and add to mixture, beating until smooth. Add sifted dry ingre-dients one cup at a time, mixing well after each addition to form a stiff ball of dough.

Place dough on a floured surface. Divide into 3 parts. Place each mound on a piece of plastic wrap. Using your hands, shape each mound into a smooth, flat, 1-inch-thick cir-cle. Wrap each flat circle with plastic wrap and allow to chill in refrigerator for 30 minutes.

Set oven temperature to 350°. Frost with Fudgy Chocolate Frosting and Sugar-Baby Frosting, recipes follow.

Note: See catalog section, page 275, for ordering cowboy cookie cutters.

Wild, Wild West Cowboy Cookies

Fudgy Chocolate Frosting

Ideal for coloring buffalo, bucking ponies, cowboy hats and boots, and for decorative accents on other special critters!

½ cup butter
6 (1-ounce) squares of
  unsweetened chocolate
7 cups confectioners' sugar,
  sifted

¾ cup hot coffee or water
2 teaspoons vanilla (Mexican
  preferred)
3 bottles chocolate sprinkles

Place a saucepan over low heat and melt butter and chocolate, mixing together until thoroughly blended. Place mixture in the bowl of an electric mixer and add remaining ingredients; beat on high until well blended. Add additional hot coffee or hot water, one tablespoon at a time, until a soft spreading consistency is reached.

Dip the cookie surface in the soft frosting and smooth with a kitchen knife. For Chocolate Buffalo shapes, immediately apply chocolate sprinkles to accent cape and tail. Pipe-on colors to accent other cookie shapes. Yields approximately 4 cups.

Wild, Wild West Cowboy Cookies

Sugar-Baby Frosting

1 (32-ounce) package
  confectioners' sugar, sifted
⅓ cup evaporated skimmed
  milk

⅓ cup white corn syrup
1 teaspoon vanilla (Mexican
  preferred)
⅓ cup boiling water

Sift confectioners' sugar and set aside. Combine evaporated milk, corn syrup, and vanilla in a small saucepan over heat; then place this hot liquid in a mixing bowl. Immediately add boiling water and blend with electric mixer on low speed.

Add sifted confectioners' sugar, blending on low speed until a smooth, soft consistency is achieved. Pour the soft glaze into five lidded containers with large openings. Leave one portion white and color the remainaing four using powdered food coloring. Decorate Cowboy Cookies by dipping the surface of cookies in the soft glaze and smooth with a kitchen knife. Accent with piped-on colors. Yields approximately 3 cups.

Wild, Wild West Cowboy Cookies

★ ★

Cowboy Cookies

1 cup shortening
½ cup white sugar
1½ cups brown sugar
2 eggs
2 cups flour
1 teaspoon baking soda

½ teaspoon salt
1½ teaspoons vanilla
2 cups rolled oats
1 cup flaked coconut
1 (12-ounce) package chocolate
   chips

Cream shortening and sugars. Add eggs, flour, soda, salt, vanilla, rolled oats, coconut, and chocolate chips. Drop onto greased cookie sheet and bake at 375° for 15 minutes.

Brisbin Community Cookbook

Wyoming Whopper Cookies

⅔ cup butter or margarine
1¼ cups packed brown sugar
¾ cup sugar
3 eggs, beaten
1½ cups chunky peanut butter
6 cups old-fashioned oats (not
   quick-cooking)

2 teaspoons baking soda
1½ cups raisins
2 cups semisweet chocolate
   chips

In large saucepan, melt butter over low heat. Blend in sugars, eggs, and peanut butter. Mix until smooth. Add oats, baking soda, raisins, and chocolate chips. Dough will be sticky. Drop onto greased baking sheet, 1 inch apart, with large ice cream scoop. Flatten slightly. Bake at 350° about 15 minutes. Remove cookies to a wire rack to cool. Yields 2 dozen.

Feeding the Herd

Wyoming is home to the world's largest single elk herd. The National Elk Refuge, located just outside the town of Jackson, is the largest established elk preserve in North America. Up to 9,000 elk winter on the refuge, and visitors can enjoy close-up views on daily sleigh rides from December through April.

Munchies

1 (10-ounce) package
 mini-pretzels
5 cups Cheerios cereal
5 cups Corn Chex cereal
2 cups salted peanuts

1 large bag of M&M's
2 (12-ounce) packages white
 chocolate chips
3 tablespoons vegetable oil

In a large bowl combine first 5 ingredients; set aside. In a microwave-safe bowl, heat chips and oil on MEDIUM or HIGH for 2 minutes; stir. Microwave on HIGH for 10 seconds; stir until smooth. Pour over mixture and mix well. Spread onto wax paper-lined cookie sheets. Cool—break apart and store in an air-tight container. Makes 5 quarts.

Recipe from Bonnie's B&B, Kalispell, Montana
Recipes from Big Sky Country

Butterscotch Ice Box Cookies

2 cups brown sugar (or 1 cup
 white and 1 cup brown)
1 cup butter (not margarine),
 softened
2 eggs, beaten

1 scant teaspoon baking soda
1 teaspoon cream of tartar
4 cups flour, divided
1 cup chopped nuts
1 teaspoon vanilla

Cream sugars and butter. Add well beaten eggs. Sift soda and cream of tartar with 1 cup flour. Add to creamed mixture. Then add nuts and vanilla. Add the rest of the flour, kneading the last of the flour into the mixture. Be sure to use all flour called for. Shape in rolls, and set in a cool place until morning. Slice and bake in a moderate, 350° oven. Check cookies for doneness between 8–12 minutes. Unbaked cookie dough can be stored in refrigerator up to 2 weeks.

The Pure Food Club of Jackson Hole

Ranger Cookies

1 cup brown sugar	½ teaspoon baking powder
1 cup sugar	2 cups oatmeal
1 cup shortening	2 cups cornflakes
2 eggs	2 cups flour
1 teaspoon vanilla	1 cup flaked coconut
1 teaspoon baking soda	½ cup nuts

Combine sugars, shortening, eggs, vanilla, soda, and baking powder. Add oatmeal, cornflakes, flour, coconut, and nuts; mix well and chill. Roll into balls and press down on cookie sheet. Bake 10–15 minutes in a 375° oven. Bake only until slightly brown.

Food for the Soul

Snow Flurries

These are my favorite holiday roll-out cookies. They are tasty and very tender.

1½ cups sugar	1 teaspoon vanilla extract
⅞ cup butter	½ teaspoon almond extract
⅔ cup shortening	½ teaspoon salt
1⅓ tablespoons lemon zest	½ teaspoon baking powder
3 eggs	4½ cups unbleached flour

Thoroughly cream sugar, butter, shortening, and lemon zest. Add eggs, 1 at a time, and stir. Beat batter until it becomes light. Add vanilla and almond extracts, and stir. Mix in salt and baking powder with the first cup of flour. Add the rest of flour 1 cup at a time, stirring after each addition.

Shape the dough into two rectangular shapes, and wrap in plastic wrap. Chill well before rolling.

Roll out on floured counter. Cut with floured cutters. Transfer to papered trays with metal spatula. Bake at 350° for about 10 minutes, until they barely start to brown. Makes 6–7 dozen.

Get Your Buns in Here

Sesame Cookies

1 cup sesame seeds	1 teaspoon vanilla extract
½ cup flaked coconut	½ teaspoon salt
¾ cup vegetable oil	½ teaspoon baking soda
1 cup brown sugar	1 teaspoon baking powder
2 eggs	2 cups unbleached flour

Preheat oven to 350°. Toast sesame seeds and coconut on a clean dry pan. Stir occasionally and don't let them burn.

Thoroughly cream the vegetable oil and brown sugar. Add eggs and beat until light in color. Add vanilla, salt, baking soda, and baking powder. Stir in toasted ingredients. Add flour 1 cup at a time and stir. The dough will be moist but not sticky. Roll into 1-inch balls and bake on papered trays until they are golden, which will be about 10 minutes. Makes about 3 dozen.

Get Your Buns in Here

Yaak Trail Bars

1 cup brown sugar	1 cup raisins
⅔ cup peanut butter	½ cup coconut
½ cup light corn syrup	½ cup raw, shelled sunflower
½ cup butter, melted	seeds
2 teaspoons vanilla	⅓ cup wheat germ
1½ cups quick oats	2 tablespoons sesame seeds
1½ cups crisp rice cereal	Dash of cinnamon or more
1 cup semisweet chocolate	
pieces	

Grease a 9x13x2-inch baking pan; set aside. Combine brown sugar, peanut butter, corn syrup, butter, and vanilla.

In another bowl, combine oats, cereal, chocolate pieces, raisins, coconut, sunflower seeds, wheat germ, sesame seeds, and cinnamon; stir in peanut butter mixture. Mix well. Press evenly into prepared pan. Bake in 350° oven for 25 minutes or until lightly browned. Cool. Cut into bars.

Yaak Cookbook

Fudgy Oatmeal Bars

2 cups packed brown sugar
1 cup plus 2 tablespoons
  softened butter, divided
2 eggs
2 teaspoons vanilla, divided
2½ cups flour
1 teaspoon baking soda
1 teaspoon salt, divided

3 cups quick cooking or regular
  oatmeal
1 (12-ounce) package chocolate
  chips
1 (14-ounce) can sweetened
  condensed milk
1 cup chopped nuts

Heat oven to 350°. Grease 15½x10½x1-inch jellyroll pan. Mix brown sugar, 1 cup butter, eggs, and 1 teaspoon vanilla in a large bowl. Stir in flour, baking soda, and ½ teaspoon salt; stir in oats. Reserve ⅓ of the oatmeal mixture. Press remaining oatmeal mixture in pan.

Heat chocolate chips, milk, and 2 tablespoons butter in 2-quart saucepan over low heat, stirring constantly until chocolate chips are melted. Remove from heat; stir in nuts, 1 teaspoon vanilla, and ½ teaspoon salt. Spread over oatmeal mixture in the pan. Drop reserved oatmeal mixture by rounded teaspoons onto chocolate mixture. Bake until golden brown, 25–30 minutes. While warm, cut into bars, about 1x2-inch. Makes 70 cookies.

Wolf Point, Montana 75th Jubilee Cookbook

★ ★ ★ ★ ★ ★ ★ ★ ★ ★ ★ ★ ★ ★ ★ ★ ★ ★ ★ ★

Chocolate Chip Bars

½ cup butter	½ teaspoon salt
¾ cup brown sugar	½ teaspoon baking soda
1 whole egg	¾ cup chocolate chips
1 teaspoon vanilla	¾ cup chopped walnuts
1¼ cups flour	

Cream butter and brown sugar. Add egg and vanilla and mix well. Add flour, salt, and baking soda. Mix. Stir in chocolate chips and nuts. Grease 9x13-inch baking dish. Spread dough in baking dish and bake at 375° for 12–15 minutes. Cool and cut into bars. Makes 10 servings.

Recipe from Fox Hollow B&B, Bozeman, Montana
A Taste of Montana

Caramel Bars

1 package butter pecan cake mix	1 (12.5-ounce) jar caramel topping
½ cup margarine, softened	⅓ cup chopped nuts
1 egg	⅓ cup flaked coconut

In large mixing bowl, stir together cake mix, margarine, and egg. Press half of mixture in bottom of 9x13-inch pan. Bake at 350° for 10 minutes. Pour caramel topping over baked crust. Sprinkle with nuts and coconut. Spread remaining half of cake mixture on top. Bake at 350° for 20–25 minutes or until lightly browned. Cool thoroughly. Cut into bars. Yields 24 bars.

Irene's Country Cooking

Hell's Half Acre, located approximately 45 miles west of Casper, Wyoming, is a 320-acre area of unusual rock formations created by the erosion of volcanic rock. Other names include: "The Devil's Kitchen," "The Pits of Hades," and "The Baby Grand Canyon."

Pecan Pie Bars

2 cups all-purpose flour
½ cup confectioners' sugar
1 cup butter or margarine,
  softened
1 (14-ounce) can sweetened
  condensed milk
1 egg
1 teaspoon vanilla extract
Pinch salt
1 (6-ounce) package toffee-
  flavored chips
1 cup chopped pecans

In mixing bowl, combine flour and sugar. Cut in butter until mixture resembles coarse meal. Press firmly into a greased 9x13-inch pan at least 2 inches deep. Bake at 350° for 15 minutes. Meanwhile, in another bowl, beat milk, egg, vanilla, and salt. Stir in toffee chips and pecans. Spread evenly over baked crust. Bake for another 20–25 minutes or until lightly browned. Cool, then refrigerate. When thoroughly chilled, cut into bars. Store in refrigerator. Makes 4 dozen.

The Pure Food Club of Jackson Hole

Pumpkin Bars

2 cups flour
2 cups sugar
2 teaspoons baking powder
1 teaspoon baking soda
1 teaspoon cinnamon
1 teaspoon nutmeg
½ teaspoon salt
½ teaspoon ground cloves
1 cup oil
1 (16-ounce) can (2 cups)
  pumpkin
4 eggs

Heat oven to 350°. In large bowl, combine all bar ingredients; beat at low speed until moistened. Beat 2 minutes at medium speed. Pour into greased 15x10x1-inch baking pan. Bake at 350° for 25–30 minutes. Cool before frosting.

FROSTING:
2 cups powdered sugar
½ cup butter, softened
1 tablespoon milk
1 (3-ounce) package cream
  cheese, softened
1 teaspoon vanilla

In a small bowl, combine all frosting ingredients; beat until smooth. Frost when cooled. Cut into bars. Store in refrigerator. Makes 48 bars.

Columbus Community Cookbook

Georgia Street Squares

This is a no-bake cookie.

FIRST LAYER:

½ cup butter or margarine
½ cup cocoa
¼ cup sugar
1 teaspoon vanilla
1 egg, slightly beaten

2 cups crushed vanilla wafers
  or graham crackers
1 cup flaked coconut
½ cup chopped nuts

Mix butter, cocoa, sugar, and vanilla in top of double boiler and cook until blended. Add egg and cook 5 minutes longer, stirring constantly. Add cracker crumbs, coconut, and nuts. Press into a 9x13-inch pan. Cool.

SECOND LAYER:

½ cup butter or margarine,
  softened
1 tablespoon instant vanilla
  pudding

2 cups powdered sugar
3 tablespoons milk

Mix thoroughly and spread on First Layer.

THIRD LAYER:

¾ cup chocolate chips
  1 tablespoon milk

1 tablespoon butter or
  margarine

Melt in top of double boiler and spread over top of cookies. Keep in refrigerator.

Irma Flat Mothers' Club Cookbook

Honeymoon Bars

CRUST:

2 cups flour

4 tablespoons brown sugar

1 cup butter, melted

Mix flour, sugar, and butter. Press in 9-inch cake pan and bake 10 minutes at 350°.

FILLING:

2 eggs, beaten

1½ cups brown sugar

1 teaspoon vanilla

½ teaspoon baking powder

¾ cup flaked coconut

¾ cup chocolate chips

½ cup chopped nuts

Mix all ingredients together. Put on baked Crust and bake another 25 minutes.

Food for the Soul

Peanut Logs

3 cups white sugar

¼ cup white Karo

⅛ teaspoon baking soda

1 cup cream, sweet or sour

Boil all ingredients to a little over soft-ball stage (about 240°). Cool, stir, and cream up like chocolate drop centers. Work with hands and shape in rolls, 1½ inches long and ½ inch thick.

CARAMEL:

1½ cups white sugar

½ cup butter

¾ cup white Karo

1 cup sweet cream

½ teaspoon vanilla

¾ cup finely chopped nuts

¾ cup melted chocolate

Cook sugar, butter, Karo, and cream slowly, stirring occasionally. Cook to 240°. Remove from heat; add vanilla. Dip rolls in hot Caramel, then roll in chopped nuts. Press nuts into caramel with hands. Top with melted chocolate.

Amish Country Cooking

Orange Gumdrop Chews

1½ cups cut-up orange gumdrop slices	2 cups sifted all-purpose flour
1⅓ cups flaked coconut	3 eggs
½ cup chopped pecans or walnuts	1 tablespoon water
	2 cups brown sugar
	½ teaspoon salt

Mix cut-up orange slices, coconut, nuts, and flour. Beat eggs with water until foamy. Gradually add brown sugar and salt, beating till light and fluffy. Stir in gumdrop mixture. Spread evenly on greased 15x10½x1-inch pan. Bake in moderate 375° oven about 15 minutes or till done. Cool. Cut in bars. Makes 4 dozen.

Home at/on the Range with Wyoming BILS

Turtles

1 cup butter, melted	1½ cups sugar
¾ cup semisweet cocoa	2 cups plus 2 tablespoons flour
4 eggs, beaten	1 teaspoon vanilla

Mix butter, cocoa, and eggs. Add sugar, flour, and vanilla; mix well. Don't chill. Bake on a medium waffle iron for 1 minute. Small portions will make 5 dozen cookies.

FROSTING:

1 square chocolate	2½ tablespoons butter
½ cup brown sugar	1 teaspoon vanilla
¼ cup water	1½ cups powdered sugar

Boil chocolate, brown sugar, water and butter for exactly 3 minutes. Add vanilla and powdered sugar.

French Family Favorites

Three hundred years ago, a horde of grasshoppers was forced to land in Montana because of a storm, and were subsequently entombed in ice. This place in the Custer National Forest is now called Grasshopper Glacier.

Beef Fudge

A must for every Montana cookbook!

1 cup ground cooked roast beef
½ pound butter or margarine
1 (14½-ounce) can evaporated
  milk
4 cups sugar

1 (12-ounce) bag chocolate
  chips
1 pint marshmallow créme
2 teaspoons vanilla
1 cup chopped nuts

Remove any hard crust from the beef before grinding. Cook butter, milk, and sugar to hard-ball stage. Stir often. Remove from heat. Stir in chips, marshmallow créme, vanilla, beef, and nuts. Beat all until firm. Pour into well-buttered 9x13-inch pan. Cut into squares. Refrigerate.

French Family Favorites

Mashed Potato Fudge

¼ cup hot mashed potatoes
1 teaspoon butter
2¼ cups confectioners' sugar
½ teaspoon vanilla

Dash of salt
1⅓ cups flaked coconut
5–6 squares semisweet
  chocolate, melted, divided

Mix potatoes and butter; gradually add sugar. Beat until thoroughly blended. Stir in vanilla, salt, and coconut. Line an 8-inch-square pan with wax paper. Pour in ¼ of the melted chocolate, then the coconut mixture, and finally the remaining chocolate for top layer. Refrigerate. Cut into 1-inch squares. Yields 64 (1-inch) squares.

The Hole Thing Volume II

Worn two to six feet into an eroded sandstone ridge by wagon wheels, the Oregon Trail Ruts provide moving testimony of the route followed by thousands of Americans in their migration westward across the Plains during the mid-1800s. The Oregon Trail Ruts National Historic Landmark is located on the south side of the North Platte River about one-half mile south of the town of Guernsey, Wyoming.

★ ★

Fast and Fabulous Dark Chocolate Fudge

This is the easiest, best-tasting fudge I've ever eaten!

½ cup light corn syrup
¼ cup evaporated milk
3 cups semisweet chocolate
   chips

¾ cup confectioners' sugar,
   sifted
2 teaspoons vanilla
1 cup chopped walnuts

Spray 8- to 9-inch baking dish with nonstick cooking spray. In 2-quart saucepan, combine syrup and milk. Add chocolate chips, stirring constantly. Cook over medium-low heat until chips melt. Remove from heat; add confectioners' sugar, vanilla, and nuts. Beat with wooden spoon until mixture is thick and glossy. Spread in prepared pan. Chill 2 hours or until firm. Cut into squares. Yields 25 squares.

Rare Collection Recipes

Chocolate Butter Fudge

The high proportion of butter is one of the reasons this fudge is so outstanding.

3 cups sugar
1 envelope unflavored gelatin
1 cup milk
3 squares unsweetened
   chocolate

½ cup light corn syrup (scant)
1¼ cups butter
2 teaspoons vanilla
1 cup chopped walnuts

Butter a 9-inch-square pan. Mix sugar and dry gelatin in a saucepan. Add milk, syrup, chocolate, and butter. Cook over medium heat (238°), stirring frequently until a few drops tested in cold water form a soft ball, which flatten on removal from water. Remove from heat and pour into a large mixing bowl. Flavor with vanilla and cool 15 minutes. Beat until candy thickens. Add nuts and spread on buttered pan. Cut into squares.

First Ladies' Cookbook

Vinegar Taffy

2 cups sugar
½ cup vinegar
⅛ teaspoon cream of tartar

⅛ teaspoon salt
2 tablespoons butter (no
   substitute)

Mix sugar, vinegar, cream of tartar, salt, and butter in saucepan. Cook to hard-ball stage. Pour onto a buttered plate. Let cool until you can handle it without burning yourself. Then butter hands and pull taffy until it becomes snowy white.

Sharing Our Best

Popcorn Balls

⅔ cup corn syrup
2 cups sugar
⅔ cup boiling water
2 tablespoons vinegar
2 teaspoons cream of tartar

½ teaspoon baking soda
2 tablespoons butter
1 teaspoon food coloring
2 gallons of popped corn

Combine in large saucepan corn syrup, sugar, boiling water, and vinegar and bring to a boil. Add cream of tartar; stir until dissolved. Boil to soft-crack stage. Remove from heat and add soda, butter, and coloring. Mix well and pour over popped corn. Stir well. Dip hands in cold water and make balls.

Irma Flat Mothers' Club Cookbook

PIES & OTHER DESSERTS

PHOTO © JOHN REDDY PHOTOGRAPHY, INC.

Fields and trees glisten in the sun on a frosty morning in the serene Wolf Creek area of Montana. Wolf Creek's name was derived from a nearby creek and the Indian phrase, "Creek-Where-the-Wolf-Jumped-Too."

Montana Huckleberry Pie

Picking huckleberries in western Montana is like going to heaven. It's hard to explain, really, what the magic is. I think perhaps it's the place where huckleberries grow. Picture a steep mountainside, with conifer woods above, and a green valley below. There's a river meandering through the valley. You are sitting in the late afternoon sun on the edge of the deep green woods. Wind is soughing in the pine trees. Listen! It is the only sound you hear. Oh yes, there are some small birds calling and chirping, but they are musical notes that blend in with the soughing of the wind. The sun is hot but there's a breeze. I could sit on that mountainside in the berry patch forever. This is as close to paradise as I can imagine.

3 tablespoons flour	Pastry for double-crust 9-inch
¾ cup sugar (more if berries	pie (do try whole-wheat
are very tart)	pastry flour)
4 cups fresh or frozen	
huckleberries (blueberries)	

Mix flour and sugar with berries. Set aside. Roll out a little more than half the pastry dough to ⅛-inch thickness and fit into a 9-inch pie pan. Pour the berries into the pie shell. (If you use commercial blueberries, sprinkle 1 tablespoon lemon juice on top.) Roll remaining pastry a little thinner than for the bottom crust. Prick with your favorite design. Brush the edge of the bottom crust with cold water, and place the upper crust on pie. Press crusts together at the rim and trim off the excess dough. Flute the edge.

Bake in a preheated 450° oven for 10 minutes. Reduce the heat to 350° and bake about 40 minutes.

Note: Montana huckleberries are really blueberries. The scientific name of the genus is Vaccinium and that is the blueberry genus. But these wild berries are a world apart from the commercial blueberry, so they deserve a distinct title. We Montanans will fight for the name "huckleberry."

The Kim Williams Cookbook and Commentary

★ ★

Montana Huckleberry Chocolate Fleck Pie

What better way to combine two wonderful foods—chocolate and Montana huckleberries! This is a great dessert to make a few days before needed, and a favorite for Christmas dinner.

PIE CRUST:

½ cup butter	1 cup flour
2 tablespoons sugar	

Combine butter and sugar. Do not cream. Add flour. Mix just until dough will form. Place ¼ cup of mixture crumbled in small pan. Press remaining mixture evenly over bottom and sides of 9-inch pie pan with well floured fingers. Bake at 375° until light golden brown. Bake crumbs 10–12 minutes, and crust 12–15 minutes.

PIE FILLING:

½ cup semisweet chocolate chips	1½ teaspoons vanilla
⅔ cup sugar	1 teaspoon lemon juice
¼ cup water	1 cup whipping cream
1 unbeaten egg white	½ cup huckleberries

Melt chocolate chips in double boiler. Cool to lukewarm. Combine in small bowl the sugar, water, egg white, vanilla, and lemon juice; beat with electric mixer at highest speed until soft peaks form when beaters are raised (3–5 minutes). Beat whipping cream until thick. Fold melted chocolate slowly into whipped cream mixture then fold into egg white mixture. Fold huckleberries into the mixture. Put into pie crust; sprinkle with baked crumbs and freeze.

Recipe by Vivian Schaap, Lone Mountain Ranch, Big Sky, Montana

Montana Celebrity Cookbook

The Montana Yogo Sapphire is the only North American gem to be included in the Crown Jewels of England. The largest cut Yogo is 10.2 carats and can be viewed in the Smithsonian Institution in Washington, D.C.

Pecan Pie

3 eggs
3/4 cup white Karo
1/2 cup sugar
4 tablespoons butter, melted
2 tablespoons water

1/4 teaspoon salt
1 teaspoon vanilla
1 cup chopped pecans
1 (9-inch) unbaked pie shell

Beat eggs; add other ingredients except pecans; mix well. Add pecans. Pour into unbaked pie shell. Bake about 1 hour at 350°. Do not overbake.

Amish Country Cooking

Pecan Angel Pie

Forget the calories. This is absolutely superb. For those who have trouble with meringues—you absolutely cannot go wrong and the taste is delicious, even better than standard meringues.

3 egg whites
1/2 teaspoon cream of tartar
1 cup sugar
1 1/2 teaspoons vanilla
3/4 cup chopped pecans

12 soda crackers, crushed
Fresh fruit such as
    strawberries, peaches, etc.
Whipped cream for garnish

Beat egg whites until stiff. Add cream of tartar; continue beating. Slowly add sugar. Beat until glossy and then add vanilla, pecan bits, and soda crackers, which you have crumbled in your hands—no need to use rolling pin to crush.

Pour mixture into greased pie plate, forming ridge around outside and depression in center. Bake at 350° for 25 minutes, until delicately browned, very delicately. Serve with a topping of fresh strawberries, fresh peaches, etc. Garnish with whipped cream. Chill overnight or all day. Best served same day. Serves 6–8.

The Fine Art of Cooking Volume 2

Pecan Pie Squares

CRUST:

2 cups flour

¼ cup sugar

½ teaspoon salt

½ cup butter, melted

Combine all ingredients and press into a 9x13-inch pan and bake for 20 minutes at 350°.

TOPPING:

3 eggs, slightly beaten

1 cup sugar

1 cup light corn syrup

2 tablespoons butter, melted

1 teaspoon vanilla

2 cups chopped pecans

Mix all ingredients well and pour over Crust. Bake at 350° for 25 minutes or until set. Cool and cut into squares.

Favorite Recipes

Sour Cream and Pear Pie

Very tasty and very easy.

1 (9-inch) unbaked pie shell

FILLING:

3 cups chopped pears

1 cup sugar

1 beaten egg

1 cup sour cream

1 tablespoon flour

1 teaspoon vanilla

Dash salt

Mix filling ingredients and pour into shell. Bake at 350° for 15 minutes. Remove from oven.

TOPPING:

⅔ cup flour

½ cup sugar

¼ cup butter

Combine ingredients. Mix to crumble. Sprinkle over pie and bake 30 minutes longer or until top turns light brown. Serves 6–8.

The Fine Art of Cooking Volume 2

Sour Cream Rhubarb Pie

FILLING:

3 tablespoons flour
½ teaspoon salt
1¼ cups sugar
1 egg
1 cup sour cream

1 teaspoon vanilla
½ teaspoon lemon extract
3 cups chopped rhubarb
1 (9-inch) unbaked pie crust

TOPPING:

⅓ cup sugar
⅓ cup flour
Pinch of salt

1 teaspoon cinnamon
¼ cup soft butter

Sift together flour, salt, and sugar. Add egg, sour cream, vanilla, and lemon extract. Add the rhubarb and pour into a 9-inch unbaked crust. Bake at 400° for 15 minutes. Reduce heat to 350° and bake for 25 minutes.

Mix all ingredients for Topping together with a fork. Sprinkle Topping over pie and return to oven for 15 minutes. Serves 6–8.

The Hole Thing Volume II

Rhubarb Custard Pie

Pastry for 2-crust, 9-inch pie
3 eggs, slightly beaten
3 tablespoons milk
2 cups sugar

¼ cup flour
¾ teaspoon nutmeg
4 cups cut-up rhubarb
1 tablespoon butter

Make pastry and line pie pan with crust. Beat slightly the eggs; add milk. Mix and stir in the sugar, flour, and nutmeg. Mix in the cut-up rhubarb. Pour into lined pie pan. Dot with butter and cover with a lattice top. Bake 50–60 minutes in 375° oven.

Simac Family Favorites

★ ★

Peaches and Cream Streusel Pie

STREUSEL:

⅓ cup firmly packed dark brown sugar
⅓ cup all-purpose flour
⅓ cup old-fashioned rolled oats
½ teaspoon ground cinnamon
¼ teaspoon ground nutmeg
¼ cup chilled butter, cut into small pieces
¼ cup sliced almonds (about 1 ounce)

Preheat oven to 350°. In a medium bowl, mix together brown sugar, flour, oats, cinnamon, and nutmeg. Using a pastry blender or 2 butter knives, cut the butter into the flour mixture until coarse crumbs form. Stir in nuts.

FILLING:

1 large egg
⅓ cup heavy cream
¼ cup sugar
1 teaspoon vanilla
1 teaspoon almond extract
½ teaspoon ground nutmeg
Pinch of salt

Mix egg, cream, sugar, vanilla, almond extract, nutmeg, and salt.

5 cups ripe, peeled, pitted, and sliced peaches (about 1½ pounds)
1 (8-inch) pie shell, baked

Arrange the sliced peaches in the bottom of baked pie shell; pour Filling over peaches. Sprinkle Streusel evenly over the cream mixture to edges of pie crust. Press Streusel down slightly. Bake pie until the Streusel is lightly browned, 30–35 minutes. Transfer pan to a wire rack to cool completely. Garnish with peach slices.

Note: If using frozen peaches, you will need 1 pound of unsweetened frozen, thawed, drained peaches.

Recipes to Make You Purr

Cookie Crust Fruit Pie

A beautiful, refreshing dessert.

½ cup sugar
3½ tablespoons cornstarch
1½ cups apple juice
1 teaspoon grated lemon rind

¼ cup lemon juice
6 cups assorted sliced or cut-up
   fresh fruit
1 (9-inch) pastry shell, baked

In a saucepan, mix sugar and cornstarch. Gradually stir in apple juice until smooth. Stir over medium heat until mixture boils 1 minute. Remove from heat; stir in lemon rind and juice. Cool completely. Gently fold glaze into fruit. Pile high into the baked and cooled pastry shell. Chill 4 hours or until set.

PASTRY:
¼ cup butter, softened
¼ cup sugar

1 egg yolk
1 cup flour

Mix softened butter with sugar and egg yolk. With pastry blender, gradually mix in flour until crumbs form. Press firmly into 9-inch pie plate. Bake in 400° oven about 10 minutes or until lightly browned. Cool.

The Fine Art of Cooking

★ ★

Chocolate-Covered Cherry Pie

1 (15-ounce) can sweetened condensed milk
²⁄₃ cup semisweet chocolate pieces
½ teaspoon salt
½ teaspoon vanilla
1 can cherry pie filling
1 (9-inch) pie shell, baked
Whipped cream for garnish
Stemmed cherries (optional)

Cook sweetened condensed milk over low heat, stirring occasionally, until mixture begins to boil. Let boil, stirring constantly until it thickens, about 4 minutes. Remove from stove; add chocolate pieces and stir until melted and well blended. Add remaining ingredients; stir until blended. Pour into cooled, baked pie shell. Chill 2–3 hours. Garnish with whipped cream and stemmed cherries, if desired.

The Best of Rural Montana Cookbook

Sour Cream Apple Pie

TOPPING:
⅓ cup sugar
1 teaspoon cinnamon
⅓ cup flour
¼ cup butter

Mix all ingredients and set aside.

3 tablespoons flour
¾ cup sugar
½ teaspoon vanilla
1 cup dairy sour cream
1 egg, beaten
2 or 3 cups finely cut apples
¼ teaspoon salt
1 (9-inch) unbaked pie shell

Mix flour and sugar; add vanilla, sour cream, and egg. Beat until smooth. Stir in apples and salt. Pour into pie shell. Bake at 450° for 15 minutes. Reduce heat to 325°; bake about 30 minutes longer. Remove from oven; sprinkle with Topping crumbs. Return to oven and bake 10 minutes more.

Amish Country Cooking

Sour Cream Lemon Pie

1 cup sugar
3½ tablespoons cornstarch
½ cup lemon juice
3 egg yolks
1 cup milk

¼ cup butter
1 cup sour cream
Baked or graham cracker crust
Whipped cream

Combine sugar, cornstarch, juice, egg yolks, and milk in heavy saucepan and cook over medium heat until thick. Stir in butter and cool to room temperature. Fold in sour cream and pour into a baked or graham cracker crust. Top with whipped cream.

Columbus Community Cookbook

Wildcat Pie
(Vinegar Pie)

In the Old West, visitors at camps where Vinegar Pie was made asked for the recipe and refused to believe the cook when he told them there was nothing in the filling except suet, sugar, water, and vinegar. They thought there was a secret ingredient. Not so. The flavor came from sugar, bubbling and caramelizing through holes in the crust, and from the vinegar which substituted for fruit acid. If the cook had a few left-over dried peaches, he might cut them small and mix them in to heighten the illusion of fruit in his Vinegar Pie.

½ pound suet
1 cup water
½ cup vinegar
Flour as needed

1 cup sugar
Dried peaches (optional)
Pastry dough (your own recipe)

Chop the suet and fry out. Discard the crackling. Add water and bring to a boil. Add the vinegar. Stir in flour slowly, creaming to form a paste. Add sugar and peaches, if desired, and pour into a dough-lined pie tin. Cover with dough, cut numerous openings for escaping steam, sprinkle sugar over top, and bake in 350° oven until the crust is crisp and brown. The result is surprisingly like a fruit pie.

Cow Country Cookbook

Chocolate Cream Cheese Pie

1 (3-ounce) package cream
  cheese, softened
2 tablespoons sugar
1 tablespoon milk
1 (8-ounce) carton whipped
  topping, thawed, divided
1 (8- or 9-inch) graham cracker
  crust in pan

1 (3.9-ounce) package instant
  chocolate pudding
1¾ cups milk
Coconut or chopped nuts
  (optional)

In small bowl, beat cream cheese, sugar, and 1 tablespoon of milk until smooth. Fold in half of whipped topping. Spread over graham cracker crust. Chill.

In large bowl, beat pudding and milk with wire whisk or hand mixer on low speed for 2 minutes. Pour pudding over cream cheese mixture. Chill.

Before serving, spread remaining whipped topping over top. Sprinkle with coconut or nuts, if desired. Yields 6–8 servings.

Irene's Country Cooking

Milk Chocolate Pie

1 cup milk chocolate chips
½ cup milk, divided
1 (8-ounce) package cream
  cheese, softened

1 (8-ounce) carton Cool Whip,
  thawed
1 chocolate crumb pie crust
Milk chocolate kisses (optional)

In a microwave dish or double boiler, combine chocolate chips and ¼ cup milk. Cook until chips are melted; stir until smooth. In a mixing bowl, beat cream cheese and remaining milk until smooth. Gradually beat in the chocolate mixture. Fold in the whipped topping. Pour into crust. Freeze for 4–6 hours or overnight. Garnish with kisses and whipped topping, if desired.

Favorite Recipes

Aunt Pat's Peach Melba

4 fresh peaches, scalded in
  boiling water, skinned,
  quartered and pitted
¼ cup white sugar

2 cups water
½ teaspoon vanilla extract
Vanilla ice cream
Vanilla wafers

Combine all ingredients, except ice cream and vanilla wafers. Cook over medium heat until peaches are soft. Drain and chill. At serving time, place 1 scoop of vanilla ice cream in champagne glass. Place 4 quarters of peach around ice cream. Top with Raspberry Sauce and serve with vanilla wafers.

RASPBERRY SAUCE:

1 cup fresh or frozen
  raspberries, unsweetened
⅓ cup orange juice

1½ tablespoons sugar
2 teaspoons cornstarch

Thaw berries if frozen. Combine all ingredients in saucepan. Cook over medium heat, stirring constantly, until sauce is thickened and bubbling. Cook at least 1 minute extra. Strain sauce to remove seeds. Cover and chill. Makes 4 servings.

What's This Green Stuff, Flo?

Magic Peach Cobbler

1 stick butter
1 cup flour
2/3 cup sugar
1½ teaspoons baking powder
3/4 cup milk

4 cups sliced fresh peaches
¼ cup sugar
Cinnamon and nutmeg
(optional)

Melt butter in 9x13-inch pan. Mix flour, 2/3 cup sugar, baking powder, and milk. Pour this over melted butter, DON'T STIR. Add peaches on top. Sprinkle ¼ cup sugar on top of peaches. Bake at 350°–375° for at least 45 minutes. Should be nice and brown.

Note: May sprinkle a little cinnamon and nutmeg along with the sugar on top.

Story, Wyoming's Centennial Community Cookbook

Skillet Cobbler

1 stick margarine or butter
1 cup flour
1 cup sugar
1 teaspoon baking powder

3/4 cup milk, enough to moisten
1 (16-ounce) can fruit cocktail,
drained

Melt margarine or butter in medium-size cast-iron skillet.

Mix flour, sugar, baking powder, and milk. Pour dough on top of melted butter. Spread out and then sprinkle top with fruit cocktail. Bake at 350° for approximately 40 minutes.

Irma Flat Mothers' Club Cookbook

In land area, Montana can accommodate Virginia, Maryland, Delaware, Pennsylvania, and New York, and still have room for the District of Columbia. Montana covers more than 147,000 square miles, making it the fourth largest state in the nation after Alaska, Texas and California.

Fresh Apple Cobbler

FILLING:

3/4 cup sugar
2 tablespoons flour
1/2 teaspoon cinnamon
1/4 teaspoon salt
1 1/2 tart apples, peeled and
  sliced

1 teaspoon vanilla
1/4 cup water
1 tablespoon soft butter or
  margarine

Combine dry ingredients; add apples, vanilla, and water. Mix well. Put in greased 8x8-inch pan. Dot top with butter; let stand while preparing Topping.

TOPPING:

1/2 cup flour
1/2 cup sugar
1/2 teaspoon baking powder
1/2 teaspoon salt

2 tablespoons soft butter or
  margarine
1 egg, slightly beaten

Combine all ingredients; mix until smooth. Drop batter in 9 portions on apples, spacing evenly. (Batter spreads during baking.) Bake in preheated 375° oven about 40 minutes or until apples are done and Topping is golden brown. Serve warm with whipped cream or plain or with vanilla ice cream.

Feeding the Herd

Shoshone National Forest in Wyoming became the nation's first national forest in 1891. With about 2,500,000 acres, Shoshone is one of the largest of the thirteen national forests in the Rocky Mountain region.

Art's Apple Cranberry Crisp

8 large Granny Smith apples,
  peeled and cored
1½ cups cranberries
⅓ cup sugar
2 tablespoons fresh lime or
  lemon juice
1 cup rolled oats
¾ cup pre-sifted flour

¾ cup brown sugar
1½ teaspoons cinnamon
½ teaspoon nutmeg
¼ pound soft butter
¾ cup chopped nuts (pecans,
  almonds, or walnuts)
¾ cup raisins

Preheat oven to 375°. Prepare a 9x13-inch pan with nonstick spray. Slice apples into ¼-inch slices. Combine apples, cranberries, sugar, and lime/lemon juice. Place in prepared pan. Combine oats, flour, brown sugar, cinnamon, and nutmeg. Add butter and mix until crumbly. Add nuts and raisins. Sprinkle over fruit mixture. Cover with foil and bake for 20 minutes. Remove cover and bake for 40 minutes. Serve warm with ice cream. Makes 10–12 servings.

What's This Green Stuff, Flo?

Bondurant Bread Pudding

1 loaf French bread, sliced
2 quarts low-fat milk
4 eggs
2 cups sugar

2 tablespoons vanilla extract
1½ cups dark raisins
¼ pound unsalted butter,
  melted

Soak bread in milk; crush by hand until well mixed and crumbled. Beat eggs in a separate bowl; gradually add sugar, vanilla, and raisins. Mix well. Pour butter into bottom of a shallow 3-quart baking pan. Add egg mixture to bread/milk combination and blend together until fully soaked. Pour into pan, allowing butter to rise to the top. Bake at 325° for 1 hour or until firm and slightly golden. Allow to cool. Serve with Whiskey Sauce.

WHISKEY SAUCE:
¼ pound butter
1 cup sugar
¼ cup boiling water

1 egg
¼ cup whiskey

In top of double boiler, cream together butter and sugar. Beat in boiling water. Stir constantly until sugar is dissolved. Beat egg separately and add slowly to mixture. Stir and cook 2–3 minutes. Allow mixture to cool before adding whiskey. Serves 8–10.

The Hole Thing Volume II

Some of the most important fossils in the world were found in Montana. Egg Mountain, in Choteau, was filled with fossilized eggs, babies, and adult dinosaurs from 80 million years ago. It was the first proof that some dinosaurs took care of their babies the way birds do now. That's how the Maiasaur, the state fossil, got its name, which means "good mother lizard."

Old-Fashioned Bread Pudding

3 cups soft bread crumbs (4 for firmer pudding)
2 cups milk
1/4 cup butter or margarine
1/2 cup sugar

2 eggs, slightly beaten
1/4 teaspoon salt
1/2 teaspoon cinnamon
1/2 teaspoon nutmeg
1/2 cup raisins

Place bread crumbs in 1 1/2-quart baking dish. Scald milk and butter together. Add to crumbs. Blend in sugar, eggs, salt, cinnamon, nutmeg, and raisins. Place baking dish in pan of water 1 inch deep. Bake at 350° for 40–45 minutes.

Variations: For Chocolate Bread Pudding, use 1/2 cup chocolate chips—omit raisins and spices.

Favorite Recipes of Montana

Shannon's Fruit Tart

CRUST:
3/4 cup butter
1 cup flour (heaping)

1/3 cup powdered sugar
Dash of salt

Combine ingredients with a fork or hands and press out on either a pizza round or cookie sheet. Spread as thin as possible without tearing. Bake 20 minutes at 325°—careful not to burn.

SPREAD:
1 (8-ounce) package cream cheese, softened
1/3 cup powdered sugar
1 cup whipping cream, whipped

Fruit
Apricot preserves
Water

Combine cream cheese, powdered sugar, and whipped cream and spread over cooled Crust. Arrange your choices of sliced fruit in an interesting pattern on the freshly prepared Crust. Brush a glaze of apricot preserves and water mixed and warmed to a syrup-like texture over the fruit, and refrigerate until ready to serve.

Potluck

Chocolate Tortilla Torte

This dessert torte is unique and uncomplicated. It looks and tastes gourmet, but is so easy!

1 (6-ounce) package semisweet
  chocolate bits
2 cups (1 pint) low-fat sour
  cream, divided
3 tablespoons confectioners'
  sugar, divided

4 (10-inch) flour tortillas
1–2 ounces milk chocolate,
  shaved (for garnish)

Pour semisweet chocolate bits into top of double boiler. Add 1 cup sour cream and 1 tablespoon confectioners' sugar. Heat over simmering water, stirring until chocolate melts. Place pan of sauce in cold water to cool, stirring occasionally.

Set one of the flour tortillas on serving plate and spread evenly with ⅓ of the chocolate mixture. Cover with another tortilla, another ⅓ of the sauce, another tortilla and remaining chocolate sauce, and then the last tortilla. Make pile as level as possible.

Blend remaining cup of sour cream with remaining 2 tablespoons confectioners' sugar, and spread evenly over top and sides of the torte. Chill, covered with a large inverted bowl, at least 8 hours or as long as overnight. Shave milk chocolate bar into curls using a vegetable peeler; pile chocolate curls on top of tortilla torte. To serve, cut in slim wedges with a very sharp knife. Makes 12 servings.

Best-of-Friends, Festive Occasions Cookbook

Festive Cranberry Torte

CRUST:

1½ cups graham cracker
    crumbs
½ cup chopped pecans

¼ cup sugar
6 tablespoons butter or
    margarine, melted

In mixing bowl combine graham cracker crumbs, pecans, sugar, and melted margarine. Press onto bottom and up sides of 8-inch spring form pan. Chill.

FILLING:

2 cups ground fresh cranberries
1 cup sugar
2 egg whites
1 tablespoon frozen orange
    juice concentrate, thawed

1 teaspoon vanilla
⅛ teaspoon salt
1 cup whipping cream
1 recipe Cranberry Glaze

In large mixing bowl combine cranberries and sugar; let stand 5 minutes. Add unbeaten egg whites, orange juice concentrate, vanilla, and salt. Beat on low speed of electric mixer till frothy. Then beat at high speed 6–8 minutes or till stiff peaks form. Whip cream to soft peaks; fold into cranberry mixture. Turn into Crust; freeze. Serve with Cranberry Glaze.

CRANBERRY GLAZE:

½ cup sugar
1 tablespoon cornstarch

¾ cup fresh cranberries
⅔ cup water

In saucepan stir together sugar and cornstarch; stir in cranberries and water. Cook and stir till bubbly. Cook, stirring occasionally, just till cranberry skins pop. Cool to room temperature. (Do not chill.) Makes 1 cup.

To serve, remove torte from pan. Place on serving plate. Spoon Cranberry Glaze in center. Makes 10 servings.

Home at/on the Range with Wyoming BILS

Linzertorte

⅔ cup hazelnuts
¾ cup sugar
1 cup butter
½ teaspoon vanilla extract
1½ cups unbleached flour

1 teaspoon baking powder
1 tablespoon cinnamon
1 cup raspberry preserves
Powdered sugar for garnish

Roast hazelnuts in a dry pan in the oven for about 10 minutes. Wrap them in a clean dry towel after they come out of the oven. After they have cooled, roll them in the towel to remove the skins.

Purée the hazelnuts in a food processor with the sugar. Add the butter and vanilla and mix until smooth. Add flour with the baking powder and cinnamon. Pulse until evenly mixed.

Press about ⅔ of the dough into a 9-inch tart pan. Roll the remainder of the dough or pat it into a rectangle about 9 inches long on a papered pan. Cut it into strips and then put the tray and the shell in the freezer. This is best because the dough is too soft to move, but after it is frozen, the strips are handled easily.

Preheat oven to 325°. Remove tart pieces from freezer. Fill the shell with raspberry preserves and lay the strips over the top in a lattice pattern. Bake about 35 minutes. The preserves will be bubbling to the center and the crust will be lightly browned. Allow to cool before removing from pan. You might dust lightly with powdered sugar before serving.

Get Your Buns in Here

The world's largest single mineral hot spring is located in Wyoming's Hot Springs State Park. Millions of gallons of water containing at least 27 different minerals flow through the spring every 24 hours, always at a constant temperature of 135 degrees Fahrenheit.

Huckleberry Creme Caramel

Be sure to have your custard ramekins ready for when your sugar has caramelized.

1 cup sugar
¼ cup water
2 cups milk
2 teaspoons vanilla

6 whole eggs
½ cup + 2 tablespoons white
   sugar
4 tablespoons huckleberries

In heavy skillet over medium-high heat, combine sugar and water; stir until like a wet sand. Cook, stirring occasionally until sugar mixture turns to caramel. Immediately pour equal portions of the caramel into 4 (6-ounce) oven-safe ramekins. Set aside.

In saucepan, combine milk and vanilla. Bring to a scald. In a mixer or bowl, beat eggs and sugar until fluffy, stirring rapidly; slowly add ¼ cup of the scalded milk. Still stirring, slowly add the rest of the milk to finish custard.

Pour custard over the caramel in the ramekins. Sprinkle 1 tablespoon of huckleberries into each custard. Bake custards in water bath in preheated 300° oven for 20–30 minutes, or until set. (To test, use a small paring knife stuck into middle of custard; it should come out clean.) Serves 4.

A Taste of Jackson Hole II

Favorite Raspberry Dessert

Excellent dessert.

CRUST:

1 cup flour	1 stick butter, melted
¼ cup powdered sugar	¼ cup chopped pecans

Mix flour, powdered sugar, and melted butter. Add pecans. Butter a 9x13-inch pan. Pat mixture to cover bottom of pan. Bake at 350° for 15 20 minutes. Completely cool Crust.

3 packages frozen raspberries, thawed	1 large tub Cool Whip, divided
2 tablespoons cornstarch	1 large package vanilla instant pudding
1 (8-ounce) package cream cheese, softened	Chopped pecans to sprinkle over top
1 cup powdered sugar	

Drain fruit juice into a saucepan. Over medium heat, thicken with 2 tablespoons cornstarch. Cool. Add fruit to mixture and set aside. In separate bowl, beat together cream cheese, powdered sugar, and ½ the Cool Whip. Spread this mixture over the prepared Crust. Now layer the fruit mixture. Prepare vanilla instant pudding and pour over fruit. Add the last of the Cool Whip to the top and sprinkle with chopped pecans. Refrigerate.

From the High Country of Wyoming

Apricot or Peach Dessert

1 cup crushed vanilla wafers, or
  1 cup graham cracker crumbs
1 (3-ounce) package lemon
  gelatin
1 cup hot water
1 (8-ounce) package cream
  cheese, softened
½ cup sugar
1 (8-ounce) carton whipped
  topping
1 (21-ounce) can apricot or
  peach pie filling
½ cup chopped nuts

Sprinkle crushed wafers or graham cracker crumbs in bottom of 9x13-inch pan. Set aside. In small bowl, dissolve gelatin in 1 cup of hot water and set aside. In large bowl, blend cream cheese and sugar. To this mixture, fold in dissolved gelatin and whipped topping. Pour over crushed wafers. Spread fruit filling over all and sprinkle with nuts. Chill. Yields 12–14 servings.

Irene's Country Cooking

Cherries in the Snow

This is our Christmas dessert.

1 (3-ounce) package cream
  cheese, softened
½ cup sugar
½ teaspoon vanilla
½ pint cream
Graham cracker crust
1 can cherry pie filling

Blend cream, sugar, and vanilla. In separate bowl, whip the cream. Mix whipped cream into cream cheese mixture. Pour into graham cracker crust. Top with cherry pie filling and chill overnight.

Note: This doubles nicely using an 8-ounce package of cream cheese.

Mountain Brook's Wacky Wonders of the Woods

The world record for the greatest temperature change in a 24-hour period occurred in Browning, Montana, on January 23, 1916. The temperature dropped exactly 100 degrees, from 44 degrees above zero to 56 degrees below zero.

Simple Raspberry Dessert

CRUST:

1½ cups graham cracker
  crumbs

⅓ cup margarine, softened
¼ cup sugar

Combine ingredients well; pat into 9x13-inch pan.

CENTER:

1 (8-ounce) package cream
  cheese, softened

1 cup powdered sugar
1 medium container Cool Whip

Combine cream cheese and powdered sugar; add Cool Whip.
Beat well and spread on Crust.

TOPPING:

⅔ cup sugar
1½ cups water
2 tablespoons cornstarch
1 small package raspberry
  Jell-O

2 small packages frozen
  raspberries, thawed and
  drained

Bring sugar, water, cornstarch, and Jell-O to boil. Cool
slightly; add raspberries, pour over Center layer.

Brisbin Community Cookbook

T Cross Ice Cream Pie
with Chocolate Decadence Sauce

Awesome and easy to make! You can buy a chocolate crust to make it even easier. The sauce makes this more than just an ice cream pie. It takes it to another level. The chocolate sauce makes great sundaes, too. I prefer the orange whisper of Grand Marnier over the plain vanilla version.

CRUST:

25 chocolate wafers, crushed, about 1½ cups

6 tablespoons butter, melted

Crush the cookies to fine crumbs and mix with butter. Press into a 10-inch pie plate and bake 10 minutes. Remove and completely cool. While the Crust is cooling, make the Filling and Chocolate Decadence Sauce.

FILLING:

1 pint coffee ice cream
1 pint chocolate ice cream
½ cup chopped pecans

½ cup chopped chocolate-toffee candy bars

Pull ice cream from freezer to soften while making Crust. When the ice cream is softened, mix ice cream, pecans, and chopped candy in a large mixing bowl. Pour into cooled Crust and freeze until hard. To serve, cut pie into 8–10 slices, place on a chilled dessert plate and drizzle pie and plate with Chocolate Decadence Sauce.

CHOCOLATE DECADENCE SAUCE:

4 ounces semisweet chocolate, chopped
1 cup heavy cream
1 cup sugar

3 tablespoons butter
1 tablespoon vanilla or Grand Marnier

Over simmering water in a double boiler, melt chocolate and stir in cream. Mix to combine, stirring constantly. Add sugar and butter and stir until sugar is dissolved. Remove from heat and stir in vanilla or Grand Marnier. Allow to cool at room temperature (refrigerating will cause sugar to crystallize and you'll have a grainy sauce. Makes 8–10 servings.

The Great Ranch Cookbook

Banana Split Dessert

Graham cracker crumbs
2 or 3 bananas

½ gallon Neapolitan ice cream
1 cup chopped walnuts

Cover bottom of 11x15-inch pan with graham cracker crumbs. Slice bananas; layer over crumbs. Slice ice cream in ½-inch slices and place over bananas. Sprinkle with nuts and freeze until firm.

TOPPING:
1 cup chocolate chips
½ cup butter
2 cups powdered sugar
1½ cups evaporated milk

1 teaspoon vanilla
1 pint whipping cream
1 cup graham cracker crumbs

Melt chocolate chips and butter in saucepan. Add powdered sugar and milk. Cook until thick and smooth, stirring constantly. Remove from heat; add vanilla. Cool. Pour mixture over ice cream. Freeze until firm. Whip cream until stiff; spread on chocolate layer and sprinkle with crumbs. Store in freezer. Remove 10 minutes before serving.

Lewis and Clark Fare

Vanilla Bean Créme Brûlée

Make the brûlée the day before to completely chill it, but only put the final sugar on top about 1/2 hour to 1 hour before you serve.

½ vanilla bean, split lengthwise, ½ cup sugar
  or ½ teaspoon vanilla extract 8 (4-ounce) ramekins
2 cups heavy cream 8 teaspoons sugar, regular or
7 egg yolks   superfine

Preheat the oven to 310°. Scrape the inside of the split vanilla bean and add the seeds (or extract) to a medium saucepan with the cream. Cook over medium heat until just beginning to boil. Remove from heat. Beat yolks with sugar in a large bowl. Add some of the hot cream to the yolk mixture, whisking constantly. Whisk the warmed yolk mixture into the rest of the hot cream. Skim the foam from the top and strain through a sieve into a pitcher.

Place 8 (4-ounce) ramekins in a roasting pan. Pour cream mixture into the ramekins, leaving ½ inch from the top. Pour enough hot water into the roasting pan to come half way up the sides of the ramekins. Cover with foil and bake for 15–25 minutes, until the edges are firm and the center only jiggles the size of a nickel when shaken. Remove from oven and cool, then cover and refrigerate 8 hours or overnight.

Sprinkle tops with 1 teaspoon of sugar and place under a preheated broiler for a few minutes (watch carefully) or use a blowtorch to caramelize the sugar. Chill again so that the burnt sugar hardens and the custard is completely chilled again. Makes 8 servings.

The Cool Mountain Cookbook

The Lewis and Clark Expedition explored the land that would become the state of Montana for the first time on April 25, 1805. The group rested and celebrated their arrival at the junction of the Yellowstone and Missouri rivers near the future site of Fort Union.

Apricot Tortoni

½ cup chopped almonds
3–4 tablespoons melted butter
1⅓ cups vanilla wafer crumbs
1 teaspoon almond extract
1 (12-ounce) jar apricot
  preserves
2 tablespoons apricot brandy

3 pints vanilla ice cream,
  softened, divided
1 cup whipping cream
¼ cup sugar
½ teaspoon almond extract, or
  1 teaspoon vanilla extract

Cook almonds in butter in skillet until toasted. Combine with wafer crumbs and 1 teaspoon almond extract in bowl; mix well. Press ⅓ of the mixture evenly in bottom of 9x13-inch glass dish. Combine apricot preserves with apricot brandy in bowl; mix well. Spoon ½ the ice cream over crumb mixture. Spoon ½ the preserve mixture over ice cream. Layer ½ of remaining crumb mixture over ice cream. Repeat layers, ending with crumbs.

Freeze several days before serving. The day before serving, combine whipping cream, sugar, and ½ teaspoon almond extract in mixer bowl; beat until thickened. Spoon over frozen mixture. Cut into 2-inch squares. Serve in champagne glasses. Yields 15 servings.

Cheyenne Frontier Days "Daddy of 'em All" Cookbook

CATALOG OF
CONTRIBUTING COOKBOOKS

PHOTO © DONNIE SEXTON / TRAVEL MONTANA

Little Bighorn Battlefield National Monument, near Hardin, Montana, is the site of the Battle of the Little Bighorn, commonly referred to as Custer's Last Stand. It was here in 1876 that Sioux and Cheyenne warriors defeated Lieutenant Colonel George A. Custer and his troops.

CATALOG OF CONTRIBUTING COOKBOOKS

All recipes in this book have been selected from the cookbooks shown on the following pages. Individuals who wish to obtain a copy of any particular book may do so by sending a check or money order to the address listed by each cookbook. Please note the postage and handling charges that are required. State residents add tax only when requested. Prices and addresses are subject to change, and the books may sell out and become unavailable. Retailers are invited to call or write to same address for discount information.

AMISH COUNTRY COOKING

by Andy & Millie Yoder
5253 W. Kootenai
Rexford, MT 59930   406-889-3588

This is a collection of favorite recipes of the Amish in Northwest Montana. There are 10 sections; over 600 recipes, 282 pages, with numerous poems, and humorous quotes throughout. All tried-and-true recipes that have been handed down for some generations.

$9.95 Retail price
$3.00 Postage and handling

Make check payable to Andy & Millie Yoder

BEST-OF-FRIENDS, FESTIVE OCCASIONS COOKBOOK

by Darlene Glantz Skees   Email books@farcountrypress.com
Farcountry Press   Fax 406-443-5480
P. O. Box 5630   800-821-3874
Helena, MT 59604   www.farcountrypress.com

A special collection of festive and holiday cuisine was perfected for hosts like herself; she created recipes "Easy and Elegant for People On-The-Go," for family meals or parties. Practical, warm and humorous—the recipes read like tips from your best friend.

$15.95 Retail price
$6.00 Postage and handling ($2.00 each additional book)

Make check payable to Farcountry Press   ISBN 1-56037-212-5

THE BEST OF RURAL MONTANA COOKBOOK

Rural Montana Magazine
Montana Electric Cooperatives Association   Email rural@sofast.net
Rural Montana Cookbook, Box 3469   Fax 406-761-8339
Great Falls, MT 59403   406-761-8333

This outstanding cookbook is compiled of the best recipes that were sent in to Rural Montana Magazine for its monthly contest over a ten-year period. This book contains over 180 winning recipes from 1990 through 2000. What readers will find here is the best of the best.

$8.00 Retail price
$1.50 Postage and handling

Make check payable to Rural Montana Cookbook

BITTERROOT FAVORITES & MONTANA MEMORIES

by Laura Green Blount
Gary Blount
576 Blodgett View Road
Hamilton, MT 59840   406-363-7078

Bitterroot Favorites are the recipes. There are over sixty recipes including many from members of my family—Bessie (my grandmother), Aunt
Fran, Gary (my husband), and myself. Montana Memories are the pictures of the Bitterroot Valley and Bitterroot Mountain.

$17.95 Retail price
$4.95 Postage and handling
Make check payable to Laura Blount

BREAKFAST AND MORE

by Carole Eppler
Porch Swing Publications   Email porchswing@juno.com
502 East 24th Street   www.cruising-america/porch.html
Cheyenne, WY 82001   307-778-7182

We have collected many unique and impressive recipes over the years
and compiled them in this 136-page cookbook. We prepare them for
our Bed & Breakfast guests, plus a few dessert and miscellaneous
recipes we couldn't bear to leave out—they will have your guests beg-
ging for more. Enjoy!

$15.00 Retail price
$4.00 Postage and handling
Make check payable to Porch Swing Bed & Breakfast

BRISBIN COMMUNITY COOKBOOK

Brisbin Women's Club
c/o Bonnie Francis   Email chimneyrock@ycsi.net
4284 US Hwy 89 South   Fax 406-222-1394
Livingston, MT 59047   406-222-3637

This is the second cookbook assembled by the Brisbin Women's Club. The
first was in the early 1960's and is a valued collector's item. This small
club of approximately twenty women is big on community service and
good recipes. Includes over 370 delicious, tried-and-true favorites.

$15.00 Retail price
$3.00 Postage and handling
Make check payable to Brisbin Women's Club

CENTSIBLE NUTRITION COOKBOOK

University of Wyoming Cooperative Extension Service
Cent$ible Nutrition Program   Email tortiz@uwyo.edu
P. O. Box 3354   Fax 307-766-5686
Laramie, WY 82071   307-766-5375

Designed to help families eat better for less, each recipe is low-cost, uses
few ingredients, is easily prepared, and is tasty. Contains tips for high
altitudes, a meal planning section with a time-management plan and gro-
cery list, nutrition facts, and kid-tested recipes. Also available in Spanish.

$19.95 Retail price
$5.00 Postage and handling
Make check payable to UW Cent$ible Nutrition

CHEYENNE FRONTIER DAYS™ "DADDY OF 'EM ALL" COOKBOOK

Chuckwagon Gourmet
P. O. Box 843   Email jerryjessen@worldnet.att.net
Cheyenne, WY 82003   307-634-4197

A cookbook with two goals: to preserve the rich culinary history of rodeo, Cheyenne and The West and to provide an educational endowment to the CFD Memorial Scholarship Foundation. Leather-like hardback cover, lay-flat double Wire-O binding contains 320 pages and 600 tested recipes.

$22.95 Retail price
WY residents add applicable county/state tax
  $3.00 Postage and handling

Make check payable to Chuckwagon Gourmet   ISBN 0-9649348-0-9

COLUMBUS COMMUNITY COOKBOOK

Brick-By-Brick   Email mschimmele@hotmail.com
P. O. Box 896   Fax 406-322-5110
Columbus, MT 59019   406-322-5250

The *Columbus Community Cookbook* is a collection of 300 recipes, 172 pages of favorite family recipes from community members of all ages. The proceeds from book sales will assist Brick-By-Brick in providing improvements to Heritage Park—everyone's backyard.

$12.95 Retail price
  $3.00 Postage and handling

Make check payable to Brick-By-Brick

COOKING WITH THE LADIES

Ladies of Redeemer Lutheran Church
1906 Garrett   Email k.lesco@worldnet.att.net
Cheyenne, WY 82001   307-634-5690

This cookbook celebrates the 50th anniversary of Redeemer Lutheran Church, Cheyenne, Wyoming. Recipes were gathered for several years from members. It is a spiralbound, hardcover book with 153 pages and almost 500 recipes.

$10.00 Retail price
  $.60 Tax for Wyoming residents
  $2.00 Postage and handling

Make check payable to Ladies of Our Redeemer

THE COOL MOUNTAIN COOKBOOK:
A GOURMET GUIDE TO WINTER RETREATS

by Gwen Ashley Walters
Pen & Fork Communications   Email chefgwen@penandfork.com
P. O. Box 5165   Fax 480-595-0890
Carefree, AZ 85377   480-488-2202

Twenty top-rated ski lodges from across the country shared their secret recipes with award-winning chef/author Gwen Ashley Walters who managed a fly fishing lodge in Southwestern Montana. Includes more than 130 recipes, menus, cooking tips, travel information and color photos.

$19.95 Retail price
  $1.42 Tax for Arizona residents
  $4.00 Postage and handling

Make check payable to Pen & Fork Communications
ISBN 0-9663486-1-3

COW COUNTRY COOKBOOK

Dan Cushman
Clear Light Publishers   Email publish@clearlightbooks.com
823 Don Diego   Fax 505-989-9519
Santa Fe, NM 87505   800-253-2747

Compiled and written by best-selling Montana author of *Stay Away, Joe*, this unforgettable book contains over 80 authentic pioneer recipes. Foreword by famed Western cowboy-writer Max Evans, and illustrations by legendary cowboy-artist, Charlie Russell. Stories, anecdotes included.

  $8.95 Retail price   ISBN 0-940666-18-9
  $.58 Tax for New Mexico residents
  $3.50 Postage and handling

Make check payable to Clear Light Publishers

DUCK & GOOSE COOKERY

by Eileen Clarke
Ducks Unlimited
One Waterfowl Way
Memphis, TN 38120   800-45-DUCKS

The most complete duck and goose cookbook ever; includes photos of recipes and illustrated game care and cutting instructions. By well-known outdoor writer Eileen Clarke of Townsend, Montana. Try Hide-Away Paté, Deep Fried Canada Goose, and more.

  $27.50 Retail price
  $5.95 Postage and handling

Make check payable to Ducks Unlimited   ISBN 1-572234-09-1

FAVORITE RECIPES

Ladies of Grace Bible Baptist
405 South Park Street   Fax
Casper, WY 82601   307-265-1339

A collection of 150 recipes. There is a wide variety of recipes, including many quick and easy ones, to choose from. Total pages, 54.

  $6.00 Retail price
  $.30 Tax for Wyoming residents
  $1.50 Postage and handling

Make check payable to Grace Bible Baptist Church

FAVORITE RECIPES OF MONTANA

Montana Farm Bureau Federation Women's Committee
Montana Farm Bureau   Email dianaa@mfbf.org
502 S. 19th Avenue, Suite 104   Fax 406-587-0319
Bozeman, MT 59718   406-587-3153

A must-have, down-home cookbook with more than 750 recipes from Montana's farm and ranch families. The cookbook, published by Montana Farm Bureau Federation's Women's Committee, boasts over 350 pages that truly represent the "flavors" of the Big Sky Country.

  $10.00 Retail price
  $4.00 Postage and handling

Make check payable to Montana Farm Bureau Federation

FEEDING THE HERD

Jackson Hole CowBelles
Valley Bookstore   Email info@valleybookstore.com
P. O. Box 590   Fax 307-733-6498
Jackson, WY 83001   307-733-4533

Compiled as a tribute to the many people who are active in the beef cattle industry and their tireless efforts to improve the quality of their product. Recipes are quick, tasty, and nutritious—perfect for today's busy cooks! Hardbound, 3-ring binder with easel. Happy Cooking!

$15.95   Retail price
  $.96   Tax for Wyoming residents
 $2.00   Postage and handling

Make check payable to Valley Bookstore

FESTIVAL OF NATIONS COOKBOOK

Festival of Nations
P. O. Box 1376
Red Lodge, MT 59068   406-446-1905

This cookbook is presented not only to honor the ethnic heritage of our coal-mining town, peopled by immigrants from many European countries, but also to acknowledge the ongoing, creative culinary expertise of our local cooks. Features both ethnic and traditional recipes.

$15.00   Retail price
 $3.00   Postage and handling

Make check payable to Festival of Nations Foundation

THE FINE ART OF COOKING
THE FINE ART OF COOKING VOLUME 2

Art Associates of Missoula and Missoula Symphony Guild
912 Polaris Way
Missoula, MT 59803   406-251-2816

Our cookbooks are a compilation of recipes collected from the members of two of Missoula's arts-related organizations, Missoula Symphony Guild and Art Associates of Missoula. Their time-tested recipes are popular for any occasion and reflect the diversity of western Montana. These cookbooks have proven to be substantial fundraisers for the organizations.

$15.00 each Retail price
Postage and handling included

Make check payable to Art Associates of Missoula

FIRE HALL COOKBOOK
FIRE HALL COOKBOOK #2

Fisher River Volunteer Fire Company
185 Lakeview Road   Email hoeltzel@libby.org
Libby, MT 59923   406-293-9845

The ladies of our community had a great time collecting and testing the recipes for these two successful fundraisers. There are many tantalizing recipes in both editions . . . Cookbook #1: Veggie Dip, Holiday Stew, and Doris' Rhubarb Cake . . . Cookbook #2: Old-Fashioned Ginger Snap Cookies, Swedish Meatballs . . . and many more. All are great.

$5.00   Book I; $6.50 Book II Retail price
$2.00   Postage and handling

Make check payable to Fisher River Volunteer Fire Company

FIRST LADIES' COOKBOOK

by Betty L. Babcock
Shodair Children's Hospital
P. O. Box 5539   Fax 406-444-7536
Helena, MT 59604   406-444-7548

This is a collection of 750 tried-and-true favorite recipes from Montana citizens, wives of U.S. Presidents, Governors, Senators, and Congressmen along with their pictures. Includes recipes from Montana Pioneers with historic notes. Beautiful Montana photographs separate the sections.

$16.95   Retail price
$2.50   Postage and handling
Make check payable to Shodair Children's Hospital

FOOD FOR THE SOUL

Grass Range Cemetery
Jeri Fortune
1855 Craig River Road
Wolf Creek, MT 59648   406-235-4362

This cookbook contains recipes from the people around Grass Range. There are 144 pages and 533 recipes. The last seven pages are all old-time recipes from parents and grandparents. The proceeds go to help keep the cemetary up.

$10.00   Retail price
$2.50   Postage and handling
Make check payable to Jeri Fortune

FRENCH FAMILY FAVORITES

French Family
Marceline French
113 Carroll Trail
Lewistown, MT 59457   406-538-3111

Our book contains lots of family history, from the earliest days of our marriage and some from two generations back. I wrote of our branding days, and canning our hunting and garden foods. The book has 194 pages, mostly recipes from family and friends.

$10.00   Retail price
$3.00   Postage and handling
Make check payable to Marceline French

FROM THE HIGH COUNTRY OF WYOMING

Flying A Guest Ranch
Debbie Hanson
771 Flying A Ranch Road   Email flyinga@wyoming.com
Pinedale, WY 82941   307-367-2385

Contains 400 recipes that combine hearty western food with nouvelle cuisine: authentic cowboy fare with a gourmet flare. Our approach to creating great meals is to focus on getting the best results with the least amount of fuss. The recipes are certain to be a hit in your kitchen.

$18.00   Retail price
$4.00   Postage and handling
Make check payable to Flying A Ranch

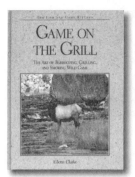

GAME ON THE GRILL

by Eileen Clarke
Voyageur Press
P.O. Box 579
Townsend, MT 59644

Grilling, barbecuing, smoking and even sausage making for your big game
and game birds. Includes 100 photos and 100 recipes, plus tips on choos
ing the right barbecue, water smoker, dry smoker, and fuel for your tastes

$23.50 Retail price

Make check payable to Eileen Clarke

ISBN 0-89658-344-9

GET YOUR BUNS IN HERE

by Laurel Wicks
Box 1470
Jackson, WY 83001   wingit@blissnet.com

Recipes for mouth-watering baked delights from the originator of The
Bunnery in Jackson, Wyoming. Recipes include breakfast treats, cookies,
quick breads, cakes, muffins, pies, breads, sour dough, and more. 142
pages. 133 recipes. Indexed. Table of contents.

$15.95 Retail price
$3.00 Postage and handling

Make check payable to Laurel A. Wicks

ISBN0-9606306-3-5

THE GREAT ENTERTAINER COOKBOOK

Buffalo Bill Historical Center
Museum Store   Email kellyw@bbhc.org
720 Sheridan Avenue   Fax 307-587-8003
Cody, WY 82414   800-533-3838

This hardbound reprint of the Buffalo Bill Historical Center's cookbook
contains 500 time-tested recipes providing a wide range of culinary
delights. Three unique sections focus on recipes from the American West,
honoring traditions established around campfires and chuckwagons.

$24.95 Retail price
$1.25 Tax for Wyoming residents
$7.95 Postage and handling

Make check payable to Museum Selections

ISBN 1-57098-408-5

THE GREAT RANCH COOKBOOK:

SPIRITED RECIPES & RHETORIC FROM AMERICA'S BEST GUEST RANCHES

by Gwen Ashley Walters
Pen & Fork Communications   Email chefgwen@penandfork.com
P. O. Box 5165   Fax 480-595-0890
Carefree, AZ 85377   480-488-2202

Cookbook/travel guide to 30 of the most exclusive western guest ranches.
Don't think of this as a "barbecue and beans" cookbook—it's not! These
ranches were chosen first and foremost for their outstanding cuisine.
Hard cover, 256 pages, 130+ recipes. Color photos of the ranches.

$19.95 Retail price   ISBN 0-9663486-0-5
$1.42 Tax for Arizona residents
$4.00 Postage and handling

Make check payable to Pen & Fork Communications

HEAVENLY RECIPES AND BURNT OFFERINGS

Women Missionary Ladies
New Life Assembly of God Church
515 7th Avenue N
Lewistown, MT 59457   406-538-3512 or 538-7095

This is a unique collection of old and new recipes. Many are unpublished, handed down from parents and grandparents. It includes some Hutterite recipes because of the many colonies here in Montana, and we love their baked goods.

$10.00 Retail price
$2.00   Postage and handling

Make check payable to Lewistown A.O.G. Church

HERE'S WHAT'S COOKING:
RECIPES USING CHUGWATER CHILI PRODUCTS

Chugwater Chili Corporation   Email chugchili@coffey.com
P. O. Box 92   Fax 307-422-3357
Chugwater, WY 82210   800-972-4454

Our cookbook contains recipes using our Chugwater Chili Products for appetizers, main dishes, salads, soups, sauces, snacks, condiments, and quick fixes. Recipes have been contributed from board members and their families, friends and neighbors—local, state and nationwide.

$4.00 Retail price
$.20   Tax for Wyoming residents
$4.95 Postage and handling

Make check payable to Chugwater Chili Corp.

THE HOLE THING VOLUME II

St. John's Hospital Auxiliary   Email scaesar@tetonhospital.org
P. O. Box 428   Fax 307-739-7507
Jackson, WY 83001   307-739-7402

The Hole Thing Volume II, is a compilation of favorite recipes from Jacksonson Hole residents. This 226-page cookbook contains over 200 recipes of the local's favorite cuisine. This is our second edition and provides an intimate glimpse of Jackson Hole through its food and art.

$12.95 Retail price
$.78   Tax for Wyoming residents
$3.00   Postage and handling

Make check payable to St. John's Hospital Auxiliary
ISBN0-9633521-1-3

HOME AT/ON THE RANGE WITH WYOMING BILS

Wyoming/PEO Sisterhood, Chapter Y
Helen Sheppard, Vice Pres.   Email sheppard@coffey.com
1558 Westridge Court   Fax 307-577-0903
Casper, WY 82604   307-234-2134

A rare book of men's favorite recipes containing 340 recipes from the spouses of PEO sisters throughout Wyoming. Attractive pen and ink drawings by two members grace the cover and divider pages. Proceeds from the sale of this book will benefit PEO educational projects.

$10.00 Retail price
$3.00   Postage and handling

Make check payable to PEO Chapter Y

HORSE PRAIRIE FAVORITES

Grant Volunteer Fire Department
c/o Yvonne Turney
11820 Hwy 324
Grant - Dillon, MT 59725   406-681-3141

Horse Prairie Favorites contains 121 pages of recipes from the "Horse Prairie" area, and most have ingredients that are common in most kitchens.

$10.00   Retail price
$3.56   Postage and handling
Make check payable to Grant Volunteer Fire Department

IRENE'S COUNTRY COOKING:
FROM FARM TO FREEWAY

by Irene D. Wakefield
Anticipation Press
5312 Westedt Road
Cheyenne, WY 82009   Email vrwakefiel@aol.com

More than a cookbook! There are 320 quick 'n easy farm recipes perfected during Irene's years as a suburban working mom. She tells her own story, enhanced with old-time farm photos and those of today's triked Gold Wing motorcycle. Irene includes dozens of her own handy household tips.

$14.95   Retail price
$.90   Tax for Wyoming residents
$3.00   Postage and handling
Make check payable to Anticipation Press   ISBN 0-96765284-3-8

IRMA FLAT MOTHERS' CLUB COOKBOOK

Irma Flat Mothers' Club
101 Lower Southfork Road
Cody, WY 82414   307-587-4028

To celebrate our organizations's 90th anniversary, we gathered 146 recipes from many past and present members. In 1909, pioneer women of the rural Irma Flat community organized the Irma Flat Mothers' Club for social enjoyment and to sponsor Sunday school at the Irma Flat school.

$7.50   Retail price
$4.00   Postage and handling
Make check payable to Irma Flat Mothers' Club

JACKSON HOLE A LA CARTE

Jackson Hole Conservation Alliance   Email info@jhalliance.org
P. O. Box 2728   Fax 307-733-9008
Jackson, WY 83001   307-733-9417

Recipes from alliance members and friends of Jackson Hole from all over America—and the world. All recipes have been rigorously tested and the dishes can be easily transported. From the land of wide open spaces, where the deer and the antelope still play, we wish you "Bon Appetit!"

$12.95   Retail price
$0.78   Tax for Wyoming residents
$2.00   Postage and handling
Make check payable to JHCA   ISBN 0-9617014-0-4

★ ★

CATALOG OF CONTRIBUTING COOKBOOKS

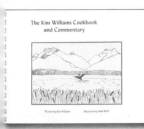

THE KIM WILLIAMS COOKBOOK AND COMMENTARY

by Kim Williams; illustrations by Janet Bush
Bitterroot Educational Resources
315 S. Fourth Street East   Email blueflax@mtwi.net
Missoula, MT 59801   406-543-6997

Combines 75 recipes with Kim Williams' unique observations, as a National Public Radio commentator, on food, health, and life. Naturalist and nutritionist, Kim introduces edible plants, natural foods, and her Montana lifestyle. 30 commentaries, 178 pages.

$10.95 Retail price   ISBN 0-915111-00-4
$3.50 Postage and handling

Make check payable to Kim Williams Cookbook

LEWIS AND CLARK FARE

Whitehall Senior Citizens
Attn: Mary Gustin
P. O. Box 248
Whitehall, MT 59759   406-287-5336

Our cookbook is compiled of favorite recipes of family, friends and seniors of the Whitehall Senior Center. We chose the name *Lewis and Clark Fare* in commemoration of the Lewis and Clark Centennial. Our book consists of 131 pages and many of our seniors' favorite recipes.

$10.00 Retail price
$2.00 Postage and handling

Make check payable to Whitehall Senior Transportation

MONTANA BED & BREAKFAST GUIDE & COOKBOOK

Janet Ollila Colberg
Summer Kitchen Press   www.helpbooks.com
314 Chaucer Street   Email jcolberg@helpbooks.com
Helena, MT 59601   800-418-5237

This lively cookbook combines 288 pages of recipes, pictures and histories of mansions along Montana's Lewis & Clark Trail. Jeff Morris, *Montana Magazine,* says, "Add class to your Montana road trip . . . this is Lewis & Clark for people who like to eat and sleep." *Idaho's Country Register* quips, "for the tenderfoot with an appetite."

$14.95 Retail price

Make check payable to Summer Kitchen Press   ISBN 0965364739

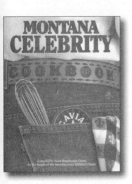

MONTANA CELEBRITY COOKBOOK

by Susie Graetz
Intermountain Children's
  Home and Services   Email development@intermountain.org
500 S. Lamborn   Fax 406-442-7949
Helena, MT 59601   406-442-7920

A chance to peek into the recipe files of 200 high-profile Montanans and those who have strong ties to the Big Sky Country. These caring people have shared recipes, anecdotes, family histories, and cooking tips to help raise money for young, severely emotionally-disturbed children.

$17.95 Retail price   ISBN 1-56037-22-X
$5.00 Postage and handling

Make check payable to Intermountain Children's Home and Services

★ ★

MOUNTAIN BROOK'S WACKY WONDERS OF THE WOODS

Mountain Brook Ladies Club
1905 Foothill Road
Kalispell, MT 59901
                   Email wlmsout@centurytel.net

A collection of 600 recipes from more than 120 cooks in the area. This publication, by the Mountain Brook Ladies Club, has over 270 pages of unusual and unique Montana recipes. Also includes 20 pages of colorful local history. This spiral-bound, hard-cover cookbook makes an excellent gift.

$10.00 Retail price
$2.95 Postage and handling
Make check payable to Mountain Brook Ladies Club

POTLUCK:
THE ARCHIE BRAY FOUNDATION ARTISTS COOKBOOK

Archie Bray Foundation for
  the Ceramic Arts   Email archiebray@archiebray.org
2915 Country Club Avenue   Fax 406-443-0934
Helena, MT 59602   406-443-3502

100 pages, spiral-bound, containing favorite recipes and artwork from over forty past resident artists and friends of the Bray, where sharing meals together has been a longstanding and tasty tradition. Taste why Josh DeWeese's Artichoke Heaven deserves its name.

$20.00 Retail price
$4.00 Postage and handling
Make check payable to Archie Bray Foundation

THE PURE FOOD CLUB OF JACKSON HOLE

Judy S. Clayton
Teton Views Publishing   Email editor@tetonviews.com
P. O. Box 832   Fax 307-734-7257
Jackson Hole, WY 83001   307-733-7161

These 150 historical recipes are a unique blend of history and photographs from Jackson Hole cooks, past and present, with 19 photos of early Jackson Hole and its residents. Each recipe includes information about its donor and their place in Jackson Hole history. 105 pages.

$12.95 Retail price
$.78 Tax for Wyoming residents
$2.50 Postage and handling
Make check payable to Teton Views Publishing   ISBN 0-9709786-0-X

RANCH RECIPE ROUNDUP IV

Wyoming Livestock Roundup
Del Tinsley - Maverick Press   Email wlr@trib.com
P. O. Box 850   Fax 307-472-1781
Casper, WY 82602   800-967-1647

A collection of beef, lamb, and ranch recipes from the Wyoming CattleWomen, the Wyoming Wool Growers, and Wyoming's finest cooks, our ranch women.

$12.00 Retail price
$2.50 Postage and handling
Make check payable to Wyoming Livestock Roundup

RARE COLLECTION RECIPES

Soroptimist International of Billings   Email ssduganz@attbi.com
P. O. Box 2322   Fax 406-652-3770
Billings, MT 59103   406-656-5819

This wonderful cookbook has "time-tested" and "taste-tested" recipes from several generations of excellent cooks. It is a delight for everyone who enjoys good cooking and good eating.

    $8.00   Retail price
    $3.00   Postage and handling

Make check payable to Soroptimist International of Billings

RECIPES FROM BIG SKY COUNTRY:
A COLLECTION OF MONTANA'S FINEST BED & BREAKFAST RECIPES

Montana Bed & Breakfast Association
Winters Publishing   Email tmwinters@juno.com
P. O. Box 501   Fax 812-663-4948
Greensburg, IN 47240   812-663-4948

Over 140 tempting recipes for every meal, not just breakfast! With everything from Cherry Puff Pancake to Stained Glass Candy, this cookbook showcases the delicious dishes of Montana's finest B & Bs. Descriptions and line drawings of the inns help you plan a perfect stay in Montana!

    $12.95   Retail price
    $2.00   Postage and handling

Make check payable to Winters Publishing   ISBN 1-883651-18-2

RECIPES FROM THE HEART

Christ Lutheran Church Women   Email clc@libby.org
200 W. Larch Street   www.libby.org/~clc/
Libby, MT 59923   406-293-3705

Compiled by members of Christ Lutheran Church, this cookbook contains many tried-and-true family favorites. Proceeds go toward church improvements. Have fun cooking up new ideas and making memories with your family. Above all, enjoy the fruits of your labor. Bon appétit!

    $9.50   Retail price
    $2.00   Postage and handling

Make check payable to Christ Lutheran Church Women

RECIPES TO MAKE YOU PURR

Humane Society of Park County
5537 Greybull Hwy
Cody, WY 82414   307-2587-9479

Recipes contributed by the members, volunteers, staff, and Board of Directors of the Humane Society. All proceeds from the book go to the care of abandoned and forgotten animals. Treat yourself to some delicious recipes—many of which have never appeared in cookbooks before.

    $12.00   Retail price
    $2.50   Postage and handling

Make check payable to Humane Society of Park County

SALAD SAMPLER FROM QUILTING IN THE COUNTRY

by Jane Quinn
5100 S. 19th Road   Email jquinn@quiltinginthecountry.com
Bozeman, MT 59718   406-587-8216

Inspired by the success of *Soup's On,* Jane Quinn, owner of Quilting in the Country, asked fellow quilters for favorite salad recipes to be included in her second cookbook. The result, Salad Sampler, is a compilation of over 250 recipes, ranging from old family favorites to salads popular today.

$20.00   Retail price
$4.00   Postage and handling

Make check payable to Quilting in the Country   ISBN 0-9664403-1-5

SHARING OUR BEST

Kalif Shrine Buckskin Horse Patrol
417 Meade Cr. Rd.   Email pw5946@vcn.com
Sheridan, WY 82801   307-672-3249

Sharing Our Best is a collection of 88 pages and 279 recipes. The cooks who submitted their favorite recipes "tried them lots of times," they swear. This book is chocked full of a variety of recipes.

$12.00   Retail price
$3.00   Postage and handling

Make check payable to Kalif Shrine Buckskin Horse Patrol

SIMAC FAMILY FAVORITES

by Jodi DeMars and Patsy Simac
P. O. Box 97
Winifred, MT 59489   406-462-5335

This second edition includes recipes from the descendents of Kuzma and Johanna Simac who came from Yugoslavia in the 1900s and raised 17 children in rural Montana. The 498 recipes in this book include many of their favorites, including some Croatian recipes. (First edition sold out.)

$9.00   Retail price
$2.00   Postage and handling

Make check payable to Jodi DeMars

SOUP'S ON AT QUILTING IN THE COUNTRY

by Jane Quinn
5100 S. 19th Road   Email jquinn@quiltinginthecountry.com
Bozeman, MT 59718   406-587-8213

These delicious soup recipes, collected from quilting students and quilters across Montana, were inspired by a quilting block design known as Soup's On. A pot of soup and a quilting party go hand in hand. This book is sure to inspire you to test your skills at both.

$16.00   Retail price
$4.00   Postage and handling

Make check payable to Quilting in the Country   ISBN 0-9664403-0-7

SOUVENIRS

Karen Leigh and Gini Ogle
611 Second Avenue East
Kalispell, MT 59901   406-257-0809

A feast of local color and home cooking from The Last Best Place, a beautiful valley just a few minutes from Glacier National Park. Includes ten full-color illustrations along with local lore, poetry, quotes, 35 pen and ink drawings and 253 tested recipes collected from family and friends.

$18.95 Retail price
$2.00 Postage and handling

Make check payable to Karen Leigh   ISBN 0-9640623-0-5

STORY, WYOMING'S CENTENNIAL COMMUNITY COOKBOOK

Story Woman's Club
P. O. Box 103   Email ausieina@fiberpipe.net
Story, WY 82842   307-683-2331

A collection of "then and now" recipes and a little history of the Story, Wyoming community. 150 pages—nearly 400 recipes.

$15.00 Retail price

Make check payable to Story Woman's Club

A TASTE OF JACKSON HOLE II

Christine Goodman
P. O. Box 3308   Email christineg@wyoming.com
Jackson, WY 83001   307-733-1199

Recipes from 32 of Jackson Hole's finest restaurants, offering a broad range of cultural cuisine. A special section features great cooks of Jackson Hole, and a collection of often-asked-for recipes from Café Christine. Wine pairings and recommendations are features for many recipes.

$19.95 Retail price
$2.75 Postage and handling

Make check payable to Christine Goodman   ISBN 0-9633566-0-7

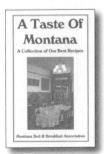

A TASTE OF MONTANA:
A COLLECTION OF OUR BEST RECIPES

Montana Bed & Breakfast Association
Winters Publishing   Email tmwinters@juno.com
P. O. Box 501   Fax 812-663-4948
Greensburg, IN 47240   812-663-4948

Inside this sensational cookbook, you'll find many tempting recipes. With everything from Angel Cookies to Spicy Chicken Casserole, this 96-page book features 90 favorite dishes from Montana's finest B&Bs. A Montana Travel Guide, inn descriptions, and line drawings add to its appeal.

$10.95 Retail price
$2.00 Postage and handling

Make check payable to Winters Publishing   ISBN 1-883651-11-5

TASTES & TOURS OF WYOMING

by Karla Steinle Pellatz and David W. Pellatz
Wyoming Homestay and Outdoors Division
Box 40048   Email whoa@coffey.com
Casper, WY 82604   307-237-3526

A galloping overview of Wyoming's fascinating history along with an in-depth look at the state, highlighting the stories, natural features, and attractions that make the area unique. The 304-page book features 182 recipes, including winning entries from the Governor's Recipe Contest.

$12.50   Retail price
$.63   Tax for Wyoming residents
$2.50   Postage and handling
Make check payable to WHOA   ISBN 0-9661976-0-7

TRULY MONTANA COOKBOOK

Bitterroot Valley Public Television   Email ghightower@cybernet1.com
P. O. Box 838   Fax 406-363-0481 or 406-961-3692
Hamilton, MT 59840   406-961-3692

A unique collection of recipes and beautiful photographs celebrating the diverse heritage of Montana. Includes recipes from the years 1800 to 2003. Dedicated to all whom contributed, sharing with love the family treasures and good food. Proceeds benefit public television in Western Montana.

$18.00   Retail price
$2.00   Postage and handling
Make check payable to Bitterroot Valley Public Television

WHAT'S COOKING, FLO?

By Jerry Palen
Laffing Cow Press
P. O. Box 1647   Email apalen@union-tel.com
Saratoga, WY 82331   307-326-9852

Flo knows just how to transform the contents of a cupboard into a tasty, creative meal to feed the hungriest child or the grumpiest husband. She knows how to run from the field to the kitchen, prepare a meal quickly, and make everyone think she's been behind the stove all day.

$6.95   Retail price
$2.00   Postage and handling
Make check payable to Jerry Palen   ISBN 0-943255-31-7

WHAT'S THIS GREEN STUFF, FLO?

By Jerry Palen
Laffing Cow Press
P. O. Box 1647   Email apalen@union-tel.com
Saratoga, WY 82331   307-326-9852

Nothing is better than fresh produce picked at the perfect moment and cooked immediately, ensuring that the natural nutrients are preserved. Flo knows this and shares with you some of her old stand-bys and just-picked family favorites.

$6.95   Retail price
$2.00   Postage and handling
Make check payable to Jerry Palen   ISBN 1-879894-03-3

WHEAT MONTANA COOKBOOK

Wheat Montana Farms
Three Forks Books, an imprint of Falcon Publishing, Inc.
10778 Hwy. 287   Fax 406-285-3749
Three Forks, MT 59752   800-535-2798

Recipes have been provided by our loyal customers and range from pancakes, waffles, muffins, biscuits, quick-breads and yeast-breads, to desserts, soups and salads—utilizing a variety of flavors and grains. Includes information and products available. 170 pages.

$16.95 Retail price
$3.00 Postage and handling
Make check payable to Wheat Montana Farms

WILD, WILD WEST COWBOY COOKIES

by Tuda Libby Crews   Email info@wildwestcookies.com
P. O. Box 1804   Phone and Fax 1-888-277-0294
Cheyenne, WY 82003-1804   www.wildwestcookies.com

Just like every cowboy needs his trusty horse, every western cook needs her cookie—or at least a great recipe for one. This delightful book offers a variety of cookie recipes and helpful tips, making these cowboy cookies as tasty as they are artistic. Unique Cowboy Cookie Cutters are also available in a variety of shapes. See website or call for details.

$12.95 Retail price for book
$.78 Tax for Wyoming residents
Make check payable to WWWCC   ISBN 0-87905-808-0

WITH LOTS OF LOVE

A. Drummond Ranch B & B
Taydie Drummond   Email adrummond@juno.com
399 Happy Jack Road   Fax 307-634-6042
Cheyenne, WY 82007   307-634-6042

A unique collection of unusual creations which are easy and awesome! 125 recipes served at our Ranch B & B over the years, inspired by family, friends, & guests from around the world, including special projects for kids!

$15.00 Retail price
$4.00 Postage and handling
Make check payable to A. Drummond's Ranch

WOLF POINT, MONTANA 75TH JUBILEE COOKBOOK

Jubilee Cookbook Committee
Wolf Point CofC & Ag   Email wpchmber@nemontel.net
218 Third Avenue S #B   Fax 406-653-2028
Wolf Point, MT 59201   406-653-2012

This cookbook has been compiled to help in the celebration of Wolf Point, Montana's 75th Jubilee. It is a collection of 735 recipes including comments from our people and highlights of our history.

$15.00 Retail price
$3.00 Postage and handling
Make check payable to Wolf Point CofC & Ag.

WONDERFUL WYOMING FACTS AND FOODS

by Judy Barbour
Judy Barbour Books
P. O. Box 1032
Bandera, TX 78003   830-796-7111 or 210-216-4149
Wonderful Wyoming Facts and Foods is a culinary jewel of the state of Wyoming. It contains not only delicious recipes representative of the state, but also a concise history of the state and a chronological historical fact on each page—two books in one! 64 pages. 63 recipes.

$7.95 Retail price
  $.65 Tax for Texas residents
$2.00 Postage and handling

Make check payable to Judy Barbour   ISBN 0-9611746-1-7

WYOMING COOK BOOK

by Karin Wade
Golden West Publishers, Inc.   Email goldwest1@mindspring.com
4113 N. Longview Avenue   Fax 602-279-6901
Phoenix, AZ 85014-4949   800-658-5830

From Yellowstone National Park to Cheyenne—homemakers, caterers, B&B owners and chefs have contributed over 130 lip smackin', palate pleasin' recipes reflecting Wyoming's unique ethnic, cultural, and agricultural makeup. Take a culinary ride through Wonderful Wyoming!

$6.95 Retail price
$3.00 Postage and handling

Make check payable to Golden West Publishers   ISBN 1-885590-33-4

YAAK COOKBOOK

The Yaak Women's Club
Winnie Canavan
1010 Vinal Lake Road
Troy, MT 59935   Email yaakcookbook@yahoo.com

Our cookbook contains over 300 mouth-watering recipes. In addition to family favorites, there are recipes native to the Yaak River Valley, such as wild game, huckleberries, grouse, etc. There are also pictures of some of the local activities. This is a cookbook you won't want to miss.

$9.00 Retail price
$2.00 Postage and handling

Make check payable to Yaak Womens Club

YOU'RE HOT STUFF, FLO!

by Jerry Palen
The Saratoga Publishing Group, Inc.
P. O. Box 1647   Email apalen@union-tel.com
Saratoga, WY 82331   307-326-9852

Flo is really on a roll. She knows her culinary skills are beyond doubt, so she has taken on a saucy, spicy, brave new taste. It's the new American cuisine! Some call it Tex-Mex, some call it Southwestern, but it's coming right out of Flo's own kitchen to you.

$7.95 Retail price
$2.00 Postage and handling

Make check payable to Jerry Palen   ISBN 1-879894-05-X

INDEX

PHOTO © WIND RIVER VISITORS COUNCIL

Ancient Indian petroglyphs (carvings or line drawings on rock) are scattered throughout Wyoming and Montana. Castle Gardens is one of the largest petroglyph sites in Wyoming, and includes depictions of medicine men, warriors, and hunters.

★ ★

INDEX

INDEX

★ ★ ★ ★ ★ ★ ★ ★ ★ ★ ★ ★ ★ ★ ★ ★ ★ ★ ★ ★

INDEX

★ ★

INDEX

281

★ ★ ★ ★ ★ ★ ★ ★ ★ ★ ★ ★ ★ ★ ★ ★ ★ ★ ★ ★

INDEX

★ ★

INDEX

★ ★

INDEX

Best of the Best State Cookbook Series

Best of the Best from **ALABAMA** 288 pages, $16.95	**Best of the Best from** **IDAHO** 288 pages, $16.95	**Best of the Best from** **MISSISSIPPI** 288 pages, $16.95	**Best of the Best from** **SO. CAROLINA** 288 pages, $16.95
Best of the Best from **ALASKA** 288 pages, $16.95	**Best of the Best from** **ILLINOIS** 288 pages, $16.95	**Best of the Best from** **MISSOURI** 304 pages, $16.95	**Best of the Best from** **TENNESSEE** 288 pages, $16.95
Best of the Best from **ARIZONA** 288 pages, $16.95	**Best of the Best from** **INDIANA** 288 pages, $16.95	**Best of the Best from** **NEW ENGLAND** 368 pages, $16.95	**Best of the Best from** **TEXAS** 352 pages, $16.95
Best of the Best from **ARKANSAS** 288 pages, $16.95	**Best of the Best from** **IOWA** 288 pages, $16.95	**Best of the Best from** **NEW MEXICO** 288 pages, $16.95	**Best of the Best from** **TEXAS II** 352 pages, $16.95
Best of the Best from **BIG SKY** 288 pages, $16.95	**Best of the Best from** **KENTUCKY** 288 pages, $16.95	**Best of the Best from** **NEW YORK** 288 pages, $16.95	**Best of the Best from** **VIRGINIA** 320 pages, $16.95
Best of the Best from **CALIFORNIA** 384 pages, $16.95	**Best of the Best from** **LOUISIANA** 288 pages, $16.95	**Best of the Best from** **NO. CAROLINA** 288 pages, $16.95	**Best of the Best from** **WASHINGTON** 288 pages, $16.95
Best of the Best from **COLORADO** 288 pages, $16.95	**Best of the Best from** **LOUISIANA II** 288 pages, $16.95	**Best of the Best from** **OHIO** 352 pages, $16.95	**Best of the Best from** **WEST VIRGINIA** 288 pages, $16.95
Best of the Best from **FLORIDA** 288 pages, $16.95	**Best of the Best from** **MICHIGAN** 288 pages, $16.95	**Best of the Best from** **OKLAHOMA** 288 pages, $16.95	**Best of the Best from** **WISCONSIN** 288 pages, $16.95
Best of the Best from **GEORGIA** 336 pages, $16.95	**Best of the Best from the** **MID-ATLANTIC** 288 pages, $16.95	**Best of the Best from** **OREGON** 288 pages, $16.95	*Cookbooks listed above* *have been completed as* *of December 31, 2003.*
Best of the Best from the **GREAT PLAINS** 288 pages, $16.95	**Best of the Best from** **MINNESOTA** 288 pages, $16.95	**Best of the Best from** **PENNSYLVANIA** 320 pages, $16.95	*All cookbooks are ring-* *bound except California,* *which is paperbound.*

Note: Big Sky includes Montana and Wyoming; Great Plains includes North Dakota, South Dakota, Nebraska, and Kansas; Mid-Atlantic includes Maryland, Delaware, New Jersey, and Washington, D.C.; New England includes Rhode Island, Connecticut, Massachusetts, Vermont, New Hampshire, and Maine.

Special discount offers available! *(See previous page for details.)*

To order by credit card, call toll-free **1-800-343-1583** or visit our website at **www.quailridge.com**.
Use the form below to send check or money order.

Call 1-800-343-1583 or email **info@quailridge.com** *to request a free catalog of all of our publications.*

Order form

Use this form for sending check or money order to:
QUAIL RIDGE PRESS • P. O. Box 123 • Brandon, MS 39043

❏ Check enclosed

Charge to: ❏ Visa ❏ MC ❏ AmEx ❏ Disc

Card # _____

Expiration Date _____

Signature _____

Name _____

Address _____

City/State/Zip _____

Phone # _____

Email Address _____

Qty.	Title of Book (State) or Set	Total

Subtotal _____

7% Tax for MS residents _____

Postage ($4.00 any number of books) **+ 4.00**

Total _____